From the Heart of the Church

From the Heart of the Church

The Catholic Social Tradition

Judith A. Merkle, S.N.D. de N.

MG

A Michael Glazier Book

LITURGICAL PRESS

Collegeville, Minnesota

www.litpress.org

A Michael Glazier Book published by the Liturgical Press

Cover design by David Manahan, O.S.B. Photo by Marie Docher/PhotoAlto.

1   2   3   4   5   6   7   8

Library of Congress Cataloging-in-Publication Data

Merkle, Judith A.
    From the heart of the church : the Catholic social tradition / by Judith A. Merkle.
        p. cm.
    Includes bibliographical references and index.
    ISBN 0-8146-5111-9 (alk. paper)
    1. Christian sociology—Catholic Church—History of doctrines—19th century. 2. Christian sociology—Catholic Church—History of doctrines—20th century. 3. Encyclicals, Papal. I. Title.

BX1753.M46   2004
261.8'088'282—dc22

                                                2003024863

To the Sisters of Notre Dame de Namur

across five continents

As we celebrate two hundred years of

Proclaiming the Goodness of God

1804–2004

Contents

PART THREE

The Future of the Catholic Social Tradition

Preface

This is a book about ownership, Catholics taking ownership of a rich tradition in the Church, the Catholic Social Tradition. This tradition is more than policies about social problems; it is a way of life in society. As a living tradition it has been fed by the blood of martyrs and simply by good people giving an honest day's work for a day's pay. The Catholic Social Tradition is about voice and responsibility in the Church and the society. It promotes conscious living and intentional choices about the commitment of energy in a modern society filled with options, yet empty of direction.

The Catholic Social Tradition is a tradition of thinking and acting. Within this tradition stand the social encyclicals since 1891 as unique manifestations of its ethical intuition and commitment to the Gospel as lived in society. The Catholic Social Tradition is about more than how to be just in society. It contains theological positions that belong to the Church that are essential to its logic. Each modern historical period of the Catholic Social Tradition can be characterized broadly as possessing an implicit understanding of faith, spirituality and the Church, along with a characteristic style of the expression of social commitment in society. We will call this a form of Social Catholicism. Social Catholicism is a form of the vision and practice in the life of the Church and its members that builds societal life and its institutions in a particular context in order to foster human dignity. While Catholics join with fellow Christians, members of other religions, and people of good will in this endeavor, Catholic life provides the context in which social commitment is expressed.

Understandings of the Christian mystery that inspire social commitment in each period of Social Catholicism stand along side other approaches and interpretations. There is always a pluralism of spiritual expression in the Church at any given time that is not captured by any single emphasis in its life. However, there is sufficient embodiment of a "social way" within each historical period that broad understandings of the relationship between the Christian life and social commitment can be detected.

North American theologian Frederick Herzog gives an historical perspective to the place faith and public concerns hold in the Church today. The primary questions of the early Church were devoted to the closeness of God to Jesus. In the Reformation era it was God's closeness to the human being. Today the concern is God's closeness to history in the struggle for justice.[1] We will talk about more than the social encyclicals as we consider the Catholic Social Tradition since the discernment of God's presence to history in the struggle for justice has many witnesses. While the Catholic social encyclicals are the center of the Catholic Social Tradition in the modern era, they join with other voices and expressions in the living Church. Theologies that relate the Christian life to society, as well as those that express the operative faith of diverse populations across the church also are expressions of the Catholic Social Tradition, faith as lived in society. We will explore political theology and liberation theology in its various forms as Latin American, black, Hispanic, feminist, African and Asian. We will study the statements of various bishops' conferences as witnesses to faith in society in a particular context. We will also assume that the Catholic Social Tradition, addressed not just to the Church but to the society at large, is strongly influenced by movements and resources outside ecclesial circles. While this book does not attempt to say everything about the Catholic Social Tradition, it aims at presenting a path through it, as a way of promoting a better understanding of its place in church life. This book is written not only for Catholics, but for all interested in a spirituality that does justice. Hopefully sharing our tradition, and in places its dialogue with similar movements in other Christian churches, will foster a deeper appreciation of the relationship of Christian faith to society for all who read it.

This book is divided into three sections. The first section presents foundational concepts regarding faith, spirituality and Church that

[1] Frederick Herzog, *God-Walk: Liberation Shaping Dogmatics* (Maryknoll, N.Y.: Orbis Books, 1988) 46.

inform the Catholic Social Tradition. The second section examines the tradition itself, emphasizing the modern social encyclicals since 1891, selected major statements of bishops' conferences in Latin America and the United States, and theologies that address the relationship of faith, culture, and society. The last section offers a proposal for community formation to foster "carriers" of the Catholic Social Tradition in the future.

This book is written for those who wish to understand the Catholic Social Tradition in its essential elements and scope. At times the references in this work alert the reader to varying interpretations of the tradition. At other times, they provide short overviews of elements of the tradition, as in dictionary articles or standard sources from scholarly reflection. The goal is to provide a "grammar" of the tradition for its further integration into Catholic life and society.

I wish to thank my students over the years who, through their questions regarding the Catholic Social Tradition, opened to me a path of understanding of its elements. I am grateful to the Vincentian Community at Niagara University for a summer grant that assisted in the research of this text. I also appreciate the hospitality of the Sisters of Notre Dame de Namur of the British Province, especially the Battersea community, during several study visits to England. I wish to acknowledge the gracious welcome and support of the community at the North American College at the Catholic University of Leuven, Belgium, during my sabbatical time that facilitated the final research on this text. I wish to thank the Liturgical Press for its interest in this endeavor. Finally, I am grateful for the encouragement of my friends, family, colleagues, and for the continuing support of my own Notre Dame community. I hope this text contributes to the deeper integration and furthering of the Catholic Social Tradition in the Church.

Documents Cited
and Abbreviations Used[1]

Rerum Novarum: The Condition of Labor (Leo XIII, 1891)	RN
Quadragesimo Anno: After Forty Years (Pius XI, 1931)	QA
Mater et Magistra: Christianity and Social Progress (John XXIII, 1961)	MM
Pacem et Terris: Peace on Earth (John XXIII, 1963)	PT
Lumen Gentium: Dogmatic Constitution on the Church (Vatican II, 1964)[2]	LG
Gaudium et Spes: Pastoral Constitution on the Church in the Modern World (Vatican II, 1965)	GS
Populorum Progressio: On the Development of Peoples (Paul VI, 1967)	PP
Octogesima Adveniens: A Call to Action on the Eightieth Anniversay of Rerum Novarum (Paul VI, 1971)	OA
Justice in the World (Synod of Bishops, 1971)	JW

---

[1] All social encyclicals and statements of the U.S. Bishops are cited from *Catholic Social Thought: The Documentary Heritage,* David J. O'Brien and Thomas A. Shannon, eds. (Maryknoll, N.Y.: Orbis Books, 2002).

[2] *The Documents of Vatican II,* Walter M. Abbott, S.J., ed. (New York: Herder and Herder, 1966).

Evangelii Nuntiandi:
Evangelization in the Modern World (Paul VI, 1975)   EN

Laborem Exercens: On Human Work (John Paul II, 1981)   LE

Sollicitudo Rei Socialis: On Social Concern (John Paul II, 1987)   SRS

Centesimus Annus: On the Hundredth Anniversary of
Rerum Novarum (John Paul II, 1991)   CA

The Challenge of Peace: God's Promise and Our Response
(U.S. Catholic Bishops, 1983)

Economic Justice for All (U.S. Catholic Bishops, 1986)

Documents of Ecclesial Conferences of Medellin (1968),
Puebla (1979) and Santo Domingo (1993):
(Bishops of Latin America)[3]

---

[3] As referenced in the text.

PART ONE

Foundations

Chapter One

Social Teaching:
A Message Lived or Professed?

St. Augustine, in his fourth-century work, *The City of God*, ponders the connection between the Christian life and political life. Today we ask the same question as we inquire as "Church" into the relationship between daily life, religion and politics. We question, not as Christians at the time of the fall of the Roman Empire, but as people of today. Since the beginning of the Church, Christians have approached problems in society in light of their faith. However, the great changes brought about by the industrial revolution stimulated a new search for the relevance of faith to public issues.

The social encyclical tradition arose as the Church sought to respond to the "social question," or how the Christian faith impacted solutions to the economic, social, and political problems raised by the industrial revolution. Different popes, in later years, addressed changing conditions of modernization, secularization, and globalization. One record of the Church's response to modern life and politics is found in the social encyclical tradition since Leo XIII (1891–present). These letters, written by the pope to the world and to the Church, are an important voice of the Church as it interprets the impact of the gospel message on social conditions. The social encyclicals continue Augustine's inquiry into the relationship between the Church and conditions in the world. In this sense, they are part of a tradition which predates them, the Catholic Social Tradition.

In Augustine's account of fourth century life in *The City of God*, he notes the variety of philosophies, schools of thought, and visions of right living in Roman society. In his account, there were currently 288 varieties![1] This might take the modern reader aback, as we think life in the "good old days" was simple and monolithic. Augustine reviews the categorization of these different ways of thinking, first by their content and then by whether the philosophy requires that the philosopher actually practices the beliefs espoused or simply professes them. For Catholics who study the social encyclical tradition, Augustine's criteria prove to be relevant to our search today. We too can ask, is the social encyclical tradition an essential element of Catholic life, or is it simply a message professed?

The social encyclicals since Leo XIII, and the literature that surrounds them, are as complex as Augustine's schools of thought. People today have diverse readings of the purpose and meaning of social teaching, as well as how it should function. Some refer to social teaching as a blueprint for Catholic action in society; others see social teaching as visionary, but supporting no specific social program. Some refer to social teaching as the "official stance" of the Church on public policy. Others feel the Catholic should find in social teaching a checklist for conscience formation regarding social responsibility.

Beyond differences regarding identity and function, there are divergent views as to how social teaching is related to other areas of Catholic life, such as the sacraments, liturgy, doctrine, and community living. Some see a relationship between social teaching and the life of the Church, and others see social teaching more as "policy" that stands independently from church life. This difference of opinion arises on two accounts. First, since Catholic social teaching, in the encyclical tradition, is addressed to the Church and to the wider society, many would not link this teaching and life in the Church. There is a message in the encyclical tradition that does not require church membership to hear. Stress on the universal message of social teaching can overshadow the question of the link between social teaching and Catholic life. However, social teaching has also been called the "best kept secret" of the Church.[2] This suggests that its role in Catholic life is not always self-evident and more exploration is required to understand its full identity.

---

[1] Augustine of Hippo, *The City of God,* Marcus Dods, trans. (New York: Random House, 1950) Book XIX.1, 669. Here Augustine quotes Marcus Varro.

[2] P. J. Henriot, E. P. Del Berri, and M. J. Schultheis, *Our Best Kept Secret: The Rich Heritage of Catholic Social Teaching:*(Washington, D.C.: Center of Concern, 1985).

Not all miss the link between Catholic life and social teaching. The following remark reflects a contrary view, that Catholic life and social involvement are not to be split. "At the age of seventeen, I heard a young *militant* of the Catholic left in France describe his regular combination of reciting the Rosary with a 'see, judge, and act' rubric orientated towards social justice and *contre le capitalisme.* It made a strong impression."[3] This book will argue that the above behavior reflects an essential link between Catholic practice and social action, and it is not simply an account of private devotion.

We will explore the connection between Catholic life and Catholic social teaching in three ways. First, we will suggest that there is sufficient unity between the encyclical tradition and Catholic life in any period of time since the beginning of the modern encyclicals that we can speak of different visions of "Social Catholicism."

"Social Catholicism," as we will use it, refers to Catholic responses both internally and externally, to economic modernization, industrialization, theories of progress and globalization, especially their effect on social classes since the end of the nineteenth century. Even though social teaching is addressed to the world, and not just to the Church, we will assume it expresses an implicit vision of Catholic life in society. Through the encyclicals Catholicism was interpreted as to how it shed light on changing social conditions. Beyond providing a vision of a better society, Catholic social teaching also interpreted how Catholic life was to be lived in society. "Catholicism" in this sense is not the Roman Catholic Church in all its manifestations, but how the Church expresses its inner life and its public presence, or its social vision, at a particular moment in time.[4]

Second, we will explore the encyclical tradition since Leo XIII as part of a broader reality that we will call the Catholic Social Tradition.

---

[3] Jonathan Boswell, "Solidarity, Justice and Power Sharing: Patterns and Policies," in *Catholic Social Thought: Twilight or Renaissance?* Jonathan Boswell, Francis P. McHugh, Johan Verstraeten, eds. (Louvain: Peeters, 2001).

[4] I use the term "Catholicism" differently than Paul Misner, *Social Catholicism in Europe* (New York: Crossroad, 1991), who gives a careful study to the particular pattern of the Church's public presence and activity from the French Revolution to World War I in Catholic parts of Europe. In this book we will suggest that along with timely principles for social reform sponsored by the Church in each period of the social encyclicals, there were patterns in images of faith, spirituality and Church that suggest, beyond issues, a vision of Catholic life in society at the time.

We will assume that the Catholic social tradition itself is a diverse language. Besides the social encyclicals and statements of bishop's conferences, we find in the social theologies of liberation and political theology important reflection on faith in society that form part of the modern Catholic Social Tradition. In addition, other aspects of secular and religious thought enter into the gestalt that we identify as Catholic social tradition. Contained within the social encyclicals and the social theologies are broader philosophical and social science preferences that are incorporated into the social vision of the Church.[5] Certainly Catholic social teaching is influenced by other Christian groups, as well as other religions.[6] We will assume that in the Catholic Social Tradition, the social encyclicals arise from a mix of resources, including social scientific and philosophical currents judged compatible and illustrative of church social values. A further indispensable element of the Catholic Social Tradition is the social movements that carry its message into society. Besides utilizing non-church sources for its analysis, social teaching is made effective by movements and groups that take the teaching into society.[7] A study of Social Catholicism cannot be isolated from the diverse elements that contribute to the response of the Church to society. We will address these in passing. However, the thrust of this inquiry will be to study, not the history of these movements, but how they reflect a particular pattern of church-society involvement in a period of Social Catholicism.

Third, we will note there are diverse images of faith, spirituality, and the Church that express the Church's social message in different periods of social teaching. For instance, the Catholic Action movement during the time of Pius XII is a different configuration of Catholic social action than the liberation and basic community style of the post-Vatican era. Different theologies within Catholicism influence various periods of social Catholicism.

We can see these different theologies reflected today. Catholics can be divided on how social teaching relates to Catholic living. Some

---

[5] See: *Catholic Social Thought: Twilight or Renaissance?* Jonathan Boswell, Francis P. McHugh, Johan Verstraeten, eds. (Louvain: Peeters, 2001) for a distinction between these concepts.

[6] This is a theme we will refer to in passing, but which cannot be developed fully in this text.

[7] Marvin L. Mich, *Catholic Social Teaching and Movements* (Mystic, Conn.: Twenty-Third Publications, 1998).

see the essentials of Catholic life expressed in doctrinal belief and sacraments, with social action an admirable but expendable extra. Others link social involvement with a particular personality profile. Someone may remark, "Yes, I want to use the social teaching of the Church more in my life as an adult Christian, in my work, parish or ministry, but does that mean I have to engage in boycotts, or walk in marches?" Others transfer to social teaching their ambivalence toward hierarchical forms of church life. They might remark, "I believe in the goals of social teaching, but I have problems with the hierarchical style of the message." These remarks reflect common questions concerning the nature of faith, church membership, and its relationship to justice. We will assume that linking social teaching and Catholic life is not merely an academic exercise. Rather, drawing the connection between social teaching and the meaning of faith and spirituality and Church is essential to understanding this profound tradition in the Church.

We know that the social encyclical tradition is addressed to society at large. However, we will argue that the social encyclical tradition is dependent on Catholic life for its uniqueness. On the one hand, Catholic social teaching is never just "secular" and in this sense, taking its place as just one theory among others in society for secular reform. Even its most universal proposals arise from the Church's reflection on Scripture, its long tradition of social thought, the logic that flows from its inner life, and its liturgy and praxis.

On the other hand, the social teaching of the Church is not a self-enclosed system.[8] Over the years it engages in a continuous dialogue with major visions for the organization of contemporary life such as Marxism and liberalism. Also, it has given its social message in various social conditions: in a world of independent nation states, to international regional institutions and in the present global situation of interdependence among nations. Social teaching is in dialogue with major philosophies of life today. It challenges contemporary worldviews, which overstate the role of personal autonomy, and separates rights and responsibilities. It listens to new voices for independence, women's rights, and racial equality. Social teaching, therefore, is an open system, being shaped as well as engaging in pubic discourse concerning major issues since the nineteenth century.

---

[8] John A. Coleman, "Retrieving or Re-inventing Social Catholicism: a Transatlantic Response," in *Catholic Social Thought: Twilight or Renaissance?* op. cit., 165.

The leading question, what is social teaching, however, is key for anyone seeking a deeper understanding of the Church's social message. So as a first step in our inquiry into this deep tradition, let us identify in broad terms approaches to Catholic Social Teaching.

Diversity of Approaches to Social Teaching

A concerned person who turns to social teaching to form a vision of social responsibility in our world today will, like Augustine in the fourth century, encounter diversity in its interpretation. Some look to the social encyclical tradition as a recipe for social reform. Others hope to find in social teaching a prophetic denunciation of social ills. A third group sees in social teaching moral doctrine that outlines the obligations of a Christian for life in society. A fourth approaches social teaching as broad principles, or rules of thumb, reflective of gospel values applied to society. While not feeling bound to the specifics of social teaching, they see it as a guideline to judge any social policy or arrangement. Let us look more closely at each of these positions.

Some see social teaching as the Church's social policy directions for the modern world.[9] From this perspective, the social teaching of the Church is analogous to the policy statements of an international organization. It offers to the world a perspective on political, social, economic and cultural issues, from the viewpoint of Christian values, as interpreted by the Catholic Church. Social teaching, in this sense, is a blueprint for achieving the common good. It can be recognized as socially constructive by all, including those beyond the boundaries of the Church. This approach emphasizes the universality of social teaching.

A second group considers social teaching as modern day prophecy. Social teaching is a prophetic statement of the Church in our time that advocates societal transformation.[10] As prophecy, social teaching

---

[9] Richard L. Camp, *The Papal Ideology of Social Reform: A Study in Historical Development 1878–1967* (Leiden: E. J. Brill, 1969) 1. Camp calls the social encyclicals "Vatican social theory."

[10] Thomas J. Gumbleton, "Peacemaking as a Way of Life," in *100 Years of Catholic Social Thought,* John A. Coleman, S.J., ed. (Maryknoll, N.Y.: Orbis Books, 1991) 304. Here Gumbleton states the prophetic role of the teaching negatively. "At a historic moment when the world needed the clear call of denunciation against horrendous crimes and when individual Christians needed the strong, clear guidelines of the teaching church, it was not there."

offers the world a utopian vision. It might be an "impossible ideal," as Niebuhr called all Christian ethics, but it serves the Church and the world as a stimulus to overcome their indifference to social sin. In this sense, social teaching is parentic, not programmatic. It is meant to stir the consciences of members of the church and the society to deal with social ills. This approach would emphasize both the biblical basis of social teaching and its normative anthropology; its vision of the nature and destiny of humankind and the purpose of society and creation as perennial tools are to criticize existing social configurations and humanize them.

A third view emphasizes social teaching as moral doctrine. Social teaching enunciates the social implications of Christian faith in secular society and communicates, if not specific behavioral norms, formal norms or values that carry with them a sense of moral obligation. In this sense social teaching teases out the implications of faith for social living. It obliges the conscience of the Christian across the same spectrum of obligation as other moral teachings. To take on the mind of the Church implies attention to this body of moral teaching and the attitudes and the behaviors it encourages. Since social teaching is moral doctrine, it should be viewed as an extension of the Ten Commandments, and other moral guides of church practice.[11]

The moral doctrine approach is most commonly linked to the identification of Catholic Social Teaching to the encyclical tradition of the last hundred years. This body of teaching reflects the Church's response to social and political matters in modern times. As a statement of the magisterium, it is an extension of the teaching office of the Church. While the linkage between the encyclical tradition and its bearing on the moral conscience would be consistent in this approach, people within it would use the word "doctrine" differently in this tradition.

For instance, at the time of the papacy of Pius XI in 1931 the word "doctrine" was used as "the doctrine" of a third way between socialism and capitalism. In other words, the doctrine of the Church was the moral encouragement to step back from the excesses of both systems, and to see the moral necessity of nonidentity with either of

---

[11] John F. Cronin, S.S., *Christianity and Social Progress: A Commentary on Mater et Magistra* (Baltimore-Dublin: Helicon, 1965) 7. The social encyclicals are described as, ". . . applications of Christian teachings and natural ethics to the complex society of their day."

them. At other times "doctrine" means simply church teaching that requires the serious attention of the faithful conscience. The *Catechism of the Catholic Church* makes this link between faith life and historical life in society in its definition of social teaching as: . . . "a body of doctrine which is articulated in the Church, interprets events in the course of history, with the assistance of the Holy Spirit, in the light of what has been revealed by Jesus Christ."[12]

In general, those who approach social teaching as doctrine, interpret its doctrinal nature broadly. While generally the Christian is left to judge the best means to arrive at the goals of social teaching, the ends stated in social teaching oblige in conscience.

A fourth approach presents social teaching as perennial moral principles to be applied in specific societal situations. Social teaching, in this sense, is a guideline, given by the Church, for social action. The teaching does not contain a direct guideline for every social action. Rather, a specific action can be discerned by reliance on the Catholic tradition's view of a just society, implicit in social teaching. In this sense Catholic Social Teaching is a set of signposts showing the way forward, or a set of questions by which we can examine the way we live.

Those who share this approach to social teaching take one of two approaches. They either explicate key themes of social teaching, or enunciate social "principles" traditionally found in social teaching.[13] Those who speak of key themes of social teaching touch on broad theological relationships regarding the dignity of persons, their need to form society, their relationship to work, the fact that creation is meant for all peoples and apply these themes, as criteria for discernment, for modern day living.

Others, who speak in the language of principle, draw these principles in different ways. Some derive these principles from the Church's classical definition of a just society as a well-ordered society governed by law. Others see principles as learnings, which emerge as a result of

---

[12] *Catechism of the Catholic Church* (Dublin, 1994) 517.

[13] The bishops of the United States use both approaches in *Sharing Catholic Social Teaching: Challenges and Directions: Reflections of the U.S. Catholic Bishops* (Washington, D.C.: United States Catholic Conference, 1998) 4. The Church's teaching offers ". . . moral principles and coherent values." They also refer to ". . . key themes that are at the heart of our Catholic social tradition."

pastoral action for justice.[14] In either case, these principles aid consistency in commitment and coherency between belief and practice.

All views, except the first, regard social teaching as having moral import for the formation of conscience. Each perspective might arrive at the nature of this obligation on conscience by different means. Some use inductive strategies of an action-reflection-action theological method and others use deductive ones of the classical model of applying principles to real life situations. Those taking a more inductive approach ground the obligation contained in social teaching in Scripture, the tradition of the Church, images of the Kingdom of God, and reading the signs of the times.

The latter three models also will have different interpretations of the level at which social teaching binds on conscience. All four views utilize the social sciences, or non-theological or philosophical information, in different ways.

Augustine's description of the great pluralism in the fourth century should be a consolation to the inquirer into social teaching as he or she confronts these different approaches to a single body of teaching. However, they might be taken back as they encounter criticisms of social teaching in theological and secular literature. We find that criticisms of social teaching often reflect the disappointment of expectations. Members of one school of thought find that the teaching does not stand up to the criteria of adequacy of their perspective.

Criticisms of Social Teaching

While each model of social teaching most likely reflects a practical way a community or school of thought sought to utilize social teaching in practice, no one model actually conveys the full identity of social teaching. Many times criticisms of social teaching reflect the inadequacy of any one model to capture its full import.

Social teaching is often cited for being "too high" or "too low." Some complain that it is so full of ideals and principles it offers no details for concrete action. Others, that it is so localized to a particular situation that it cannot be applied elsewhere. However, when we apply the above models of thought to categorize schools of criticism, we get further insight into common complaints about social teaching.

---

[14] Donal Dorr, *The Social Justice Agenda: Justice, Ecology, Power and the Church* (Maryknoll, N.Y.: Orbis Books, 1991) 83.

Social teaching is not simply a listing of principles for social action or strategies for solving policy questions of poverty, environment, warfare and the like across the globe. When social teaching is judged only in this light, it must answer criticisms that it reflects mainstream progressive political platforms, lacks an adequate social theory or relies on a pre-modern concept of society.[15] Social teaching is also more than an action arising from the institutional Church. When seen mainly as the action of the magisterium and less connected to the life of the Church as a whole, it is often dismissed as unattached to real social movements, and thus politically impotent. Lastly, social teaching is not merely the social implications of the faith. One knows that faith cannot be captured solely in social behavior. The early Church rejected this as Pelagianism. Common sense tells us that appropriate social action is often the result of prudential judgment or discernment, thus rarely can be equated solely with a simple behavior. While the Church must be open to honest criticism regarding the adequacy of its teaching on many fronts, the full identity of social teaching is often not captured in these partial critiques.

Identity of Catholic Social Teaching

Brian Hehir suggests the identity of social teaching is more complex than the above approaches indicate. Social teaching refers to the twentieth-century effort to provide a systematic, normative theory relating social vision of the faith to the concrete conditions of the twentieth century.[16] Social teaching then is a hybrid of moral doctrine, societal criticism, and social vision. Social teaching is dependent upon a living body. It is an act of the Church in context.

Because social teaching is an act of the Church in context, it carries with it the ambiguities of historical knowledge. Social teaching addresses ethical problems whose solutions require information beyond the scope of revelation. It utilizes other forms of knowledge besides Scripture and theology, like the social sciences and philosophy. These other forms of knowledge do not secularize social teaching or strip it of its identity in the Gospel. Rather they serve to aid it to explore the

[15] Paul F. Lakeland, "Ethics and Communicative Action: The Need for Critical Theory in Catholic Social Teaching," *Thought,* vol. 62, no. 244 (March 1987) 60.

[16] J. Brian Hehir, "Personal Faith, The Public Church, and the Role of Theology," *Harvard Divinity Bulletin,* vol. 26, no. 1, 1996.

real human condition of the world today and achieve its rightful place in the alleviation of suffering and injustice. Social teaching also requires a community as a carrier of its import into society as a whole. Hence, social teaching has no identity without the commitment of the members of the Church to its ideals. For these reasons, the social teaching of the Church is more than one social theory among others in the world; it is teaching that comes directly from the heart of ecclesial life.

Social Teaching and the Public Church

Social teaching, as the Church's social encyclical tradition, has in the last hundred years shifted the image of the public Church. Brian Hehir reflects that over time attention to Catholic social teaching has moved the Church from an institution without an explicit social expression of its faith in the modern age to one that in its pastoral practices, institutions, and programs shows more attention to the social dimension of Christianity. While today there is more consensus on the public role of the Church in social policy, we find less agreement on how social activism is linked to the nature of the Church and the place of social Catholicism in personal faith formation.

There are two ramifications of this gap of understanding regarding the public Church and social teaching.[17] First, while religion is a strong and growing force in the way Americans think about politics, activists are often not noticeably influenced by the positions church leadership takes. Hehir notes that this divide can be based on moral, empirical or communication issues, but it also raises the theological question of what resources we use to think about a public conception of the Church and how these resources shape personal conceptions of faith in practice. The key question raised by social teaching is the nature of living faith and its relationship to society.

Second, it is not uncommon to meet in public policy debates the limits of the ethical and purely moral argument to address underlying dimensions of public policy disputes and decisions. These debates often involve deeper issues than knowledge of what is the right thing to do or empirical understandings of the nature of the problem. The deeper issues behind these technical questions are never pressed or pursued. Questions such as to whom are we responsible and for what

[17] Ibid., 248.

are we responsible frame the extent to which a group even pursues a solution to a social problem.

This type of question relies on premoral values often formed or not formed in places like a church community. Premoral values are attitudes and dispositions toward what is good and what is evil in life. Often these goods are taught and held sacred within real communities, not just in abstract systems like philosophies. An important link between social teaching and the life of the Church comes with the recognition that premoral values, as transcendent data, influence the extent that social teaching is even "heard" or received in the Church. When social teaching is seen as policy guidelines, abstract principles or simply moral rules alongside others, its link to a faith vision held and fostered in a community can be forgotten.

An additional factor that links social teaching to church life is its relationship to evangelization. The connection between social involvement and the growth and quality of church life is often not made in first-world countries. Paul VI in his exhortation on Evangelization in the Modern World, *Evangelii Nuntiandi* (1975) stresses that evangelization has a social dimension (EN 29). Human rights, family life, peace, justice, development and liberation involve social conditions "without which personal growth and development is hardly possible" (EN 31). The person "who is to be evangelized is not an abstract being but is the subject of social and economic questions" (EN 17).

Evangelization is the proclamation of Christ to those who do not know him, which involves preaching, catechesis and conferring baptism and other sacraments (EN 18). Yet the document states that the church also seeks to convert both the personal and collective consciences of people, the activities in which they engage, and the lives and concrete situation that are theirs (EN 22.1). In other words, evangelization involves action by the Church to upset the criteria of judgement used in a society.

Evangelization is not aimed only at individuals; it also seeks to transform culture. Today this process is called inculturation. Here we find an important link between social teaching and the life of the Church. The work of evangelization is not just "informational." Evangelization involves the measure of how the points of interest, lines of thought, and sources of inspiration and models of life are in line with the Gospel. Paul VI stresses that no culture can be penetrated with the Gospel without the visible witness of how adherence to Jesus Christ influences how one lives in community (EN 23). This witness is to be grounded in church life: acceptance of the Church, participation in the sacraments and continual investment in the "new state of things" inaugurated by faith in Christ.

Evangelii Nuntiandi depicts the Church's work of evangelization as more than mere social reform. Evangelization involves yet transcends the social, political, economic, and cultural changes the Gospel stirs. The liberation of the evangelizing process is to meet the whole person, including a person's openness to the absolute, or the religious. Changed structures are not enough; individuals within the structures are to undergo a change of heart. The document also argues that this evangelization, which involves the realm addressed by social teaching, cannot be done without the action of the Holy Spirit (EN 75).

Approaching Social Teaching

John Paul II clarifies that the identity of Catholic social teaching is more comprehensive than the common approaches acknowledge. The core of social teaching is a statement about human meaning, or what it means to be human at the beginning of a new millennium. He asserts, ". . . the complete truth about the human being constitutes the foundation of the Church's social teaching and the basis also of true liberation.[18] The Pope's view here is dialectical. The human person is understood in social teaching, not just in himself or herself, but vis-à-vis the complex social systems of the day. Yet, the human person is not just one subjected to economic or political processes. These processes are also to be directed to the good of the human person. The utility of economic and political processes in our postmodern world is measured by how they build community.

The Pope stresses that the human person is the primary and fundamental way for the Church, meaning the promotion of human dignity is essential to the identity and the direction of the Church. In the encyclical *Redemptor Hominis* (1979), John Paul II remarks, this "way" is "traced out by Christ himself," the mystery of the incarnation and the redemption is grounded in God's love for human beings (RH 14). Christ's own model of living through the paschal mystery is the model that the Church herself is to follow.

---

[18] John Paul II, "Puebla Address," *Origins,* 8 (Feb. 8, 1979) 535.

For John Paul II the defense of human dignity and human rights, which is taken up by the Church in social teaching, is more than significant human and moral endeavors, it is for the Catholic Church an ecclesiological imperative.[19] There is need for social teaching, because the Church, by its nature, must engage in the defense of human dignity. Social teaching and the ethic that arises from it, specifies the challenges confronting the Church in mission at a particular period of history. The Church will engage in all four responses as discussed above: in social policy suggestions, in prophecy, in moral guidelines and principles. But the meaning of the Church's social ethic transcends "teaching" as social policy or enunciation of moral principles. It is inseparably linked to the inculturation of the gospel and reflects the heart of the mission of the Church.[20]

The social transformation the Church envisions is grounded in its doctrine of grace. It is founded on the belief that without the Spirit the most convincing dialectic has no power over the heart. Implicit in social teaching, therefore, is the message that its social mission involves the continued conversion of the Church and its members.

Summary

We began by suggesting that there is no uniform approach to social teaching, as the social encyclical tradition. People bring different expectations to this body of literature and subsequently criticize it by application of different criteria. However, John XXIII, in *Mater et Magistra,* Christianity and Social Progress (1961), reveals the true identity of social teaching, as inseparably linked to the life of the Church, in a simple statement. "If it is indeed difficult to apply teaching of any sort to concrete situations, it is even more so when one tries to put into practice the teaching of the Catholic Church regarding social affairs. This is especially true for the following reasons: there is deeply rooted in every person an instinctive and immoderate love of his own interests; today there is widely diffused in society a

---

[19] J. Brian Hehir, "John Paul II: Continuity and Change in Social Teaching of the Church," in *Readings in Moral Theology No. 5: Official Catholic Social Teaching,* Charles E. Curran and Richard A. McCormick, S.J., eds. (New York: Paulist Press, 1986) 255.

[20] Michael Paul Gallagher, S.J., *Clashing Symbols: An Introduction to Faith and Culture* (London: Darton, Longman, and Todd, 1997).

materialistic philosophy of life; it is difficult at times to discern the demands of justice in a given situation" (MM 229). John XXIII goes on to say one only understands the social teaching of the Church about economic and social life when one practices it (MM 232). The Church has a central role in fostering and sustaining this practice.

It takes a converting and transformed heart not only to carry out the imperatives of social teaching but to understand its logic in the first place. For this reason, the social teaching of the Church is only fully understood within the matrix of living the life of the Church, the sacraments, prayer, community, and doctrine. Social teaching requires a social conscience to be understood, and such a conscience is fed by service, prayer, worship, and the example of community one finds within the Church. While it is true that social teaching is written also to all people of good will, its logic, and practice finds an echo in those who share church values, albeit from different supports and practice.

Social teaching finds its true identity linked to church life because its practice is an authentic mark of that life. Authentic Christian faith needs the concreteness of its social doctrine. Christianity is not a modern form of religion that promises to protect one from the pain and evil we find in society. It is not a religion that removes one from human existence insofar as it is imperfect, full of risk, and open to pain. Faith in Jesus Christ, who became human, opens us to his way. This way is not a way out of the conditions of human existence, but a way through them that leaves one basically intact. Followers of Christ ask to be saved from the contamination of evil, not to be delivered from this world or from the human condition. The theologian Karl Rahner defines Christianity in these terms: "Jesus Christ, faith and love, entrusting oneself to the darkness of existence and into the incomprehensibility of God in trust and in the company of Jesus Christ, the crucified and risen one, these are the central realities for a Christian."[21] Social teaching is a public voice of the Church, which calls it to concern and action for those aspects of society and the world that culture can ignore but followers of Christ cannot.

As Augustine long ago, we inquire into the relationship between faith and life in society. We see that social teaching provides us with one way the Church has responded to society since the time of the industrial revolution. As we look closer into the nature of social

---

[21] Karl Rahner, *Foundations of Christian Faith* (New York: Seabury, 1978) 324.

teaching, we can see that all four models of social teaching: social policy, prophecy, moral doctrine, and social principle mirror functions of social teaching. Yet, no one model alone retrieves social teaching's full ecclesial identity, which we will name, as the Catholic Social Tradition. Catholic Social Tradition is found in the living Church, the believing Church, the worshipping Church, the converting Church, the prophetic Church, the suffering Church, and the serving Church. All these dimensions of church life are involved in the full tradition. Hence, before we inquire into the history of social teaching in the second part of this book, we will examine how a vision of faith, spirituality and the Church are always involved when the Church shares its social thought.

Chapter Two

The Faith to Walk

The crisis of faith today is not disbelief; it is paralysis before the question, what is worth my effort? Too often the answer to this question is limited to material success. It is not uncommon today to feel positive about one's own life, but hopeless about the problems of the wider society. Some feel nothing of significance can be done to change our world. The systems and power of the globe are beyond our control. The hope that we can make a difference is dulled by the feeling that there are no alternatives. Our choice seems limited to the search for a niche, a fit, where we can be immune to the problems of the world and work out some private version of peace and happiness.

This crisis is fueled for some by a sense of estrangement from the moral-spiritual power to do and be what we might be. Powerlessness before anything except the most banal choices stands in paradox to a modern life steeped in options. This new situation of faith challenges the significance of faith today. Is faith, as Marx held, just an opium, a fantasy with no impact or substance? The lyrics of the song, "we walk by faith and not by sight" suggests the contrary. The Vatican II document *Gaudium et Spes,* The Pastoral Constitution on the Church in the Modern World (1965) claims that faith offers a vision of life for walking (GS 11). Just as Jesus asked the paralyzed man in the Gospel of Mark 2:1-12 to get up and walk, when he "saw the faith" of those who brought him for healing, the church links faith to the power to walk, or love. Yet what is faith and how does it fuel the work of justice?

Summons to Faith in Social Teaching

Social teaching calls all human beings to have faith and act from faith. It offers this message not just to members of the Church, but to the whole world. Through social teaching the Church does more than raise consciousness about social issues, it calls all people to transcendence. What is the faith to which social teaching calls the world? How do our understandings of faith in Christian theology help us understand a faith that does justice?

Medieval and early modern theologians defined faith in terms of the spiritual faculties of intellect and will. However, contemporary theologians are inclined to see faith centered in the whole personality.[1] Faith is a free-centered act, which has ramifications in all the dimensions of our human existence, including the cognitional, the volitional, and the emotional.

Faith is an experience, which is defined by its affinity with and distinctness from other human experience. The British philosopher Ian T. Ramsey suggests religious experience involves disclosure experiences, which evoke discernment and commitment. A disclosure experience is a human experience from which insight into the meaning of human life can be derived. Revelation itself can be viewed as a series of disclosure experiences, from the patriarchs, through Moses and the prophets, down to God's full disclosure in Jesus Christ.[2] The disclosures contained in the Scriptures fall into a pattern in which there are recurrent themes that highlight the nature of the God-human relationship. As the Christian community prays the Scriptures, they gain insight into their current relationships with God, others, and the world through the lens of the constants portrayed in Scripture. The disclosure of God's relationship to us occurs then in light of our relationships in real life, and there it takes on meaning. These disclosures continue to be meaningful to Christians today as we use them as clues to understand our current situation.

The reality that the ultimate power by which our lives are ruled is the personal reality of God, whose loving mercy surrounds and sustains us, is a central and recurrent theme of these biblical disclosures. The center of life is not empty but contains the presence of the goodness of God, loving us, sustaining us, and calling us to share in and to create

[1] Avery Dulles, S.J., "The Meaning of Faith in Relationship to Justice" in *The Faith that Does Justice*, John C. Haughey, ed. (New York: Paulist, 1977) 12.

[2] A. Richardson, *History Sacred and Profane* (Philadelphia: Westminster, 1964).

life. Key to this religious experience is a reciprocal sense of the ultimate meaning and ultimate value of human life that is grounded by God's presence in it.

Faith is response to this disclosure. The act of faith involves discernment of ultimate meaning of life and commitment to its relevance in our world. Faith evokes not only this conviction and commitment but also a trusting obedience to God as one who loves, who wills, and who acts.[3] Faith is a response of the human self in face of the Absolute. It is a conviction, a commitment, and a trust.

The Church sees faith as a call to transcendence that both grounds human life in a horizon beyond itself and opens to human beings a path to holiness through the call of conscience (GS 41). We experience the call to transcendence in the summons to accountability by our conscience, and the call to "more" in our lives. Here we mean not more money or a better position, but the "more" of quality and depth. The psychologist Gerald May claims all people share this search for meaning. While people may call this search by many names, the longing for wholeness, completion or fulfillment, it is ultimately a desire for God.[4]

Faith is a response to this longing and willingness to open ourselves to its meaning in our lives. The experience of the call to transcendence is also the experience of God as mystery, intimate and involved in one's life, even if this experience is fleeting and transitory. At the level of moral experience, faith manifests itself as the acceptance of the invitation to move out to others and the world in love, rather than to turn into oneself in egotism. At a religious level, faith is our mode of participation in the Kingdom of God, the Kingdom that we earnestly seek in the Our Father, "Thy kingdom *come*."

In Christian understanding, faith is more than a detached contemplation of a truth external to ourselves, nor trust in a power external to the world in which we live. Faith, writes Peter Hodgson, is "a liberating power that 'saves' life, giving it wholeness and efficacy in the midst of bondage, estrangement and guilt."[5] Social teaching calls members of the Church and all people of good will to faith. The call to faith implicit in social teaching is both human, or anthropological and religious.

---

[3] Dulles, "The Meaning of Faith in Relationship to Justice," 13.

[4] Gerald May, *Addiction and Grace* (San Francisco: Harper, 1988) 1.

[5] Peter Hodgson, *New Birth of Freedom* (Philadelphia: Fortress, 1976) 333.

Human Faith

Faith is essential to hear the message of social teaching. Faith is the courage to trust in the possibility of meaning in a world of fatalism. It is confidence that human action makes a difference before nihilism, the cultural attitude that nothing matters. Faith spurs the freedom to believe in a better world before the deterministic forces of the market, international systems, and the deadening force of cultural habits. Faith is required to know not only that my life has meaning but also that the world has meaning. Faith at a human level is the act of risk by which I seek to go beyond myself to seek the truth and to love.

Reflection on our capacity to take responsibility for our lives and the world is a window on the experience of faith. As we experience ourselves free to make choices, we also know that we can reject a possible opportunity and simply settle for what is. We can open ourselves and try what is better, or we can make remaining comfortable in the present our main goal and objective. Money, power, status quo, class interests, or ethnic superiority can take precedence over opening ourselves to a new plan or program, which threatens our self-interests.

In theological terms we can use our freedom to open ourselves to Mystery, or to love, or we can make some finite object in the world our ultimate concern. As no finite reality can satisfy the dynamism of transcendence in the human spirit, this not only blocks efforts toward the common good; it frustrates the human spirit. The Church holds that no finite reality can satisfy the dynamism of transcendence. Because the human person is spirit, he or she is oriented to nothing less than God. This orientation is a constitutive element of human person.[6]

Faith links the human heart to the fundamental call of social teaching, to work toward a more just world. This call, which stirs our hopes and elicits our faith, could not be heard unless there was a fundamental openness to it within the human spirit. Contemporary theology holds that this openness is basic to being a human being and is possessed by all people, regardless of their formal religious identity.

Faith and Transcendence

The fact that human beings can ask questions about themselves, their relationships, and their world is an indicator of their transcen-

[6] Karl Rahner, "The Concept of Mystery in Catholic Theology," *Theological Investigations* IV (New York: Crossroads, 1982) 36–76.

dence. Social teaching assumes this experience of transcendence deep within the human person. The theologian Karl Rahner understands the human being primarily in terms of this potential to question. Questioning is at the root of the human search for meaning and fulfillment.

Rahner reflects on the human experience we often observe in children. A child asks why, and this question leads to another. At an adult level this fundamental questioning attitude goes beyond the realm of childhood inquiry. By coming up with one answer and solution, one opens oneself to another, and yet another. Even the Church does through this process. The history of social teaching shows the Church and society searching for solutions to some of the worst ills of industrialization and modernization. As each possibility and solution is surpassed, a previous solution shows itself to be only a finite horizon of question. For Rahner, the experience of expanding the horizon of possibility in modern life grounds us in the awareness that the human person is someone with an infinite horizon. "The infinite horizon of human questioning is experienced as an horizon which recedes further and further the more answers man can discover."[7] Modern life itself can lead the human person to experience themselves as transcendent.

Transcendence explains why the human person is not static, rather is dynamic, a process, on the way toward a goal that is nothing less than the infinite itself. Despite the fact we are immersed in the world, we experience ourselves as transcending the world of our immediate experience. Even the experience of living in a rapidly changing culture, changing social patterns, new discoveries of science reinforce this insight. Yet, we experience our transcendence most fully when we use our freedom to love. Modern theology suggests that every time we know or choose anything in particular, we do so against a horizon of limitlessness. We experience the absolute mystery as the term of our transcendence.[8]

A final evidence of the human call to transcendence is in the modern experience of indignation. Through various media, observation and listening to others, we are aware that things are not in order in the

---

[7] Karl Rahner, *Foundations of the Christian Faith* (New York: Seabury Press, 1978) 31–32.
[8] Karl Rahner, "The Experience of Self and the Experience of God," *Theological Investigations* XIII (New York: Crossroad, 1983) 123–24.

world. Good people, however, are unwilling to give evil an equal footing with good. Indignantly we say, "This shouldn't be!"

This "no" to the world, as we find it, hides a deeper "yes." It discloses a better world of our hopes. This better situation, yet unknown, engages our energies and imagination. We devise plans to carry out our intent to make changes in the world. We invest in this vision and act as if love is worth the effort. Both believers and nonbelievers have this contrast experience of a "no" and that of an open "yes."[9] Implicit in human transcendence is the call to hope for a better world.

If transcendence is such a deep dimension of human life, why do not all human beings have religious faith? On the one hand, the experience of a sense of the Absolute, of transcendence, of hope, or even the call of conscience is more basic and more inescapable than any other type of thinking or reflection; on the other hand, recognition of God's existence does not automatically flow from it. The experience of the Absolute or of our transcendence does not impose itself upon us like a concept or sense experience or even a deep feeling. We do not automatically make the transition from the experience itself to a recognition and interpretation of it at a conceptual level. This accounts for the fact that good people can read, learn from, and actually implement the values and ideals of social teaching without consciously embracing the religious faith that motivates them. Yet modern theology holds that even those who expressly deny God may also implicitly experience God in their efforts to be faithful. In the words of Rahner,

> Wherever there is selfless love, wherever duties are carried out without hope of reward, wherever the incomprehensibility of death is calmly accepted, wherever people are good with no hope of recognition, in all these instances the Spirit is experienced, even though a person may not dare give this interpretation to the experience.[10]

---

[9] Edward Schillebeeckx, *Church: The Human Story of God* (New York: Crossroad, 1990) 22.

[10] Karl Rahner, "How is the Holy Spirit Experienced Today?" in *Karl Rahner in Dialogue: Conversations and Interview, 1965–1982*, Paul Imhof and Hubert Biallowons, eds.; Harvey D. Egan, trans. and ed. (New York: Crossroad, 1986) 142, as quoted in Declan Marmion, *A Spirituality of Everyday Faith* (Louvain: Peeters, 1998) 117.

Rahner defines religious faith in terms of the human search for meaning, not only of my life but of all life. The experience of faith in the Spirit of God is the positive and unconditional acceptance of one's own existence as meaningful and open to a final fulfillment, "which we call God."[11]

How does someone come to know that God is the face of what one knows as mystery in life? Theologians remind us that the experience of God is not to be thought of as merely one experience among others. Rather it constitutes the ultimate depths and radical essence of all spirituality and personal experience of love, faithfulness, hope.[12]

Both positive and negative experiences can engender an experience of God in modern life. We can awe at the greatness, goodness and beauty of everyday life, and the advances of our modern culture. We can marvel at the daily acts of faithfulness, responsibility, love and hope that sustain the social level of human living. However we can also sense the darkness of modern culture and fear that we are going to sink into chaos internationally and a culture of death in our national realities. We can ask, are we simply surrounded by absurdity and death? Does the apparent lack of choices in a single world economic system condemn us to continue on a path where 20 percent of the world population consumes 80 percent of the goods of this world? All of these questions pose to us the quandary, in whom and in what do we trust?

Religious Faith

Religious faith is the act of trust by which I surrender myself and my meaning to God. I hear the Christian revelation about who God is because in my heart is the question of the meaning of my existence. If I receive my meaning from culture alone, from money, from upward mobility, receiving meaning in God may prove to be "unnecessary" in my life. For many years we spoke of the phenomenon of atheism. Yet, in modern life the choice between acceptance and rejection of religious faith may not be a particularly dramatic choice. Today, rejection may take the form of evasion or postponement. Acceptance, on the

---

[11] Karl Rahner, "The Certainty of Faith" in *The Practice of Faith* (New York: Crossroad, 1983) 32.

[12] Karl Rahner, "The Experience of God Today," *Theological Investigations* XI (New York: Crossroad, 1982) 154.

other hand, involves an act of surrender and trust, and ultimately of investment. Religious faith is in the end an act of trust.

We cannot come to knowledge of God without this trust. We cannot come to the meaning of life simply by accessing the progress of our lives. Life accounts never quite "add up." Looking over their lives, many will find happy experiences to record and difficult ones. If we were to do a "balance sheet" there would be good will, mistakes, sin and disasters, repentance and forgiveness. God can never be inserted just as an individual entry in order to strike a balance between debit and credit. In religious faith we find ourselves ultimately unable to balance our life's accounts, and prove once and for all that life has meaning, rather we must simply surrender. Religious faith requires surrender to God. Rahner claims that in religious faith, people surrender, ". . . to the hope of an incalculable final reconciliation of their existence, marked by the presence of the One whom we call God."[13]

No one comes to religious faith simply through the drives of human life. Rather God communicates in grace within the structure of human knowing and loving, as limited, yet open to what is ultimate. It is in everyday existence where men and women listen for the possible Self-manifestation of God in a human word.[14] God reveals God's own Self as personal and loving and acting.

Revelation, in this sense brings awareness that the horizon encompassing all human life is the saving God. This is the primary perspective of all social teaching. Human life is the abiding presence of God in which God offers to humanity God's Self and the possibility of the free response of faith. In social teaching this free response involves commitment to the transformation of culture and society.

Through special revelation, and through the person of Christ, the believer knows that God is more than the metaphysical condition of the possibility of human knowing and loving. Rather this field of knowing and loving can now be interpreted through faith as the presence of God and the ground of Christian hope and love. Religious faith in the Christian community is the identification of the ultimate possibilities and limits of human life and the world with the revelation of Jesus Christ. While the challenges of human growth are ex-

---

[13] Karl Rahner, "Experience of the Holy Spirit," *Theological Investigations* XVIII (New York: Crossroad, 1983) 200.

[14] Stephen Duffy, *The Graced Horizon* (Collegeville: The Liturgical Press, 1992) 209.

perienced and faced through human faith, religious faith interprets the process in relationship to God. We see now that believers and nonbelievers share the experience of wanting the world to be a better place and both struggle for justice. Believers, however, see the face of God in this experience and name the unfolding of a better history as God's gift.[15]

Human faith and religious faith work together. We see the concreteness of faith recorded in the Bible. In Exodus there is a human process of liberation whereby the Israelites liberate themselves from the hands of the Egyptians, a real evil in their lives. It took human faith to risk leaving Egypt. However, as believers reflected on this experience they understood that YHWH saved people from Egypt. Before events are seen in the light of religious faith, they are first experienced as meaningful events in themselves. Often it is difficult to distinguish these two types of faith, since they are intertwined in everyday experience. Social teaching calls on both kinds of faith. It calls on all people of good will to address the most urgent problems of society, and it manifests and fosters the living faith of the Church as it does this.

Religious faith, then, grasps the religious significance of human action that in fact liberates, heals or establishes communication. Religious faith makes clear how an experience relates to God's promise to save. Missionaries often ask if they are working in a poor country, should they simply provide better living conditions for people, or should they also preach Jesus Christ? We believe, as Church, that even if better living conditions are provided, something is missing, if people do not have the opportunity also to know Jesus Christ. While Christians acknowledge that God's Spirit acts beyond the boundaries of the Church, they also hold that God's promise to save is most fully grasped through Jesus, whom Christians testify is the Christ. No one can make this leap between Jesus and the Christ except in the power of the Spirit. The work of the Church simply serves this encounter between God and the person.

Faith is a grace, not just a personal decision. Yet the "leap" of faith is not something extrinsic to the human person. Nor is it something just based on the attractiveness of Jesus Christ, as if Jesus is presented as a personality purely extrinsic to the person, like George Washington

---

[15] Juan Luis Segundo, *Faith and Ideologies,* John Drury, trans. (Maryknoll, N.Y.: Orbis Books, 1984) 81.

or a movie star or great historical figure to be admired. To be led to
faith is always to be assisted to understand what has already been
experienced in the depth of human reality; in other words, human beings in their very structure of knowing and loving are oriented to this
revelation.[16]

Faith in this sense is the supernatural elevation of the transcendence of the human spirit, thanks to God's self communication in
grace. Rahner understands this communication given to every human
person and is thus not dependent on prior evangelization. Both human
faith and religious faith open one to the ethical challenges to transcend what is, and work toward a better world order. This is the challenge and call to faith of social teaching. However, for Christians,
a deeper meaning of this struggle can be fostered by probing the full
meaning of the doctrine of salvation.

Social Teaching and the Meaning of Salvation

For many Catholics and other Christian believers, the vision of
what it means to be saved is often restricted to a notion of personal
salvation. God frees me from sin and enables me to share with God
happiness in heaven. This is echoed in formal teaching. The magisterium teaches that the act of faith is a complete surrender of the human
person to God, one which includes acceptance of revealed doctrine,
voluntary submission to grace, and trust in God's promises (D 798,
1989; Vatican II Constitution on Revelation, art. 5).[17] Faith is seen as
knowledge of revealed truths, *fides quae creditur;* and trusting obedience to God in a personal encounter with him; *fides qua creditur.* Faith,
in this sense, is the disposition for justification and ordination to final
salvation in the beatific vision, or participation in the life of the glori-
ous Christ, the salvific, and eschatological dimension of faith. The
Christian community holds that Christ is the center, the foundation,
and the final goal of faith. However, the salvation that Jesus Christ
brings is not only salvation from sin on a personal level but a Lord-
ship over all social structures and systems of the world.[18]

---

[16] This is a traditional teaching of the Church found in Aquinas, *De Veritate,*
q. 14, a. 2, and reformulated in transcendental Thomism by Karl Rahner.

[17] Karl Rahner, "Faith" in *Dictionary of Theology: A Concise Sacramentum Mundi.*
Karl Rahner, ed. (London: Burns and Oates, 1975) 500.

[18] Philip Land, *Catholic Social Teaching* (Chicago: Loyola University Press, 1994)
131.

Social teaching helps us to see the link between the real evil from which we are freed in baptism and the social evil that pervades our society. The Council of Trent, in line with the early Council of Carthage, affirmed the solidarity of every person with the sin of Adam, or original sin. Even though recent reflection has modified the understanding of original sin to more easily address modern ways of thinking, the teaching of the council is a permanent witness to the fact that there is a reality of evil behind particular sins of individual persons.

In contemporary times, the Church has taken a journey deeper into the mystery of sin and evil and of faith, to plumb its social dimension. Today the human condition is also characterized not just by the situation of being born with original sin but as a condition of massive human suffering, caused not just by human ineptitude, but by sin. While the New Testament writings of John and Paul testify to a sin of the world, sin as embroiled in the conditions of life itself, the Church put less emphasis on this type of sin and how it pertained to society in its earlier history. In the past we perceived our social structures something like nature itself, a "given" over which we had little influence. Our justification, which flowed from the justice of God, made us just, and renewed us in mind and spirit. However, its application to social structures was not developed, nor was our responsibility to change them. The world in this former system was a place of temptation that distracted us from the tasks of holiness.

Today however we have more tools to understand the human influence on society, and the influence of society on individuals. We realize that structures and institutions affect the acts of individuals and in a large measure enter into the morality of individual acts.[19] *Gaudium et Spes* reminds us that an individualistic ethic is no longer enough. Rather each person is charged, ". . . to promote and assist the public and private institutions dedicated to bettering the conditions of human life" [GS 30]. The salvation brought to us by Jesus Christ is also to free us from all forms of alienation, whether social, economic, or political. The council states that we should not reduce the salvation brought by Christ simply to an impetus for social reform, but we should find in its freedom the commitment to social responsibility.[20]

---

[19] Judith A. Merkle, "Sin" in *The New Dictionary of Catholic Social Thought*, Judith A. Dwyer, ed. (Collegeville: The Liturgical Press, 1994) 883–88.

[20] "Earthly progress must be carefully distinguished from the growth of Christ's kingdom. Nevertheless, to the extent that the former can contribute to the better

The bishops at their Synod on Justice in the World in 1971 remind us that the Church should engage itself with justice and the transformation of the world, for its mission concerns the "redemption of humanity and its freedom from every condition of oppression" (JW 6).

Most Christians formulate their ideas concerning from what and by whom we are saved through their understanding of doctrine. Doctrines are fundamental beliefs about the God-human relationship, passed on through the tradition of the Church. The need for formal doctrine and church tradition is a fundamental consequence of being persons who are oriented toward spiritual realities yet within everyday life. We cannot grow spiritually except by being and acting in the world, and relying on very concrete constructs that attempt to mediate the divine. In other words we can only seek God, pursue the mystery through rituals, rites, doctrines, prayers and the concrete community of religious activity.[21] In this sense, the entire life of the Church, including its formal teachings, are important in understanding the full message of social teaching.

Faith as Vision

Traditionally, the Church has seen faith as an illumination of the human heart. Augustine saw the human soul as blinded by sin. Through the healing grace of God the soul was drawn from the imprisonment of sin to a connatural attraction to know God and be in union with God. Without faith, one could not know or love God. Faith was the beginning of wisdom, the first step toward the beatific vision. For Aquinas faith was the light of the soul, a light that was between the light of natural reason and the light of glory. Faith, as a gift of God, was already a participation in the life of God and the beatific vision.[22]

These views of faith, while upholding the deep personal union that faith effects between God and the human person, suggest the kind of faith better developed in detachment from the world than in involvement in it. Since through faith we experience an illumination and see what we cannot see on our own, it is important to ask the

---

ordering of human society, it is of vital concern to the kingdom of God." *Gaudium et Spes,* 39.

[21] Rahner, *Foundations of the Christian Faith,* 140–42.

[22] Dulles, "The Meaning of Faith," 14ff.

nature of this illumination. Is faith given to know God in anticipation of heaven alone, or also to find meaning in our lives on earth and to bring about the Kingdom of God?

Faith as conviction, discernment, commitment has often in the tradition been developed as conviction alone. In this sense, faith was seen as an assent to a body of revealed doctrine. Faith is a firm assent to that which the Church authoritatively teaches in the name of God. In this approach, faith is equated with belief.

Why would such an assent be considered faith? Revelation is accepted not because it is seen to fulfill any yearning for communion with God, but simply out of reverence for the authority of God the revealer. Faith in this sense is an act of religious submission, an obedience of the intellect. Vatican I depicts faith as a supernatural virtue by which, through the grace of God, "we believe the things that he has revealed to be true, not because of their intrinsic truth perceived by the natural light of reason, but because of the authority of the revealing God himself, who can neither deceive nor be deceived."[23] Faith here is expressed in articulated beliefs, and involves an assent to formulated truth guaranteed by a revealing God.[24]

However, when faith is perceived only as assent to revealed truths, it is seriously threatened by rapid cultural change. Believers can equate faith with clinging to formulations handed down from the past, without any consideration of the time-conditioned character of their formulations. Even Catholic Social Teaching must be understood within the context in which it was written. When faith is equated only with assent to revealed truths, one's understanding of faith is incomplete. When new experiences in society need to be integrated into one's faith vision, these experiences can appear to fall outside the categories of a traditional worldview, and therefore beyond the sphere of faith. Salvation can be sought only in the sphere in church and worship while the secular sphere of economic, social or political life can be left unaddressed. A limited view of faith can miss the challenge to inculturate the gospel in modern culture. If faith's sole grounding is in a sense of the authority of the past, such authority

---

[23] Denzinger-Schonmezer, *Enchiridion Symbolorum* (32nd ed., Freiburg, 1963) no. 3008. See Josef Neuner, S.J., and Heinrich Roos, S.J., *The Teaching of the Catholic Church,* Karl Rahner, S.J., ed. (New York: Mercier Press, 1967) nos. 35, 32.

[24] Juan Alfaro, "Faith," in *Sacramentum Mundi,* vol. II, Karl Rahner, ed. (London: Burns and Oates, 1968) 314–15.

can be an anomaly in a postmodern society, tentative about all systematization. The consequence is the relevance of faith for modern life is dismissed. The assent of faith is important. However, the assent of faith involves not only acceptance of meaning about sacred truths handed down in the tradition but also the significance of those truths for the contingencies of daily life and the challenges of global society.

The traditional approach to faith as assent is of value to those who approach social teaching. It upholds the fundamental character of faith as a personal assent to the invitation of God. In the New Testament we observe a series of individuals encountering Jesus and choosing either to believe, or not. The believer today does not encounter Jesus Christ directly, as did people of old. However, if God's revelation in Christ is expressed in human language, which in the church is the language of doctrine, acceptance of this revelation must involve an assent of our minds. Only by such means can we know the message of Christ and respond to God's ongoing revelation.

Doctrinal propositions do objectify the message of Christ, yet through the doctrinal message, faith connects with the revealed reality. The fact that faith involves our minds as well as our hearts is inseparable from its ecclesial character. The social teaching of the Church, as moral doctrine, is part of the Church's doctrine. When we take seriously the revelatory character of all doctrine, it is easy to see that social teaching cannot be the Church's "best kept secret." As moral doctrine social teaching reveals the eschatological nature of faith, how the hope established through the Gospel sustains us to transform and humanize our world. Faith not only looks beyond the world and death in eager expectation of eternal life in the encounter with the risen Christ (1 Cor 1:7-8), but faith also seeks the Kingdom that has not yet fully realized in time. Work for justice is the passion to bring this Kingdom with Christ into every dimension of human life.

Modern culture has its own "doctrines" or teachings about the meaning of life. Modern theories of progress suggest life will get better and better with each succeeding generation. Cultural attitudes toward success claim that upward mobility will bring about such an individual autonomy that citizens will be rewarded with having to depend less and less on others or be influenced by their wills.[25] Yet we

---

[25] Robert Bellah, *Habits of the Heart: Individualism and Commitment in American Life* (Berkeley: University of California Press, 1985) 143.

realize that modern culture lacks a language of meaning when life's negative experiences occur.[26] The rosy outlook of secular culture makes faith, salvation, and church extra baggage on a non-conflicted secular life journey. In contrast, the call to faith implicit in social teaching provides believer and nonbeliever alike with the vision of human existence that is consistent with its call to transcendence.

In conclusion, in common practice we do connect faith in its essential connection to love. We expect people to "practice what they preach." Yet in modern times we must emphasize that faith also provides a vision of hope regarding this life, as well as the next. Faith can bring meaning to many aspects of life that otherwise might appear unintelligible, including negative experiences of poverty, death, and the self-denial of sacrifice. Perhaps more than any other experience, faith before the cross in modern life illumines that faith is "given" and graced, and not simply continuous with cultural optimism. In this sense faith gives vision for the journey depicted by social teaching. A puzzling problem, however, is how one links this faith vision with the calculations and information necessary to actually engage in society and bring about social change.

Transcendent Data

Faith is not just an intellectual pursuit, but a movement of the entire personality that affects how one thinks, acts and feels. Another way to say this is a person of faith operates by a different set of data over life, transcendent data.[27] Transcendent data can be compared to a store of utopias within each person. "They are meaning-structures that would come to occupy first place if reality were not what it is or seems to be."[28] When we work for "a better world," "global peace," or "sustainable community," we are engaging with transcendent data. These data do not transcend human experience, but generally exceed direct verification because their fulfillment occurs less often in life than their opposite. Transcendent data point to the fact that reason itself is influenced by values in moral decision-making.[29]

[26] Christopher Lasch, *The True and Only Heaven: Progress and its Critics* (New York: Norton, 1991) 40–81, 529ff.

[27] Segundo, *Faith and Ideologies*, 23, 74–75, 84–85.

[28] Ibid., 73.

[29] Juan Luis Segundo, *Berdiaeff: Une reflexion chretienne sur la personne* (Paris: Montaigne, 1963) 333, 338, 341.

Transcendent data are different than scientific data in that they are not able to be proven empirically, instead are self validating. We cannot prove that "honesty is the best policy." We simply act on it. Instead of empirical reality being the measure of deciding the truth or falsity of transcendent data, *they* are the measure for judging reality.

They are values in the deepest meaning of the word, yet values that function in our moral experience as "reasons" for behavior. Transcendent data do not stem from anything that science or reason can decide. "Experiential reality by itself can do little to alter them since they determine what is perceived and how it is perceived."[30] We use these data to justify our behavior. Transcendent data are decisive for the acceptance or rejection of specific values because they have to do with the possibilities for satisfaction that those values can or cannot provide. We learn these life beliefs from others.

For example, a young doctor, after a five-year practice, decides to give up her position in her medical office and go to Africa to help with refugee needs. One group of her colleagues thinks she is crazy to leave her place in her profession. Another group of colleagues tells her she represents the best of their profession. Obviously, these two groups of people are acting from different sets of transcendent data or beliefs about the possibilities for satisfaction that values can or cannot provide. Transcendent data influence our perception of empirical reality by forming our hierarchy of values, or our ontological premises, and our "filters" on reality, or our epistemological premises. We rely on both in making moral decisions.

Ontological premises measure the order or structure we place on reality. They form the structure of our hierarchy of values through which we perceive the concrete possibilities and limits in a particular situation. They insure that values are not just juxtaposed, but rather are structured in a meaningful hierarchy by each person.

On the other hand, epistemological premises determine the way we will get to know reality. They filter my cognitive field and determine what is going to penetrate my perception and how it is going to do it. We can understand the nature of epistemological premises by pointing to their function.

> Far from being a neutral photograph, cognition can present one and the same reality to me as either a triumph or a defeat—be it death, money,

[30] Segundo, *Faith and Ideologies*, 108.

imprisonment, or whatever. It is not so much that I start right out evaluating them as such, but rather that I already perceive them in that way. They enter my cognitive field as data which, straight out of reality, either oblige me to revise my way of acting or confirm the latter as consistent with the data.[31]

Ontological and epistemological premises affect reason in a manner prior to reason's function. They are premises that are operative in one's personal world-view but also have their source in a person's faith. While they exist as assumptions about life in general and in this way function as an aspect of rationality, they are learned in faith through the witness of others.

These premises about what is worth our effort, for whom are we responsible, what is necessary for our happiness, influence our decisions. They account for the human experience that ratiocination seems to be able to do very little to "convert" human beings from one meaning structure to another. These transcendent data, their transmission and their logic are as much a part of social teaching as its policies and suggestions for shaping the world order. Because these data are learned primarily in relationship, this is another reason why social teaching is meant to be understood and "carried" not just as one position among many on a continuum of social programs in society, but also as a lived tradition in the Church.

Faith and Ideology

A final consideration of the faith implicit in social teaching is how to apply the insights of faith to concrete problems in society. Because the world operates by different laws than the creative values of love, human beings must calculate how to make their values effective in the human condition. We need to know the best and most economical way to combine the meaning of existence with the know-how to manipulate reality. We employ two types of knowledge in this discernment: faith and ideology.[32]

Faith is a type of knowledge that is not based on any direct or scientifically verifiable experience, but depends on the witness of others.[33] Faith enables us to structure our life around some specific

[31] Ibid., 92.
[32] Ibid., 71.
[33] Ibid., 25.

meaning.[34] This function of faith holds true whether it is anthropological or religious.

Faith in this context is more than a relational sense of confidence regarding eschatological salvation.[35] Rather, faith is the act of risk through that one devotes the use of one's freedom to the positive task of love.[36] Thinking and acting from the stance of faith is something that produces tangible results. A life ordered by the "bet" of faith can be compared and contrasted to others. The human choices generated by faith can be experienced as satisfactions and weighed alongside others. Faith, in this sense, is more than a religious act. It is an epistemological structure that orients the total meaning structure of life.[37] Faith involves how one perceives reality and how one will respond.

Religious faith is related to this more fundamental human faith. Through basic human faith people form relationships, create values, and respond to the problems in society.[38] Religious faith, in the Christian sense, builds on this more fundamental type of faith. It is an identification of the ultimate possibilities and limits of human life and the universe with the revelation of Jesus Christ. As one theologian puts it, "Faith is the surrender of one's whole being to the person, community and teaching of God, who strictly speaking saves men and women with his grace from the evils which, here and now in this life, point toward absolute paralysis, absolute enslavement, absolute

---

[34] Ibid., 5. Segundo's concept of anthropological faith is not contentless. He assumes this faith is a commitment in varying degrees to change and improve the world. *The Liberation of Theology,* John Drury, trans. (Maryknoll, N.Y.: Orbis Books, 1976) 81.

[35] Since Segundo understands faith in a more general manner than the *initium fidei* of the act of Christian faith, he considers anthropological faith itself as an expression of the supernatural and as having a place in morality. This faith has its origin in the universal call to salvation. As anthropological faith it defines the common moral road of all men and women. The project of human freedom is synonymous to the obligation of love against which all human beings will be judged. *Grace and the Human Condition,* John Drury, trans. (Maryknoll, N.Y.: Orbis Books, 1973) 111. This type of faith, albeit in different language, is also suggested in the encyclical tradition. See the 1987 encyclical of John Paul II, *Sollicitudo Rei Socialis*, 38.

[36] Juan Luis Segundo, *De la sociedad a la teologia* (Buenos Aires: Carlos Lohle, 1970) 92.

[37] Segundo, *Grace and the Human Condition,* 111.

[38] Segundo, *Faith and Ideologies,* 50.

death."[39] Social teaching calls forth both human faith and religious faith.

Social teaching makes clear that the transcendent quality of religious faith is marked by its concern for history and the task of love. True religious faith is evidenced in a concern to establish the divine will as the Kingdom of God on earth. It always involves a greater facility, because of the conscious God-human relationship it involves, to enter into a process of growth or change in values. In other words, religious faith leads to ongoing conversion. "Religious faith in the fullest sense of the word is a faith which is the source of a new meaning structure."[40]

Faith relates us to a God who is concerned about the problems of our history. Through faith we are called to grow in our capacity to interpret the events of our human experience in the light of God's intentions for the world.

However, to allow faith to impact the problems in society, the Christian requires another kind of information. Christians need data about politics, economics, trade, and culture and turn to other tools, the social sciences, economics, anthropology, and environmental studies. The social action called for in social teaching requires a combination of faith and ideology.

Ideology is a way of knowing related to efficacy.[41] The word "ideology" can designate any system of "ideas" about the world and how it works. In contrast to the empirical world, ideology is the systematization of our perception of what we observe. It is an interpretation of the concrete tools and mechanisms operating in a situation at any given time. We rely on our ideology to make our values operative within the structures of everyday society. Ideas as to why people are poor, what are appropriate careers for men and women, why and when it is legitimate to wage war, are part of our ideology. Another name for ideology is "world-view," our current ideas as to how the world works.[42]

---

[39] Segundo, *Grace and the Human Condition,* 156.

[40] Segundo, *Faith and Ideologies,* 71.

[41] Ibid., 16, 109.

[42] Sometimes the world ideology is used in a pejorative sense as a distortion of the truth. This is not its meaning in this text. Yet, an adequate ideology would include an understanding of the ideological mechanisms and distortions in any given society. See Segundo, *The Liberation of Theology,* ch. 2.

Social teaching calls for a faith that requires both faith and ideology. Faith and ideology mix when our faith provides vision and our ideology specifies the concrete options open for our action. In the interplay between faith and ideology, we grow in our capacity to engage in effective social action. On the one hand, faith provides the vision to see new possibilities and the motivation to carry out a plan. It provides the political will to take action. On the other hand, ideology can make demands on our faith. When a negative social experience shakes us into reformulating our view of the world, we realize that we must respond differently. Faith without ideology is ineffective since ideology provides us with the knowledge and skills of a particular situation.

Conversion is a process of constantly revising our ideologies so they better conform to reality. Social teaching calls us to know current approaches in politics, economics and the sciences to select efficacious ways to bring about social change. It also asks us to correct our views of the world when they are wrong, such as biases, prejudices and overly nationalistic attitudes. To do this requires both faith and ideology.

Church membership, as upheld in social teaching, involves not only belonging to a community of faith and worship but also taking up a value stance toward life. The Church calls her members to take on certain "premoral" values or beliefs about the dignity of human life, the right to work, to participation, the inherent equality of all men and women, the right to food, clothing and shelter, education, and health care. The belief that love is worth our effort, sacrifice is indigenous to life, creation is for the good of all, and belief in solidarity are "transcendent data" that form the social identity of church membership, and in this sense, constitute part of its faith.

Church membership, in the social teaching tradition, involves the transmission and acceptance of such transcendent data as expressions of the ultimate possibilities and limits of life as revealed through the person of Jesus Christ and decisive for everyday social living. Members are called to be witnesses and follow the witness of those who practice this "way" of being people of faith in society. Lastly members are called to adhere to a tradition of faith and practice that gives them access to God, as the ground of those data, and the human dignity they support.[43] Social teaching in the Church arises from a tradi-

---

[43] Segundo, *Faith and Ideologies*, 81. It is important to note that this approach emphasizes the Church as a "tradition" of human beings who have learned how to

tion of faith that provides a "way" of being in society and reveals in the process more than a social theory or even a teaching. Rather, it is also a way of faith to God and connected to the deepest mystery of the Church.

---

learn from God. In this sense, the Church as a "tradition" is a living reality, not just a school of thought. A tradition is borne along by a chain of witnesses to certain values. A school of thought establishes continuity in the logic of preferred arguments, not in the quality of the people and their experiences. We are suggesting that the social tradition of the Church involves its encyclical tradition, but also the witness of its martyrs, its social action and community life, its sacramental and mystical tradition.

Chapter Three

Spirituality for the World

Spirituality is the "way of living" we adopt to respond to God and to integrate our lives. Our spirituality fosters our intention to know God, to find freedom in our lives, and to love. Through these means we seek to transcend ourselves and participate in God's life, or in what we understand to be Ultimate reality.[1] The word "spirituality" does not occur often in Catholic Social Teaching, but its meaning does. Social teaching offers a vision of God's intention for the world and God's involvement with it. It testifies that God acts in the world through humans, and humans are called to discern and respond to God's initiative. Most strikingly it does this, not in a manner that ignores the world we face each day, but in light of its most profound challenges.

When Christians call on their faith to respond to social issues many spiritual questions arise. Are we righteous if we live a "good life" but do not reach out to the poor and the oppressed? Does it make a difference if we try to build a more just world, or should we leave all in God's hands? What role does seeking justice have in the spiritual life? Do we need the Church? How do we balance prayer and social action? Among these questions in Christian spirituality, two are central in the Catholic Social Tradition. The first is whether we need the Church. The second is the role of working for justice in

---

[1] Michael Downey, *Understanding Christian Spirituality* (Mahwah, N.J.: Paulist Press, 1997) 15.

standing in right relationship with God. Let us explore these two questions by beginning with the meaning of spirituality.

What Is Spirituality?

Spirituality is the response of the individual heart to the call and summons of God, as mystery, and one's expression of and search for that experience in one's relationship with God, self, others, and the world. Spirituality is the experience of the transcendent that is expressed in one's world. Christian spiritual experience involves awareness of God, the mystery that grounds life, as one who is in love with us and wishes to communicate with us. Christians believe that God's self-communication reached its fullest expression in history in the person of Jesus.

Christian spirituality is centered in the reality of the mystery of Jesus Christ and the Trinity. Christian faith is grounded in the acceptance of what revelation affirms about Jesus. It lives by the reality of God's saving intervention in history in Jesus Christ. Without the reality of Christ, faith is all process, ungrounded process at that, and has no content. In other words Christian spirituality is a process of growth grounded in Jesus Christ. If Jesus' death and resurrection are not real, it would be impossible to live Christ's death and resurrection as a reality in Christian spirituality (Gal 2:20). Later social teaching, especially that of John Paul II, is grounded on this Christ-centered foundation.

The incarnation of Jesus Christ marks Christian spirituality indelibly. The Word of God spoke to us through Jesus Christ was revealed, not in some mysterious way, but through human words. Christian spirituality is centered on belief in the incarnation. Christians believe that human words can express Divine Words, that Jesus' human body can assume the Son of God, and that human reality is the stuff of Christian spirituality. When social teaching addresses the problems of society, the Church assumes society is the place where we will meet God and discern God's intentions.

These essential beliefs about Christian spirituality also support the spiritual search of the individual Christian. We too are situated in a real world. We are bound by time and space, yet concerned over the conditions of our world. We are excited by new discoveries and capacities, yet ponder our capacity for destructiveness. We are deeply steeped in humanity, yet radically open to what is Absolute. Chris-

tians believe that Jesus Christ, who was both human and divine, reveals the mystery in which we find our true fulfillment. Jesus is the
"light" who shows us and enables us to be in this world and yet participate in God's life at the same time. Jesus Christ is the mystery
that grounds Christian spirituality, and the spirituality of the social
mission of the Church.

The Church

Just as Jesus Christ gives us access to God and to our full humanity, for the Catholic, the Church gives us privileged access to Jesus
Christ.[2] The Church is the community formed around Jesus Christ
and receives its meaning and structure from him. The Church is those
who believe in the self-communication of God and who explicitly pro-
fess this in historical and social form. This belief is future-oriented,
and follows a "way" of life. This community believes and hopes, yet
awaits the revelation of this self-communication at the end of history,
of both the individual and of the world.[3]

While there is great interest in spiritual matters in contemporary
culture, there is tension regarding the role of the Church and official
religion in this search. We see as far back as the twelfth century people
in disagreement as to how the human person relates to God. A spiritual
movement, the Waldenses questioned the mediation of the Church in
the spiritual quest. They noted the worldly interests and political
power of the Church, rejected the hierarchical priesthood and thought
of the pope as the Antichrist. Dissatisfaction with the Church led to a
questioning of its relevance for the spiritual life. This debate continued through the time of the Reformation and later in rationalism.[4]

Today the question still remains: do we need the Church to be
spiritual? Does Christian spirituality have an ecclesial dimension?
Questioning of the role of the Church in the spiritual life is an icon of
post-Vatican II unrest in the Church. The unsettling effect of Vatican II,
rapid change with insufficient catechesis, left some wondering where

[2] Richard McBrien, "Roman Catholicism: *E Pluribus Unum*," in *Daedalus: Journal of the American Academy of Arts and Sciences* (Winter, 1982) 77.
[3] "Faith" in *Sacramentum Mundi*, vol. 2, Karl Rahner, ed. (London: Burns and Oates, 1968) 313.
[4] Marie-Joseph le Guillou, "Church," in *Sacramentum Mundi*, vol. 1, Karl Rahner, ed. (London: Burns and Oates, 1968) 313–17.

their Church had gone. Those accustomed to a more traditional Church felt that it had changed beyond recognition. Others were affected by the impression given after Vatican II that the hierarchy was reluctant to acknowledge the ecclesial responsibilities of women and eager to keep them in roles that are complementary, and by the same token subordinate, to those of men.[5]

For others, disagreement over moral stances in the Church surfaced mixed feelings toward the role of church identity in personal spirituality. Recent scandals in the Church have caused some to question its integrity. First-world culture does not support church membership. It stresses the autonomy of the individual, making community involvement optional and unnecessary for spiritual well being. For these reasons among others some look less to the Church's hierarchy for spiritual leadership. The search for spiritual inspiration is displaced from the Church to other areas of experience, as in music, art, poetry or fiction, and the new picture of the universe emerging from contemporary astronomy.[6]

Another factor in this ambivalence regarding the Church is the rise in communications in the world. The growing availability of immediate communication, as well as more opportunities for travel and cross-cultural education at home through exposure to "new peoples" in our local environments, introduces interested Christians to spiritual concepts, methods, and practices that have their origin outside of the Judeo-Christian cultural matrix. Direct exposure to the spiritualities of other great religions, new philosophies, new methods of meditation and contemplation, new tools for personal understanding coming from Indian lore and the Sufi tradition, all have become part of the modern experience of Christian spirituality. These experiences have both positive and negative effects on the maturation and deepening spiritual identity of Christians.[7]

[5] George Tavard, "The Ecclesial Dimension of Spirituality," *The Gift of the Church*, Peter Phan, ed. (Collegeville: The Liturgical Press, 2000) 228.

[6] See, for example, Briane Swimme and Thomas Berry, *The Universe Story: From the Primordial Flaring Forth to the Ecozoic Era: A Celebration of the Unfolding of the Cosmos* (San Francisco: Harper, 1992).

[7] See, for example, "Report on the Sects or New Religious Movements: Pastoral Challenge," *Information Service/Secretariat for Promoting Christian Unity* 61:3 (1986) 144–54. Letter of the Congregation for the doctrine of the faith to the bishops of the Church on "Some Aspects of Christian Meditation," 15 October 1989, *Origins* 19:30 (1989) 492–98.

When there are shifts away from a church-centered spirituality, people can mistakenly identify spirituality with the interior life or the inner dimension of the person, dissociated from groups or the community. This can set the stage for a weakening of links between spirituality and justice, or at least remove action for justice from its grounding supports in the church tradition.

A holistic view of spirituality considers not just intimate experience of "the Other" but the effect of this search and encounter in one's relationships.[8] This wider view is captured in the Old Testament where the people of Israel learned that right relationship with God involved not just cultic worship but relationships with their neighbors that reflected the covenant that God had with them.[9] Today, many accept that spirituality involves a loving response to others in service and love but question whether they need others as companions on the spiritual journey and the supports that the practice of a religion offers.

Do We Need Religion?

Karl Rahner treats the meaning of church membership by going back to his understanding of the human person. The human person is an incarnate spirit, someone oriented to transcendence yet living in a material world. The human person is not just a "being," but rather a "being in the world." A consequence is that the human person must seek God, pursue mystery through ritual, rites, dogmas, prayers, etc. Faith in God, as personal and mysterious as it is, is always entered into historically, in a time and place.[10]

Vatican II assures us that the spiritual or the supernatural does not happen in some plane apart from life, but by entering more deeply into life and history. God's communication happens in history, and in the "signs of the times." A consequence of the incarnation is revelation, and redemption enfolds in our own lives and in those of whole peoples in everyday life.

[8] "Spirituality," in *The New Dictionary of Catholic Social Thought,* Judith A. Dwyer, ed. (Collegeville: The Liturgical Press, 1994).

[9] See George Lobo, S.J., *Guide to Christian Living: A New Compendium of Moral Theology* (Westminster, Md.: Christian Classics, Inc. 1985) 23–65.

[10] Declan Marmion, *A Spirituality of Everyday Faith: A Theological Investigation of the Notion of Spirituality in Karl Rahner* (Louvain: Peeters Press, 1998) 57.

Rahner explains that religion is necessary, not just because it arises from a felt human need and thus can be dismissed as a need if not felt. Rather, the only way to enter into one's own transformation to fulfillment, or follow a spiritual path, is in time, in history. If God shares God's Self through revelation, Scripture, then we must ask where is the group in time that lives by this revelation.[11]

J.M.R. Tillard takes this argument one step farther. The letters of Paul imply that reconciliation with God is inseparable from entrance into the unity of sisters and brothers in the body of Christ. The self in this way has been absorbed into Christ. The new way of life "exists in the space opened by Christ on the cross," and this space is the ecclesial body.[12] The Christian way of life is a way of life in solidarity. Others are essential to it, not simply because, by going toward others, believers exercise their generosity or gain merit. Rather, others are radically essential because life "in Christ" is that of a body, the body of reconciled humankind vivified by the Spirit of the living God.[13]

A Catholic Way to God

The Church is composed of many churches. The Church universal is the communion of local churches, and the Body of Christ is composed of denominations. If we examined the Methodist, the Lutheran, the Anglican and the Baptist tradition in social mission, we would find common themes in biblical spirituality and shared concerns about social issues. There are many churches, but one Body of Christ. The Catholic Church understands itself as that which embodies and manifests all the institutional elements that are necessary for the integrity of the whole Body. *Lumen Gentium 14* states:

> They are fully incorporated into the society of the Church, who, possessing the Spirit of Christ, accept her entire system and all the means of salvation given to her, and through union with her visible structure are joined to Christ, who rules her through the Supreme Pontiff and the Bishops. This joining is effected by the bonds of professed faith, of the sacraments, of ecclesiastical government, and of communion.

---

[11] "Faith," op. cit., 313.

[12] J.M.R. Tillard, *Flesh of the Church, Flesh of Christ: At the Source of the Ecclesiology of Communion* (Collegeville: The Liturgical Press, 2001) 11.

[13] Ibid., 12.

Within this communion of churches, the Catholic way to God can be distinguished from other forms of Christian spirituality in broad terms. Richard McBrien finds three principles that are characteristic of Catholicism, mediation, sacramentality, and communion. Since Catholic social teaching is rooted in Catholic faith, these characteristics are implicit in the social tradition.

The spirituality of a Catholic is based on the principle of mediation. Catholics hold that the invisible, spiritual God is present and available to us through the visible and the material. Belief in Mary, the Mother of God, and the communion of saints, the role of intercessory prayer, all reflect this distinctive Catholic approach to spirituality.[14] Catholic spirituality places an importance on the ordained ministry of the priest, as a mediator, not only between the person and God, but also between persons in the Church to build the community at large.

Catholics hold that these material things are made holy by reason of divine presence. For this reason, the mystery of the Church has always had a significant place in the theology, doctrine, pastoral practice, moral vision, and devotion of Catholicism. The Church itself is a sacrament. Sacramentality marks the second characteristic of Catholic spirituality. Sacraments are not just signs of faith. God is not just in the sacramental action, God achieves something in and through that action. Created realities not only embody the presence of God; they also make that presence effective for those who avail themselves of these realities. We meet God, not just in the recesses of our consciousness, or in the integrity of our conscience. The encounter with God is a mediated experience, transmitted in the historical, and affirmed as real by the judgment that God is truly present and active here, in this event, in this person, and in this object. The liturgy, especially the Eucharist, is central to Christian life.[15] Sacramental celebration expresses an ethical horizon for Christian living. In celebrating the sacraments, believers express their hope for how the world

---

[14] See, for example, two books by Elizabeth Johnson, *Friends of God and Prophets: A Feminist Theological Reading of the Communion of Saints* (New York: Continuum, 1998); *Truly Our Sister: A Theology of Mary in the Communion of Saints* (New York: Continuum, 2003) and Mary Hines, *Whatever Happened to Mary?* (Notre Dame, Ind.: Ave Maria Press, 2001).

[15] Michael Downey, *Understanding Christian Spirituality* (Mahwah, N.J.: Paulist Press, 1997) 81.

should be, and how human beings should conduct themselves in the Church and in the world.[16]

John Paul II has extended the concept of sacramentality to the actions of the baptized Christian in the world. All human life has a sacramental dimension that he explains in three ways. First, the human person is self-determining through action; we become ourselves through our choices. Second, the redemption of Christ recovers the dimension of "mystery" for all humanity; Christ frees us to own our spiritual identity. Third, the experience of faith in Christ shared by the Church uncovers a sacramental dimension of human action. For John Paul II human action can be both a sign and an instrument of God's presence in the world.

Ethics itself is a terrain for the realization of sacramentality.[17] Belief in the sacramental dimension of human living creates a relationship between liturgy and life, worship and work, and sacraments and spirituality. It also marks the Eucharist as the heart and soul of a Christian ethic. In its celebration Christians commit themselves to building a world rooted in community and justice. Christian spirituality takes seriously in everyday living that which is said and done in liturgy.

A third characteristic of Catholic spirituality is communion. Catholics believe that the God who works through secondary causes wills to bring us many into a final unity, without destroying the individuality of any of the creation. A Christian spirituality rooted in the mystery of the Trinity emphasizes community rather than individuality. The invitation to enter into the life of God is lived out in building up the communion of all peoples in justice and peace.

The call for communion is coming from various sectors of life today. Ecologists alert us to the communion we are to have with the earth. This vision of communion challenges an approach to nature that exploits it and dominates it for human use alone. New peoples are calling us to build a new communion in our parishes as multicultural and multi-racial realities. Women are asking the Church to be more inclusive of their experience in ethics and liturgy, administration and the call to ministry. Today we seek a global ethic as religions

---

[16] See Louis-Marie Chauvet, *The Word of God at the Mercy of the Body* (Collegeville: The Liturgical Press, 2001).

[17] Gerard Beigel, *Faith and Social Justice in the Teaching of Pope John Paul* II (New York: Peter Lang, 1997) 55.

search to find a common denominator of ethics in natural law principles that foster the building of community.[18] Principles of mediation, sacramentality, and communion are expressed differently in various historical periods in the Church. Yet they are implied in the spirituality of each period of social teaching.

Spirituality and Justice

There is a cultural belief today that if God is in one's life, then the human desire to be self-determining is undermined. People reject a relationship with God today through the fear that union with God means a diminishment of human autonomy. They believe to have a spiritual relationship with God is to remain a child. However, Karl Rahner takes a different view. God is not a force competing with others in the world. Rather, God is primarily the ground that establishes the world in its own reality. Consequently drawing closer to God "does not absorb the creature but makes it more independent."[19] The spirituality of social teaching assumes that union with God makes one more able to take action in the world. Doing justice is to be done through relationship with God. Our human action is significant in bringing about God's Kingdom on this earth. In fact, we address the realities of salvation in and through a commitment of freedom to a way of living in this world.

Latin American theologians have contributed greatly to the understanding of the significance of action for justice in the Christian life, through their notion of praxis. "Praxis," or intentional historical activity aimed at justice, is essential to understanding Christian spirituality. Christian faith is itself a doing, not merely a being or an experiencing.[20] Praxis as the following of Christ is an act of faith by which the Christian participates in Jesus's own liberating ministry in this world. Theologian Jon Sobrino writes that by our very practice of justice we reach God as mystery: "The mystery of God, who is always greater is reached through the *greater* which is found in the demand to

---

[18] Jean Bethke Elshtain, "Really Existing Communities," *Review of International Studies,* 25, 1 (1999) 141–46.

[19] Karl Rahner, "Jesus Christ," in *Sacramentum Mundi,* vol. 3, Karl Rahner, ed. (London: Burns and Oates, 1968) 207.

[20] Rebecca S. Chopp, "Praxis," *The New Dictionary of Christian Spirituality,* op. cit.

humanize humankind, to re-create it."[21] The choice for God, in the choice for justice against injustice, is a choice to be with Jesus, or against him. Acting because of the demand for justice arises from the needs of others mirrors the radical call to faith given by God, and not arising simply from our own consciousness.

Justice and the Church

It would be wrong to see concern for justice in Christian spirituality simply as a product of this century. Social consciousness belongs to the very essence of Christianity. The salvation Christians proclaim affects not only the individual but the whole of society and creation. In this way justice has always had a role in the spirituality of the Church.

We see the roots of the integral role of justice in spirituality in biblical times. The people of Israel were called to a moral responsibility that transcended that of proper cultic worship, as practiced by others. Living in covenant with YHWH demanded special relationships with others and with the world. The moral code of Israel was not just a code for individual conduct but the expression of the will of God for the entire community of Israel. The unity and cohesion of the community was to be maintained and fostered by the observance of the commandments and separation from idols.[22]

In Isaiah 42:1-4 we see justice as a core concept in Old Testament:

> Behold my servant, whom I uphold, my chosen, in whom my soul delights. I have put my Spirit upon him, he will bring forth justice to the nations. He will not cry or lift up his voice, or make it heard in the street; a bruised reed he will not break, and a dimly burning wick he will not quench; he will faithfully bring forth justice. He will not fail or be discouraged till he has established justice in the earth; and the coastlands wait for his law.

Scripture scholars tell us that these verses were written to a people who were about to form a new community, close to or after the fall of Babylon. The prophet encourages the people, telling them that YHWH is supreme and works in history. In the face of their discouragement,

[21] Jon Sobrino, S.J., *"La promocion de la justicia come exigencia esencial del mensaje evagelico,"* Diakonia, no. 12 (December 1979) 45.
[22] Lobo, *Guide to Christian Living*, 23–43.

they are reminded that the unfolding of history is guided by YHWH in his servant, and YHWH's power surpasses the power of the nations. YHWH will guide the future of those who now feel they have no future. The prophet calls the people to commitment, and promises as always with his election, YHWH's power to accomplish this future.

Israel's role, in the image of "servant," is linked to the establishment of *mispat* or justice, the acts of YHWH that bestow salvation within a community-covenant context.[23] Israel here is both the servant and the ones to whom the Servant is promised. Justice is God's action, as well as a call to Israel to be the agents of God's action.[24]

The servant is an image of the true Israel and the true Israelite. The servant, one "in whom my soul delights," has a task to bring forth justice, despite all opposing forces. Yet the manner in which the mission is to be fulfilled provides a corrective to Israel's concept of how justice will be established. The servant's methods are not those of force like the tyrant's. Rather, the servant is to reveal God's own power. Justice in this way is integral to the conception of YHWH's covenant with his people.

When the New Testament writers spoke about Jesus, they used the language and terminology of Second Isaiah. It is likely Jesus used this same language to understand himself. At his baptism and transfiguration Jesus is the one in whom the Father is well pleased. Luke's Gospel links Jesus' ministry with that of the servant. The Gospel of Mark conveys that the disciple is to be like Jesus, not a person of power, but a servant of all who gives his life for others (10:35-45). The passion of Jesus is also interpreted within this image of the suffering Servant who establishes God's justice. Jesus' death exposes and unmasks the powers (1 Cor 1:18).

The gospel writers and St. Paul testify that it is through Jesus' cross and resurrection that we experience redemptive liberation. Love in the New Testament is the central social principle. Love however is God's justice that surpasses human justice.[25] Love is not just a posture toward one's friends and intimates but also extends to one's enemies.

---

[23] W.A.A. Beuken, "*Mispat*. The First Servant Song and its Context," 22 *Vetus Testamentum* (1972) 8–11.

[24] H. H. Rowley, *The Servant of the Lord and Other Essays on the Old Testament* (London: The Lutterworth Press, 1952) 49–57.

[25] Peter C. Phan, *Social Thought: Message of the Fathers of the Church* (Wilmington, Del.: Michael Glazier: 1984) 17.

Since God's own relationship to humanity is one of indiscriminate, gratuitous mercy and compassion, so this posture is to be that of the Christian.

In Paul we see an integral link between salvation and justice. Salvation is found in the event of the incarnation and the cross and resurrection of Jesus. This is the revelation of the justice of God, God's expression of his fidelity to his creation and the saving victory over the evil in creation. The Christian life involves entering into the New Passover, being lead out from oppression and slavery.[26] Faith in Jesus, in turn, involves a personal sharing in the life and death of Jesus and his work of justice. The "justice of God" comes through faith in Jesus Christ (Rom 3:22). These links between faith in Jesus, justice and life in the Christian community are throughout the New Testament.

Early Church

The community of the church from its earliest times sees itself as a community called to do justice. The justice and love as taught by the Old Testament and fulfilled in the life of Jesus are the principles that shaped the early Church's understanding of particular issues of social justice and guided its involvement in the surrounding society. While more or less prominent in different periods, there is no time in the history of the Church where we do not find a sense of its relationship to justice.

In the first centuries of the Church, the practice of Christianity was illicit and persecuted. The social concerns of the Church were mainly directed toward its own members. However, after the time of Constantine, Christianity became an integral part of public life. Its concept of charity then had to assume a social dimension, and it had to begin to work out its own relationship with the state. Powerful gaps between the rich and powerful and the poor and weak were addressed as part of church discipline. In its early days the Church saw oppression in the society as part of the consequence of original sin and simply to be endured. The Church reached out in charity but did not see the call to be just as a call to change social structures. The Church accepted slavery. However, it also worked to teach that slaves

---

[26] John R. Donahue, S.J., "Biblical Perspectives on Justice," in *The Faith That Does Justice,* John C. Haughey, S.J., ed. (New York: Paulist Press, 1977) 93.

and masters were equal in God's eyes. In this way it tried to improve the conditions of slaves, yet accepted the social structure as it was in the society.

The early Fathers were concerned about the social conditions in the world at their time. They developed a general framework for understanding what we see as early social doctrine. They took up the responsibility to interpret the requirements of justice and love in Scripture in the new historical circumstances in which they lived. General themes found in their teaching show an ideal of justice and equality in the economic and social promotion of the oppressed and destitute classes. We find a critique of the exploitations and injustices perpetuated by the ruling and wealthy classes. They also proposed concrete actions to remove these unjust situations, including the obligation to share "wealth," either material or personal gifts, at the service of others. "Having" for the Fathers has a social function; it is meant to serve the community.[27] They taught the social purpose of private property, that material goods are destined by God for the use of all human beings to satisfy their basic needs.

The early Fathers did not produce a comprehensive and autonomous system of social thought. Instead, they developed views on the person and society and gave their social critiques in light of Scripture, the teaching of Jesus and those of the apostolic Church. Platonism and Stoicism did influence their thought, but they only appropriated philosophy to the degree it coincided with what they found in Christian revelation. Many of their specific teachings no longer apply in a secular democratic society. However, their method of not just repeating Scripture but interpreting its meaning in new circumstances grounded the Church in the responsibility to interpret the world of its time in light of the Gospel and its call to justice. In this way they conveyed the solidarity and hope that is at the heart of the message of the Gospel and formed the spirituality of the Church in their times.

Middle Ages

In the Middle Ages St. Thomas reformulated the teaching of the Fathers to deal with the problems of a society moving away from the feudal system. This gave the Church a new language to interpret its call to justice in this changing situation. Aquinas based his teaching

---

[27] Phan, *Social Thought*, 29.

on justice mainly on the teaching of Aristotle. The thought of Aristotle entered the West at this time and proved to be more secular and positive than those of the Fathers.[28] Aquinas' reflection on justice flows from his entire moral system. He believes the same moral norms that govern individual human actions and choices should also regulate social, economic, and political activities.

For Aquinas, justice is "a habit whereby a man renders to each one his due by a constant and perpetual will." (II-II Q 58.1). Justice concerns the recognition of what is objectively due another, their "right." Justice concerns what we actually do to another, rather than our intentions. It is always directed toward another, and it is one of the few general virtues capable of imposing a new orientation on all actions. While other virtues have as their goal the perfection of the person, justice focuses on the good of the other.

Thomas taught that the end or goal of general justice was the common good. Injustice, in turn, is contempt for the common good. It is the refusal to recognize the debt owed to another person or the debt owed to the common good. Often this debt is expressed in civil law. Thomas gave a special role to authority to form law in the manner that is just.

Justice is also "particular" meaning it involves specific behaviors toward other individuals. Justice concerns external actions of one person with another in what concerns external deeds and things. Justice is what you do, not just what you say or think. Justice can be distributive or communitative. Distributive justice directs the distribution of the common goods of a society among members according to their merit. Communitative justice is concerned with exchange, that which governs individual's dealings with one another (II-II Q. 61.1,3). Stealing and cheating are obvious sins against communitative justice. General justice is expressed through the particular actions of communitative or distributive justice.[29]

In Thomas, justice is a virtue that can orient the whole of the Christian life, yet it relates particularly to the ordering of relationships in society. The basic solidarity owed to others is more than a

---

[28] Robert Barry, O.P., "Contribution of Thomas Aquinas," in *The New Dictionary of Catholic Social Thought*, Judith A. Dwyer, ed. (Collegeville: The Liturgical Press, 1994) 940.

[29] Jeremiah Newman, *Foundations of Justice: A Historico-Critical Study in Thomism* (Dublin: Cork University Press, 1954) 70–85. Jean-Yves Calvez and Jacques Perrin, *The Church and Social Justice* (Chicago: Henry Regnery Co., 1961) 141ff.

feeling of "togetherness" or shared consciousness. Rather, it is an objective order of rights and duties considered both from the perspective of the responsibility of individuals to one another and of the responsibility of the whole to individuals.

Aquinas' thought shaped Catholic social thought from the late Middle Ages until the early days of the Industrial Revolution, and even to the Vatican Council. His teaching on justice is a centerpiece of this contribution. Concepts like distributive justice were used to discern and delineate problems that far surpassed the conditions of his own time.

Aquinas' teaching on justice and other social-ethical theories also gave the Church powerful tools to interpret how the common good was a guiding principle for society, economics, and politics as it moved from a feudal system to a new form of society. Later, Thomas' distinctions served as a means to approach emerging capitalism and to provide an alternative vision to the "invisible hand" of the market mechanism. It gave the Church a language to call for a social order that was just, charitable, and virtuous in changing circumstances. It provided a vision beyond the piety of the day to link Christian spirituality to emerging issues in modern society. As we explore each period of modern social teaching, we will see how these core concepts of the role of justice in Christian spirituality are reinterpreted in light of contemporary problems. The justice tradition of the Church has been carried by a believing community to the present. To belong to this tradition as a Christian and a Catholic is to be more than an individual believer, it is to be a member of the community called the Church.

The Coming of the Kingdom of God

The *Our Father* is perhaps the most universal prayer in Christian spirituality. When Christians pray "Thy Kingdom come," they pray for more than a place in heaven. They state that salvation is not just something about the next world. Rather, redemption is an ongoing mystery, and God's Kingdom comes in everyday life. There are three ways this is evidenced in Christian spirituality. The Kingdom is a project; the Kingdom is a social reality, and the Kingdom is a concrete sign in the world. In these ways, among others, the coming of the Kingdom is central to Christian spirituality.

In Christian spirituality the Kingdom is not just information about the next life; it is a reality in this one. The Kingdom is the value judgment of God. It characterizes the relationship between God and human beings as one in which typically first place is given to those who suffer. Certainly the life of the Beatitudes upholds this mystery of the Kingdom. The Kingdom is not just a mystical reality, something that will happen at the end of the world. It is a political and this worldly one as well. The Kingdom is integrated into Christian spirituality appropriately as we respect its ultimate source in God, and its implications for human living. These two poles are held in tension in Christian spirituality.

First, the Kingdom is a project; the Kingdom of God is not just the final and ultimate judgment of God, now and in the future, but also the project of human life itself. The "new earth" where justice will abide (2 Cor 5:2; 2 Pet 3:13), will be brought about by God, however, "the expectation of a new earth must not weaken but rather stimulate our concern for cultivating this one" (GS 39).

Human actions have a part in creating the Kingdom, but humans cannot accomplish what belongs only to God. Human action can create the conditions where God's Kingdom can come, but God brings about the Kingdom. The experience is that we work not only to bring about social change but also experience in the process that God is with us bringing the change about. The prayer "Thy Kingdom come" challenges us to transform human relationships in favor of the values of God's reign.

God's final judgment has certainly been a central issue in the Christian spiritual imagination. The image of keeping God's law is first and foremost in this vision. However, social teaching also brings before the conscience the image of Matthew 25. In this biblical image human beings will be judged by whether they helped or refused human need and by whether they did so in a climate of mutual love. If all passes away except love (2 Cor 13ff.) love is what will endure in the new earth. The final action of God will be in fire and justice. God's fire will consume that which has not served the building and enrichment of human life according to God's plan. God's justice will restore what could not be accomplished through human effort.

Christian spirituality maintains a tension between God's transcendence and human action in history. On one hand we use initiative to improve human society; on the other hand we acknowledge and receive the fruitfulness of the results as God's gift.[30] We can never

---

[30] Segundo, *Grace and the Human Condition*, 73.

identify a human project with the Kingdom of God. Rather, we only partially and practically approximate it. The Kingdom in Christian discernment lies in that zone between what ought to be and what is at any given time in history. Vatican II teaches that "earthly progress must be carefully distinguished from the growth of Christ's kingdom" (GS 39). This raises several issues for Christian discernment.

First, there can be no strictly Christian realization of the Kingdom. There are no "Christian solutions" to problems in history, as if knowledge of Christian principles translates immediately into prescribed actions. Rather Christian faith animates the search Christians make with all people of good will for effective programs of social reform. Second, the value of the imagination is brought into the very fabric of Christian discernment and conscience.[31] Moral living involves more than keeping the boundaries of common moral norms. To be effective change agents Christians must be able to evaluate the relative value of some courses of action over others. In Christian discernment this calls for the added focus of the creation of effective solutions to historical problems rather than the single search for just one right thing.

The perspective of the Kingdom in Christian discernment opens our minds to see beyond limitations and frustration. We realize that many human decisions must be made in the direction of an ideal good rather than assuming we can directly accomplish a major change in one try. It respects the fact that evil, often in structures, mindsets, and conditions of life, acts as a limiting factor in any action on behalf of the Kingdom. Sometimes even responsible compromise becomes a means to bring the Kingdom closer to reality. This does not mean compromise of values, but the ability to choose between goods in the accomplishment of limited historical goals and the acceptance of unavoidable evils in the accomplishment of the good. It brings to action for the Kingdom an acceptance of the relative merit of one course of action over another, but not relativism.

The perspective that the Kingdom is a social reality brings the insight that God's reign extends over the personal and social life of human beings, not just individual actions. In Christian spirituality we are concerned whether an action is one of love or egotism. However, this aspect of the Kingdom adds a criterion of what will last or endure

---

[31] Brian Johnstone, "Solidarity and Moral Conscience: Challenges for Our Theological and Pastoral Work," *Studia Moralia* 31 (1993) 65–85.

in human life because of an action. For this reason social teaching urges us not just to perform good deeds but also to build structures, to establish better cultural systems, to safeguard legal protections of human rights. These are serious conditions that govern the possibility of the Kingdom growing in real situations.

Because action for the Kingdom in history is often overcome by evil, human action on behalf of the Kingdom must be both constructive and resistant. Both the possibilities and constraints facing one in any social situation have to be taken into account. Belief that the Kingdom takes root socially maintains the Christian in the often slow and complex process that action for the Kingdom involves. This belief gives new value to planning as a strategy for effective action.

Christian vision for social change admits that the "threshold" theory proves true in many situations. In evolutionary language passing over a threshold means a quantum change. A major change occurs in evolution only after a number of smaller changes. Seen from the perspective of the present, a quantum is not usually perceptible. Rather, it is seen as an increase of what was before. Seen over an extended amount of time, there is newness. The newness of the Kingdom of God often is not a huge social change. The image of the threshold is a more realistic image of its reality in many circumstances.

Also, the social quality of the Kingdom points to the fact that impersonal conduct can be coherent with the reign of God. It recognizes that significant changes in human society proceed from more than personal decisions alone. Collaboration, cooperation, and participation become expressions of Christian spirituality. Factors such as legislation, group action, and constructive use of power, actions that can obscure the distinctions and awareness of individual differences maintained on a more personal level are capabilities that are fostered by spirituality for justice. In other words besides personal initiative and creativity, we need the skills to act communally and in movements. All of these factors contribute to a realistic change in social relationships.

Finally, Christian spirituality assumes that the Kingdom of God is to be a concrete sign in the world. The Kingdom is meant to be known and experienced in this life and not merely to be a motivation for the next life. The Christian "way" of spirituality involves the inculturation of the Gospel, that is, relating the truth of the Gospel to the processes and systems in which people live their lives and become fully human. Key to the inculturation of the Gospel is bringing about unity amid differences in society. The Christian community itself is a sign of the Kingdom. Essential to Christian spirituality is the building of the Church as a community and the establishment of community in society. Through its public institutions, the visibility of the Church is fostered. Service to the world through these institutions is a meaningful expression of spirituality for justice.

Christian spirituality that prays "Thy Kingdom come" is grounded in the belief that what human effort cannot accomplish God will bring about at the end of the world. Yet, the final meaning of the world through the action of Christ will involve the culmination of all human constructive efforts to bring about the Kingdom (2 Cor 13).

The core then of the Christian spirituality that grounds social teaching is a life of faith, hope, and love.[32] Faith is in God's salvation, which, through the death and resurrection of Christ, saves history and each life from dissolution and failure. History cannot now be basically a nightmare. The basic Christian attitudes are not anxiety, skepticism, and nihilism but calm, courage, humor, and alertness.

Hope opens our hearts to the ever-changing newness of history, instead of clinging to the past, or to structures that no longer serve human flourishing. Hope also maintains patience, willingness to wait, and persevering action. It holds onto a confidence in God that excludes the cultural trust in progress, as well as the fanaticism of violence.

Last, love and solidarity feed a daily investment in collaboration, cooperation, and willingness to participate. This translates into dutiful cooperation in the humanizing and pacification of the world. Christians testify by word, life, and suffering that love is worth the effort, relying on God to confirm this life stance at the end of time and in time.

In last analysis whether the Christian will assume personal responsibility for community and history, for progress and decline, for justice and oppression, for culture and cultural decline is in no small part a function of spirituality. The social encyclical tradition can only speak to those who are "hearers of the word," who, through the darkness of the great inequalities of our global society can see and respond to the light of God's Kingdom about to dawn. In this sense social teaching is not just a theory about society and how it should function; it offers a vision of a living spirituality.

---

[32] Walter Kasper, "History," in *Sacramentum Mundi*, vol. 3, Karl Rahner, ed. (London: Burns and Oates, 1968) 44–47.

Chapter Four

The Church in Society

The mere idea of the involvement of the Church in public affairs evokes in some a degree of concern, consternation, and disapproval. They question the appropriateness of such involvement. The Church is a religious body. Can the Church engage in civic and public affairs, outside its primary realm of competence? Does "mixing in politics" weaken its primary religious nature? Can the Church really make a difference in the formation of the social values of its members or in the societies in which it is immersed? Or is the Church so immersed in each culture itself that such a critical perspective is impossible? Over the years the Church developed its response to these questions, as it explained itself and its action. It also formed its social response, not just by what it taught about society but also through how it defined itself as a community before the State and other authorities.

In this process the Church has expressed the biblical value of justice in changing historical contexts. It is a community that carries a tradition. By responding to real issues, it has taken an active role in its own interpretation of justice, and in turn this discernment and action has shaped the Church. Across time we see development in the way the Church views itself in the world, how action for justice is carried out in the Church and in the understanding of justice itself.

Church: A Challenge to Itself

After the time Christianity was accepted as part of the Roman Empire under the rule of Emperor Constantine, "Church" tended to refer the universal, worldwide Church, organized like the civil society. The Church and the state were closely identified through cultural, social, and political forces. As the empire became Christian, the Church became identified with the empire, and perceptible distinctions between Church and state were dimmed. By the eighth century in the West, Charlemange (742–814), the first Emperor of the Holy Roman Empire, called himself the *caput ecclesiae,* or head of the Church. In different ways both in the East and the West, Church and state merged into one.[1] There was at times resistance to this process of identifying Church and empire. There were schisms in the Church, and crises when whole churches broke off communion with what was perceived as the Church of the empire.[2]

From 1300 on a slow breakdown occurred in the medieval consciousness of the Church and its unity with the state. This shift called the Church to vigorously reflect on its nature. As society changed, the Church shifted its reflection from the perspective of a unified Church and state to the new problem of how the power of the Church and the state were independent yet related. Theologians reflected on how the Church as mystery existed in institutional form and how this form related to the civil society at large. They analyzed how the Christian people, its councils, and its hierarchy were to interact in its mission. All of these understandings affected how the Church understood itself and its mission and how it carried it out. Thus, the Church worked out its mission to justice against the backdrop of the question how the Church, as a religious society, related to society and the state. This involved clarifying the nature of the Church itself, as an entity separate from the state.

Church: Mystery and Human Reality

The Church is both mystery and human reality. What distinguishes the Church from other societies is that is it more than a visible organization in society; it also has a religious nature. It is a mystery or sacrament. Its unique relationship with God gives it a unique relationship to the world. The Church in this sense is the Body of Christ endowed

[1] August Franzen, "Church History," in *Encyclopedia of Theology,* Karl Rahner, ed. (New York: The Seabury Press, 1975) 258.
[2] Edmund Hill, O.P., "Church," in *The New Dictionary of Theology*, Joseph A. Komonchak et al., eds. (Wilmington, Del.: Michael Glazier, 1989) 198.

with the Spirit of the Father and the Son. God through the Holy Spirit is the primary ground of the Church. God imparts to the Church the created gifts of the Holy Spirit, faith and charity, which are oriented toward the life of Trinity itself. The mystery of the Church is God, its source and life.

The Church in this sense is the community of those who share in this mystery in Jesus Christ because the object of their lives is the same as that of the life of God. In this sense, the mystery of the Church is inseparably linked with the mystery of the Trinity. It is a visible sacrament of the revelation of the Trinity in the world. It is a sign or instrument of intimate union with God, and of the unity of the whole human race.

However, the community of the Church is more than a shared spiritual consciousness, it is a visible institution. The institution of the Church, understood by its elements, the deposit of faith, the sacraments, the apostolic powers of priesthood, teaching, and governing are all derived from its mystery and grounded in its life in Jesus Christ.

The Church is also a human reality. The Church is the people who adhere by faith to the means of salvation that comes from Jesus Christ and to the means of salvation offered by him. This shared belief forms the community of the faithful. In its human form, the Church is first this community. In this sense the people are the Church.

The theologian Yves Congar claims the Church as a human reality needs God's help. She needs, "in common with all imperfect things" to be helped toward her end and guided. The Church "on the way" is of necessity militant; it is of necessity also governed. God calls us as human beings and hence deals with us in this world as all men and women. As well as calling us to share God's life, the Church on earth assumes the human and social form of any community of men and women bound together in pursuit of a common purpose. Its purpose to "the fulfilling of Christ, who is our peace" makes it unique.[3]

All persons are not part of the Church in the same way. While all persons belong to the faithful and receive the faith, grace, and salvation within the Church, certain individuals are bearers to a certain degree of one or more powers instituted by God and which constitute the Church in the first way as mystery. The structure of the Church in

[3] Yves Congar, *Divided Christendom: A Catholic Study of the Problem of Reunion* (London: G. Bles, 1939) 67–68.

this sense refers to the divine gifts that are bestowed upon the Church through Christ (LG 8). These divine gifts, as participation in Christ's ministry, are exercised through human institutions and structures. Human beings, however, play a role in the exercise of the threefold function of sacraments, teaching, and governing. Inasmuch as fallible people carry out the work of a pilgrim Church both grace and sin play a part. When parts of the Church or people in it fail in their mission, the mystery of the Church remains, although clouded by sin.

The sacraments, teaching, and governing functions of the Church are means of God's self-communication in grace. At Vatican II the Church reflected on its own nature, not with a discussion of its structures and government as its starting point but with the notion of the Church as a people with whom God communicates in love. In this sense God's own self-communication is prior to the grace-bearing structures that are means for the transformation and sanctification of humankind.[4]

Development within the Church arises because, while grounded in mystery, it lives in the flow of history. The Church must follow humanity in its expansion and its movement. The Church always lives "in the world." It draws its concrete structures and forms from history and receives questions from the world. The Church is also transformed by the world as it recognizes authentic values contained within it.

The Church as the Body of Christ

The Church is not just like any human organization in that it is the Body of Christ. This image of the Church unites its life as mystery and the Church as a human reality, the People of God. The divine-human reality of the Church is grounded in the divine-human reality of the person of Christ.[5] Thus, its justice activity is a continuation of Jesus Christ's role as servant. The Church that resides in the mystery of the Trinity and the Church that resides in humanity are joined and united in the Body of Christ.

[4] Timothy I. MacDonald, *The Ecclesiology of Yves Congar: Foundational Themes* (Lanham, Md.: University Press of America, 1984) 280.

[5] "Just as the assumed nature inseparably united to the divine Word serves Him as a living instrument of salvation, so, in a similar way, does the communal structure of the Church serve Christ's Spirit, who vivifies it by way of building up the body," *Lumen Gentium* 8.

The Church in this sense is also constituted by its mission, a mission derived from the mission of Jesus Christ and Holy Spirit. It is a mission to all nations. The Church shares in Christ's role of being mediator between God and humankind. It identifies with him and shares in all his roles and offices, especially in his call as servant to bring justice to the world. After centuries of grappling with the identity of the Church in the modern world, Vatican II defined the Church as a sacrament, a sign and instrument of the intimate union with God and of the unity of the whole human race (LG 1).

After the Reformation, how the Catholic Church was related to other churches and religions became an issue. Are the Body of Christ and the Roman Catholic Church identical? Pius XII in his encyclical *Mystici Corporis* identified the Body of Christ, the Church as mystery, precisely and exclusively with the Roman Catholic Church. Vatican II however stated that this Church, as mystery, *subsists in* the Catholic Church governed by the pope and the bishops in communion with him (LG 8). Vatican II recognized that many elements of sanctification and truth are to be found outside the Church.[6]

Shifts in Understandings of the Church

By the 1890s and the time of Leo XIII, the first Pope to write a modern social encyclical, how the Church understood itself had impact on its understanding of its mission to justice. The notion of the Church that he inherited was formed in previous centuries through the controversies with Protestantism. It was apologetic in tone, defensive of the Church's independence, identity, and mission in society. Roman Catholic theologians defended those institutional structures and offices that Protestant theologians denied, such as the teaching authority of the pope. The mystery of the Church, was "protected" mainly by identification with its institutional life.

In contrast by the 1960s Vatican II placed the theological and pastoral treatment of the Church at the forefront. It emphasized the religious nature of the Church through images of the Church as the people of God, the Body of Christ, and the sacrament of salvation.

The shift from an institutional to a theological understanding of the Church proved significant for defining the Church's social

[6] George H. Tavard, *The Church, Community of Salvation* (Collegeville: The Liturgical Press, 1992) 86.

mission.[7] Its social mission acquired new meaning. When the Church is seen in its religious nature and understood as a sacrament, rather than simply in its institutional structures as a hierarchical organization, its work for justice is also reinterpreted. The social mission is no longer one of the tasks that the institution performs. Instead, the social mission is a symbol and sacrament of the religious nature of the Church. The Church expresses and symbolizes itself in doing its social mission. The Synod of Bishops in 1971 claimed justice is a constitutive dimension of the Church. "Action on behalf of justice and participation in the transformation of the world fully appear to us as a constitutive dimension of the preaching the Gospel, or, in other words, of the Church's mission for the redemption of the human race and its liberation from every oppressive situation" (JW, 36).

The Church and Public Issues

The role of the Church in public affairs is an ecclesiological question, or a question about the nature of the Church. It is not just a question about justice. Brian Hehir claims that social teaching did not have a strong ecclesiological basis until Vatican II.[8] Perhaps the reason for this is the Church focused primarily on its moral influence in society and assumed its own identity. It was only later that the Church found itself facing a complex modern world whose secularized atmosphere tended to dismiss it. This pushed the Church to clarify its identity in the world. When the Church engages in public issues in modern society, the secular society usually questions the appropriateness of its response.

Two practical questions arise when the Church takes part in political life or when religion and politics mix. First, does the Church, primarily a religious reality, have a right to speak on socio-economic and political realities? Second, how should the Church act in public affairs? Since 1891 each pope has answered these questions from a variety of philosophical, common sense, and theological positions.

---

[7] Francis Schussler Fiorenza, "Social Mission of the Church," in *The New Dictionary of Catholic Social Thought*, Judith A. Dwyer, ed. (Collegeville: The Liturgical Press, 1994) 151–71.

[8] Brian Hehir, "The Social Role of the Church: Leo XIII, Vatican II and John Paul II," in *Catholic Social Thought and the New World Order*, Oliver F. Williams, C.S.C., and John W. Houck, eds. (Notre Dame, Ind.: University of Notre Dame Press, 1993) 33.

Leo XIII . . . 1890s

Leo XIII, in the early years of social teaching, worked to move the Church beyond the mentality of his predecessors. Gregory XVI and Pius VI placed the Church in a position over and against modern states through their rejection of the validity of the democratic revolutions of the eighteenth century. When Leo addressed "the social question," or the social problems created by the Industrial Revolution, he shifted the Church's posture toward the world.

Leo used a variety of arguments to explain that the Church did have a right to speak on public problems. He appealed to the memory of medieval Christendom as historical verification of the power of the Church to transform society (RN 27). The Church could teach social doctrine because of its teaching authority. He states in *Rerum Novarum,* that ". . . the responsibility of the apostolic office urges Us to treat the question of set purpose and in detail, in order that no misapprehension may exist as to the principles which truth and justice dictate for its settlement"(RN 2). He added, "It is We who are the chief guardian of religion and the chief dispenser of what pertains to the Church. . . ." (RN 15).

Critics countered Leo's position. They argued that social problems do not pertain to the Church, they pertain to society, and the Church has no validity in the public realm. However, Leo protested that the Church cannot be left out of the discussion because it is concerned with morals and a sense of what is ultimate. Without this focus, the problems cannot be solved (RN 16).

The natural law tradition gave Leo XIII a basis to speak to public questions. Natural law is based on a commonality in origin, nature, and destiny of the human family. Social teaching based on a natural law ethic could relate to a pluralistic secular society that remained unmoved by religious arguments. Natural law was open to rational discussion with persons of diverse beliefs.

Leo XIII, however, did not see the Church's voice as one among many in the public realm. While he felt that many needed to address the problems of the Industrial Revolution from their particular capacity as rulers, employers, and the working classes, he claimed a unique role for the Church: ". . . all the striving of men will be in vain if they leave out the church" (RN 16). The Church's aim was not confined to the religious and moral interest of the people. Rather it was committed to use the moral and dogmatic principles of Christianity to address public issues that may affect the social, intellectual and mutual well-being of all people.[9] In contrast to philosophical approaches that focused simply on the reordering of external social structures, Leo insisted that religion alone addresses the heart of the problem in its appeal to the conscience and the moral duty of each individual.

How should the Church respond to the social question? Leo XIII sought to respond by rebuilding a Christian worldview in an increasingly secular society. His goal was to Christianize modern life and modernize Christian life.[10] He did this intellectually by responding to modern movements in a different mode than his predecessors, who condemned modern movements but did not provide well-constructed alternatives. For Leo neo-scholasticism provided a way for Catholic intellectuals to consider modern problems, but from a natural law perspective and a vision of an organic society. Concepts such as the common good, the intrinsic dignity of work, the positive role of the state and the principles of distributive justice were the basic elements by which the Church defended workers and responded to the multiple problems posed by industrialization.[11]

While Leo stressed the primary spiritual concern of the Church, he did not minimize the obligation of the Church to care for the suffering of the workers (RN 28). This responsibility came through the Church's distinctive, divinely established mission to preach the Gospel and promote Christian virtue.[12] The Church acted in society through its members. People were to live virtuous lives in society (RN 34). The Church also had the charge to sponsor charitable institutions. Relief of the poor was not to be handed over purely to the state or secular society. Leo claims, ". . . no human expedients will ever make up for the devotedness and self-sacrifice of Christian charity" (RN 30). Leo's connection between social charity and church life were clear. "Charity, as a virtue pertains to the Church; for virtue it is not, unless it be drawn from the Most Sacred Heart of Jesus Christ;

---

[9] Edward Cahill, S.J., "The Catholic Social Movement: Historical Aspects," in *Readings in Moral Theology, No. 5 Official Catholic Social Teaching* (New York: Paulist Press, 1986) 1.

[10] Oskar Kohler, "The World Plan of Leo XIII: Goals and Methods," in *History of the Church: Vol. IX The Church in the Industrial Age,* Hubert Jedin, ed. (London: Burns and Oates, 1981) 10–11.

[11] Hehir, "The Social Role of the Church," 35.

[12] Stephen J. Pope, *"Rerum Novarum,"* in *The New Dictionary of Catholic Social Thought,* Judith A. Dwyer, ed. (Collegeville: The Liturgical Press, 1994) 835.

and whosoever turns his back on the Church cannot be near to Christ" (RN 30).

Finally, Leo XIII sought to bring Christian principles to the social realm by forming Catholics into autonomous groups within an increasingly secular society. Some call this "ghetto Catholicism." However, it is an approach of the Church to social problems that lasted well into the 1950s. Leo's ideal was to create a parallel society where Catholic belief could be lived and practiced in light of the challenges of secular society. In the United States the Catholic school system, implemented at the Council of Baltimore, arose from this vision. Catholic unions, political parties, associations of Catholic lawyers, doctors, newspapers, and Catholic hospitals were agents of culture and means to plant Catholic values in what was viewed as a degenerating society.

Leo XIII's ecclesial and social perspective was thoroughly hierarchical.[13] In his view, society was shaped by princes and popes in a top-down fashion. The Church had a role in societal change, but it was to act in a strictly non-political manner. The Church was attached to no political party and had no preference for any particular form of government, provided that the functions of government are fulfilled. In Leo's view, the Church was outside and above all party politics. It could promote legislation and administration in accordance with Christian principles. It could use pressure on governing authorities. However, the main influence of the Church was on people individually. Leo's strategy placed strong emphasis on individual charity, benevolent associations, and charitable organizations in alleviating the misery of the poor. To reestablish Christian morals (RN 82), promote renewed commitment to religion and virtue were goals on par with calling the state to enact protective labor legislation to enforce the natural rights of workers (RN 16).

Leo XIII provided hierarchical support to the Catholic social conscience. The morality of life in society was underdeveloped in the moral theology of the time. Leo XIII did not stress the initiative of the individual Catholic or see their creative contribution apart from formal church structures. But he did provide a fairly coherent and ecclesially authorized body of moral and social teaching to guide social activism.

---

[13] Hehir, "The Social Role of the Church," 36.

Pius XI . . . 1930s

In many ways Pius XI followed Leo XIII in his position on the right and competence of the Church to speak on social questions. His major social encyclical, *Quadragesimo Anno* (1931), affirms that this right rests on the "deposit of truth entrusted to US by God," and the duty given to the papacy by God "to proclaim the moral law in its entire compass." The interpretation of the moral law extended to "both the social and economic sphere" (QA 41). With the world on the brink of the Depression, moral issues were at stake. Pius XI saw the Depression in moral terms. The economic order had to do with the just distribution and use of goods that were provided by God for the good of all and to help people "attain their ultimate end" (QA 41–43, 136–37).[14]

Pius XI asserted the Church had the right to speak and act on socio-economic and political matters yet also nuanced this right in three ways. First, society and economics could not be considered apart from the moral law. Popular economic theory denied this claim, asserting that economics followed its own invisible hand of the market. Second, the Church did not have expertise in technical matters, nor did it have a mission in this area, but it did have the right to judge everything in the public realm as to its moral import. Third, the Church had the authority to speak on public issues based on the authority of its teaching office, which did not just extend to Catholics, but concerned the good of all. Pius XI made this point because many in the world resented the Church's outspoken posture to the world economic crisis. The Church countered this was not an unjust claim to power.[15]

In face of the economic and social problems of the Depression, Pius XI's actual contribution to social teaching called for a radical re-ordering of society into vocational groups. Pius XI was convinced that in the conditions of Fascist Italy only religious association of Catholics was possible, political association was not. He wanted to establish

---

[14] Richard P. McBrien, "An Ecclesiological Analysis of Catholic Social Teaching," in *Catholic Social Thought and the New World Order,* Oliver F. Williams, C.S.C., and John W. Houck, eds. (Notre Dame, Ind.: University of Notre Dame Press, 1993) 153.

[15] Wilhelm Weber, "The Diversity of the Inner Life of the Universal Church," in *History of the Church: Vol. X The Church in the Modern Age,* Hubert Jedin, ed. (London: Burns and Oates, 1981) 233.

in the whole Catholic world the conditions for Catholics to be involved in social concerns as Catholics. He established what we know today as Catholic Action. "Life is action" was one of Pius XI's favorite maxims.[16]

The aims of this movement were to repair or reconstruct Christian civilization where it has been injured or destroyed. The movement called Catholic Action did this in three ways. First, the movement disseminated among people a better knowledge of Catholic social principles and ideals. Second, it sought to reorganize the public life of individual nations in accordance with Catholic standards. Third, it attempted to apply these principles to counteract the poverty, insecurity, and material misery of the laboring population.[17]

Catholic Action was seen as the best way to implement social teaching. Yet, there were limitations to this approach. For example, Catholic Action called for the formation of separate Catholic labor unions, which divided the labor movement. Instead of creating the Church within the labor movement, the Church tended to stand outside this movement through a concern to evangelize it.[18]

A second limitation was that the lay apostolate, at this point in church thinking, was at root, a participation in the apostolate of the hierarchy and was to be carried on always in subordination to it (QA 96). Pius XI recognized a special role of the laity as workers. They served as apostles to their fellow workers. But he described those lay "apostles" as "auxiliary soldiers of the Church." The Church here was clearly the hierarchy.[19] Despite limitations in scope and theological grounding in church life, the Catholic Action movement was a powerful carrier of the social message of the Church.

Pius XII—1940s and 50s

Pius XII followed the thinking of his predecessors. It was legitimate for the Church to speak on public affairs because of its "intrinsic involvement" in the world. He used the controversial formula that

---

[16] Hubert Jedin, "Popes Benedict XV, Pius XI, and Pius XII," in *History of the Church: Vol. X The Church in the Modern Age*, Hubert Jedin, ed. (London: Burns and Oates, 1981) 26.

[17] Cahill, "The Catholic Social Movement," 5.

[18] Peter Hebblethwaite, "The Popes and Politics: Shifting Patterns in Catholic Social Doctrine," in *Daedalus. Journal of the American Academy of Arts and Sciences.* Winter 1982, vol. 111, no. 1. 87

[19] McBrien, "An Ecclesiological Analysis of Catholic Social Teaching," 153.

the Church was the "vital principle of human society."[20] It was the "undeniable sphere of the Church" to judge those principles "of the eternally valid order" that God has made known through natural law and revelation.[21]

However, Pius XII never wrote a major social encyclical. He implemented the thought of his predecessors, commenting on the world situation before and during World War II through a series of allocutions and addresses (1,367 in his eighteen-year pontificate). Pius XII obviously saw the Church as an actor in the international arena as he worked diligently on a peace program between 1939 and 1942.[22] We see in Pius XII a recognition of movements as essential to the Church's social mission. For example, in 1952 he gave *Pax Christi International* its status as an international peace movement. Although *Pax Christi* maintained the church practice of having a bishop as its international president, this movement was founded by lay people and basically run by lay people.[23]

Pius XII contributed to the empowerment of the laity in social ministry. He continued and reinforced the Catholic Action movement of Pius XI. His encyclicals on the Mystical Body and on the liturgy (*Mystici Corporis Christi* [1943] and *Mediator Dei* [1947]) affirmed both the role of the lay apostolate as members of the Mystical Body of Christ and linked liturgical reform to its meaning for the reconstruction of the social order.[24] Yet, he challenged the activity of priests in social reform. The "worker priests" of France ministered to alienated factory workers by actually going into the factories and working side by side with them. Pius XII questioned the compatibility of this lifestyle with the vocation of the priest. How to minister in an increasingly secular society was a concern and a debate in the Church after World War II.

Pius XII was the first to use the term "social teaching of the church." The Church of his day was conservative according to our post-Vatican II standards. The "ultramontane" Church was highly centralized. Its

[20] Weber, "The Diversity of the Inner Life of the Universal Church," 233.

[21] Weber, 234.

[22] Steven M. Avella, "Pius XII," in *The New Dictionary of Catholic Social Thought*, Judith A. Dwyer, ed. (Collegeville: The Liturgical Press, 1994) 741–44.

[23] Mary Evelyn Jegen, S.N.D. de N., "Peace and Pluralism," in *100 Years of Catholic Social Thought*, John A. Coleman, S.J., ed. (Maryknoll, N.Y.: Orbis Books, 1991) 293.

[24] Avella, "Pius XII," 743.

strengths were clarity, unity, and power over the conscience. Its weaknesses were its inability to deal with the pluralism, diversity of culture, and the new problems and mentalities of modern culture. This new situation required openness to the sciences, a capacity to enter into politics, and a more positive view of the achievements of modern society.

Scholars today question whether the centralization of the Church during this period made it so powerful in people's lives that social teaching itself has never recovered from its loss.[25] Even though Pius XII did not create formal social teaching, the organization of the Church that he fostered "carried" social teaching with great clarity. It is a style of church life that has not been repeated in the post-Vatican Church. Today some feel that social teaching itself has lost its influence since the Church has yet to replace this ecclesial situation with an equally powerful social carrier of its message. The next decades represent the attempt to create a Church more open to the world and to allow both the theological shifts and changes in its structures to facilitate this new openness. It was to be an openness of service.

Purpose of the Church

During Vatican II theological reflection on the Church shifted its focus from the institutional structures to its religious nature and purpose. Previously, Roman Catholic theologians, before Protestant denials, had to assume an apologetic tone in defending the institutional structures and offices of the Church. However, at Vatican II, it was time to move beyond institutional defense and retrieve the Church's religious nature. This had been prepared for by theological work during the century.[26] Vatican II emphasized the religious nature of the Church by employing images of the Church as the people of God, the Body of Christ, and the sacrament of salvation.

[25] Staf Hellemans, "Is There a Future for Catholic Social Teaching after the Waning of Ultramontane Mass Catholicism?" in *Catholic Social Thought: Twilight of Renaissance?* J. S. Boswell, F. P. McHugh, and J. Verstraeten, eds. (Leuven: Peeters, 2000) 13–32.

[26] Michael Fahey, "Church," in *Systematic Theology: Roman Catholic Perspectives,* vol. II, Francis Schussler Fiorenza and John P. Galvin, eds. (Minneapolis: Fortress Press, 1991) 33. Fahey claims this reflects one hundred years of theological preparation in the works such as Johann Adam Mohler's "spiritual" ecclesiology (1796–1838), Yves Congar's work from the 1930s–1950s on ecumenism, the mystery of the Church and the laity, and Lucien Cerfaux's study on the Church in the theology of St. Paul (1942).

This shift in the understanding of the Church had significant consequences for grounding its claim to speak and act beyond spiritual affairs. As pointed out earlier, the social mission of the Church is no longer one of the tasks of the institution. Instead social action becomes a symbol and sacrament of the religious nature of the Church as such. Social teaching, social action, and work for justice are not just tasks of the Church, but the Church in action, expressing and symbolizing itself in practice.

By the 1960s people accepted change in society as normative. Society, social status, and occupational roles were no longer seen as static or unchangeable. People therefore understood societies to be changeable and open to the moral and political will of its members. Social class was not permanent, and racial and ethnic barriers could be changed.

The Church's mission to call the world to conversion took on new importance. This call was not just to individuals, a call to personal conversion and virtue. The call to conversion was beyond transforming just the leaders of society. The Church sought to transform societies. To do this it had to think of society as it was, not in its ideal form. It had to turn to the social sciences as a tool to study society concretely. Hence, social teaching had to go beyond its claims in natural law. In order to bring a distinctive contribution to the developing world order through linking the Christian Gospel and practice to social and political life, the Church had to present its social teaching in a new way. Both John XXII and the documents of Vatican II laid the foundation for this new approach.

John XXIII—1960s

John XXIII claimed the Church's right to speak on social problems as did his predecessors, yet his own approach was a turning point in social teaching. The encyclical *Pacem in Terris* reaffirmed the teaching that "the Church has the right and the duty not only to safeguard the principles of ethics and religion, but also to intervene authoritatively with her children in the temporal sphere, when there is a question of judging about the application of those principles to concrete cases" (PT 160). This document was published between the first and second sessions of the council, and it influenced the council by its message of hope and confidence in the midst of the new situation of the postwar world.

John XXIII took a new turn in social teaching when he addressed *Pacem in Terris* to the whole world, and not just to the Church. Why was this so significant? If the audience of the Church's social teaching is to be wider than the Church, its language, arguments, and logic have to be persuasive for those outside as well as inside the Church. When an encyclical is addressed to the pluralistic world, there is more at stake than communicating a sense of absolute, changeless truth, interpreted by the Church in a world that is ideologically fragmented. Truth also has to be communicated as a concrete entity and encouragement given to the fact that knowledge of the truth grows in the veracity of human relationships. John XXIII believed in the possibility of rational understanding and love among people. He held that trust in relationship is the basis of the feasibility of all knowledge of truth. Truth is no longer only the authoritatively interpreted objective deposit of faith, truth occurs also in the freedom of humankind as a social process of truth finding (PT 38).

John XXIII's position was continued at the council. At Vatican II revelation was understood no longer as simply a "deposit" of truth given over once and for all and then handed over to the proprietary care of the hierarchical magisterium, but as a continuing process of divine self-disclosure and self-communication through the "signs of the times."[27]

While the Church still grounded its "right" to speak on social affairs on much the same footing as before, this right was set in a climate of dialogue and cooperation with those in society. Even though John XXIII in his encyclicals *Pacem in Terris* and *Mater et Magistra* drew heavily on the neo-scholastic philosophical categories of his predecessors, his affirmation of human rights and dignity were placed in a democratic context. The Church stressed that individuals and states had the obligation to share responsibility for constructing institutions in which these rights could be protected.[28]

John XXIII shifted the traditional approach as to how to implement the social message. He believed that the new international community could cooperate and work together for peace, justice, and human rights across the globe. This could be done, without insisting, like earlier popes, that only acceptance of Christianity and the Church

[27] Richard P. McBrien, *"E Pluribus Unum,"* in *Daedalus: Journal of the American Academy of Arts and Sciences.* Winter 1982, vol. 111, no. 1. 80.

[28] David J. O'Brien, "A Century of Catholic Social Teaching," in *One Hundred Years of Catholic Social Thought,* John A. Coleman, ed. (Maryknoll, N.Y.: Orbis Books, 1991) 23.

could enable the human community to find its proper political and cultural form. *Pacem in Terris* also anticipated the council's affirmation of the laity's proper sovereignty in the temporal order because they "live and work in the specific sectors of human society in which those problems arise" (PT 160).

In *Mater et Magistra* the emphasis on lay involvement in social affairs is particularly strong (MM 1–6, 178–84, 218–41). "The Church" is still connected mainly with the hierarchy. It is stated that in the implementation of social teaching, "the Church especially asks the cooperation of the laity" (MM 256).[29] Yet John XXIII set the context for the "emerging layperson" in the Church, and set it in the midst of society not just as a teacher or judge, but as a brother, sister and friend. The Church moved out of the Catholic subculture to a stand within the human community. Instead of thinking of the Church and the world, John XXIII thought of the Church in the world.

Vatican II

Social encyclicals before John XXIII and the Vatican Council presuppose an organically Christian world as the basis and horizon of the Church's social teaching. An organic society is a philosophical ideal where all the parts work together to achieve the common good and the personal fulfillment of each member. With the pontificate of John XXIII and Vatican II, the horizon for the Church's social teaching expanded to embrace a modern pluralistic worldview. Insofar as the organically Christian world was the basis of the social teaching before John XXIII, the acceptance of the pluralistic world meant that the foundation of the Church's social teaching also had to be reformulated. This new foundation was begun at Vatican II and continues to the present day.

The development of a new foundation for the Church's social teaching involved both an anthropological component and an ecclesial component. An organically Christian world was the sociological ideal of pre-Vatican social thought. If acceptance of a modern pluralistic world made this no longer possible, then the new basis had to be constructed on the human person or the meaning of human dignity. The charter of personal rights in *Pacem in Terris* begins this anthropological vision. Yet *Gaudium et Spes,* Vatican II's document on the Church in the Modern World, expands this affirmation of human dignity as

---

[29] McBrien, "An Ecclesiological Analysis of Catholic Social Teachings," 154.

the center of the Church's social message. It acknowledges the personal and communitarian dimensions of the human person and the type of human activities proper to human dignity. It also lays this foundation by placing Jesus Christ at the center of this anthropology. "In reality it is only in the mystery of the Word made flesh that the mystery of man truly becomes clear"(PT 22). Every section of the document concludes with a reflection on how the life and revelation of Jesus Christ enlightens understanding with respect to the human problem being considered (PT 22, 32, 38, 45). *Gaudium et Spes* effects a decisive synthesis in the development of an anthropological foundation for the Church's social teaching through its clear presentation of a Christocentric humanism.[30]

The second advance in *Gaudium et Spes* is the ecclesial foundation it gave to social teaching. Brian Hehir claims that the distinctive contribution of Vatican II was not that it addressed a specific social question. Rather, "it was the way in which it joined the entire social ministry to the center of the church's life."[31] The council placed the Church as a sign and a safeguard of the transcendence of the human person (GS 76). This takes the center of the anthropological foundation of social teaching, human dignity, and gives it ecclesial standing. The fulfillment of this role is tied to the Church's nature and mission.

How is the Church to fulfill this role? *Gaudium et Spes* 40–42 spells this out. The Church is to remain a religious institution, directed toward the Kingdom and in service of the life of the Kingdom. Since the Kingdom is partially realized in history, the Church must fulfill its religious ministry in a way that protects human dignity, fosters human rights, and contributes to the unity of the human family. *Gaudium et Spes* provides us with a servant church model of active involvement in society. The Church is to be "a leaven and as a kind of soul for human society as it is to be renewed in Christ and transformed into God's family" (GS 40). This image is of the Church *in* the world. The Church is to learn *from* the world by reading the signs of the times. The Church is to put *at the disposal of the world* its own saving resources that it has received from Christ. The Church exists for a spiritual purpose, yet situated in and committed to serve a temporal world. The relationship between the two worlds is one of

[30] George Beigel, *Faith and Social Justice in the Teaching of Pope John Paul II* (New York: Peter Lang, 1997) 84.
[31] Hehir, "The Social Role of the Church, " 37.

"compenetration," a reality that is "accessible to faith alone" (GS 40). We can see that, beyond the moral categories of earlier teaching, Vatican II grounded the social teaching of the Church in ecclesial and anthropological themes.

Paul VI—1970s

Paul VI's distinctive contribution to the development of Catholic social teaching is his insistence that the social question has become global and that political action is a necessary form of Christian discipleship. In *Populorum Progressio,* On the Development of Peoples (1967), he affirms the Church's right and duty to shed "the light of the gospel on the social questions of their times" (PP 2). In *Octogesimo Adveniens,* A Call to Action (1971), he notes that the complexity of the world order makes it impossible for Rome simply to "hand down" solutions to social problems. Rather local churches have to apply the Gospel and the social teachings of the Church to its own particular situation. The role of the Church is greater than being one actor among others in the solving of social problems. The Church offers "a global vision of man and of the human race" (OA 40). The Church is to inspire people to attack social ills and to promote the innovations required to make the structural changes necessary to meet real needs (OA 50).

Making political action a necessary aspect of social ministry is a huge shift in social teaching. Far away from a spirituality of "withdrawal from the world," the call to political involvement is not a lessening of Christian discipleship. Rather, it is a necessary ingredient of action in society. Political action is another form of responsibility that human beings need to take for their lives, as a concrete exercise of their freedom. Paul VI recognized that an increasingly global economic system did not have a comparable governing body. While the Church could not replace world government, it could provide a vision for correctives to decision making by economic incentive alone.

Paul VI also linked the process of evangelization with the Church's concern for social transformation. In *Evangelii Nuntiandi,* Evangelization in the Modern World (1975), he affirmed that evangelization cannot be "complete" without social action (EN 29). Yet he also noted that the Church's mission cannot be reduced "to the dimensions of a simply temporal project" (EN 32).

Evangelization, as the proclamation of a transcendent salvation in Christ, is linked to action for justice in three ways in Paul VI. The anthropological link is that the person evangelized is subject to social and economic factors. The theological link is one cannot "dissociate the plan of creation from the plan of Redemption" that is addressed to "concrete situations of injustice." The evangelical link to such outreach is "that of charity" (EN 31).

How does the Church engage in its social mission? The Church is to inspire others to devote themselves to the liberation of peoples (EN 38). People are to be engaged on the parish, diocesan, family level, and even in specialized communities such as the *comunidades de base* of Latin America (EN 58–64). Besides collaborating with the local bishop and the bishops of the universal church, their efforts should not be limited to Catholics, but should extend to other Christians and others of good will (EN 53–55, 77). Paul VI held that the laity do have a ministerial role in the life of the church itself, ". . . in the service of the ecclesial community" (EN 73).[32]

The anthropological and ecclesial basis of social teaching grounds Paul VI's assertion that the basic criterion of a just social order is the complete development of the human being (PP 6–42). The essence of the Church is to evangelize, however, it must also begin "by being evangelized itself" (EN 15). To be the visible sacrament of salvation, it must give witness to it. This involves "ensuring fundamental human rights" and seeing this action as connected to the "just liberation which is bound up with evangelization" (EN 39).

John Paul II

John Paul II saw the year 2000 as a "New Advent" for an increasingly interdependent world. He defined the Church's role as distinct from political institutions, yet he intensified its social mandate. The Pope grounded his vision of the right and competence of the Church to teach in the socio-political arena on much the same basis as his predecessors. Yet he goes beyond them in scope and specificity.[33]

John Paul II distinguishes between the ecclesial and the political. He denies a political role for the Church, but he declares that the core of the Gospel is the proclamation of human worth and dignity. The affirmation of human dignity, "determines the Church's mission in the world and, perhaps more so, 'in the modern world'" (RH 10).

The human dignity that the Pope envisions, includes, yet goes beyond the human rights agenda of the secular arena. Rather, human

---

[32] McBrien, "An Ecclesiological Analysis of Catholic Social Teaching," 162.
[33] Hehir, "The Social Role of the Church," 39ff.

dignity is grounded in the mystery of Christ who reveals to human beings the full measure of their dignity. In this way John Paul II continues the theological shift in social teaching begun at Vatican II. His social vision is built upon four interlocking themes of anthropology: a vision of the human person; Christology, or what difference Jesus Christ makes to the meaning of humanity; ecclesiology, or what is the church in this God-human mystery; and social ethics, or what decisions should flow from the perspective that this God-human relationship gives us. The person is the foundation of the Church's social concern, but the full meaning of human dignity is only understood in Christ.

The Church's social teaching is essential to the Church's evangelizing mission. In *Centesimus Annus,* On the Hundredth Anniversary of *Rerum Novarum* (1991) John Paul II remarked ". . . this doctrine points out the direct consequences of that message (Christian message) in the life of the society and situates daily work and struggles for justice in the context of bearing witness to Christ the savior" (CA 5.5). John Paul II mirrors Leo XIII in his assertion that even in these times of a "new evangelization" there is no solution of the "social question" apart from the gospel (CA 5.6). While John Paul II has a more nuanced understanding of the role of the Church in the world than was available to Leo XIII, his affirmation reflects his theological approach to social teaching.

John Paul's grounding for the Church's right to engage in social teaching is centered in his understanding of the relationship of faith to justice.[34] The theological horizon of the Church's action for justice is located within the revealed plan of God for humanity, where Christ reveals man to himself "in the very revelation of the mystery of the Father and of his love" (CA 54). One must understand the "mystery" that grounds each human being to fully understand the human person. Each human being has an anthropological dimension and a theological dimension, and to miss the theological dimension is to fail to grasp the full identity of being human. Social justice is part of this theological order. The Gospel carries a light and power that demands a social witness that transforms the social order. While Christian action for justice takes place within the autonomy of the secular sphere, it can never be done, apart from the Church's mission to proclaim

---

[34] See Beigel, *Faith and Social Justice in the Teaching of Pope John Paul II,* 107ff.

"God and his mystery of salvation in Christ to every human being" (CA 54.2). Social justice must be informed by mature faith.

The Church's social concern is a function of its mission to order all reality to Christ (SRS 31). In this sense, the Church's approach to social justice is not just one theory among others on the continuum of social theory. The transforming effect of seeking to place an evangelical order on all of human life extends to every dimension of the human person, including the economic, political, and social. When Christians participate in this transforming work, they not only transform the secular but further the salvation and unification of the human race that is accomplished in Christ. In this sense both the acts of the Christian and that of the Church has a sacramental dimension.

The Church's service to the Father's plan specifically obliges it to become the sacramental expression of that mystery by which all human reality is ordered to the Father in Christ (SRS 31.5). This vocation to be sacrament flows from the Church's unique *communio* that unifies her members and unites her to the triune God.

The specifically Christian dimension of social action is solidarity that overcomes the fragmentation caused by sin (SRS 40). Going beyond the secular language of rights and equality, John Paul II uses theological language to point to the ultimate mystery that encompasses Christian social action. One's neighbor is "the living image of God the Father." Being all under God brings a new criterion to interpret the world (SRS 40.3). "Beyond human and natural bonds, already so close and strong, there is discerned in the light of faith a new model of the unity of the human race, which must ultimately inspire our solidarity." This unity is not only horizontal, urging a fragmented global world to a new unity, but also is a "reflection of the intimate life of God" and what Christians mean by "communion." The specifically Christian dimensions of this solidarity are total gratuity, forgiveness, and reconciliation.

The Pope then points to how the Church and the Christian, when engaged in social action, are sacrament. "This specifically Christian communion, jealously preserved, extended and enriched with the Lord's help, is the soul of the Church's vocation to be a "sacrament," in the sense already indicated (SRS 40.3). This sacramental dimension of Christian social action is not simply a luminous symbol of God's love; it is also an efficacious presentation of God's love to others. The efficacy of the sacramental activity of Christians is not such as to make others recognize God's love in action. It is a true human presentation of God's redeeming love, which invites others to recognize and receive that same love.[35]

The social works of Christians and non-Christians that are materially the same are formally different because of the distinctive human relationships that the Gospel establishes. To view others as redeemed by Christ and called to full participation as members of his body is a matter of new and real relationships, not merely a matter of motivation or attitude. While there is an analogy between Christian and non-Christian social action since Christ has unified all love in his work of salvation, there is a distinction in kind between each. The sacramental dimension of Christian activity is rooted in the fact that the Christian is a member of the Church, and in this sense his or her acts are ordained to God in Christ. "Through this ordination Christian activity possesses a special dimension that involves the offer to the world of the unique sacramental presence of Christ found in the Church."[36]

How does the Church carry out its social mission? It does not offer technical solutions to world problems, but a wider moral framework concerning the dignity of the person. Neither is the Church's economic position a "third way" between liberal capitalism and Marxist socialism (SRS 41.7). John Paul II focuses on the international system, but does not offer social teaching as one competing ideology among others. The Church has no models to present, yet it seeks not just to generalize but to address specific human situations across the globe. It is open to social science, respectful of the autonomy of the secular, yet insistent on its unique contribution to social transformation.

The Church Today

We have considered what the Church says about itself as to its right to teach about social reality. But it is also important to ask what this might mean for us. How can the Church influence our own faith as we respond to social issues? Three insights arise as to what the Church's role in its social mission might mean for our own spiritual journey. First, we do learn our values from others. Values and ethical ideas about what is good, just, and right, and the sense of obligation

---

[35] Ibid., 97.
[36] Ibid., 102.

and ways of thinking on which they are based, are socially embodied in particular social traditions and communities. In other words, there is no way of thinking independent of a tradition, no "view from nowhere."[37] It makes a difference not only what kind of person we are, but what communities we invest in. Second, people do not think of their own rights or moral duties in the abstract. For example, they do not think of themselves as subjects of international duties and rights. Most people experience the moral life, within virtues, social practices, and traditions of communities grounded in the world's main religions, however imperfectly it is lived out.

Third, we form our idea of what is good and evil in community. In the moral order, there are no set of rules or principles that will commend themselves to all independent of their conception of the good.[38] What makes it "rational" to act in one way and not in another way often involves images of the "good," success, "justice" embodied in a particular social tradition or community. This means that social or humanitarian practices of charity to the poor, hospitality to strangers, justice in fighting, and fairness to prisoners of war, as well as conceptions of the justice and of the good, can only be lived out and experienced in really existing communities. For this reason John Paul II affirmed that communities focused on the transcendent are those sacraments of *communio* not only necessary to proclaim the social message but to learn it in the first place. Part of understanding the Church and its social teaching is to grasp the possibilities of moral formation that come from sharing in its life.

[37] Jean Bethke Elshtain, "Really Existing Communities," *Review of International Studies*, 25, 1 (1999) 141–46.
[38] Josef Fuchs, *Moral Demands and Personal Obligations* (Washington, D.C.: Georgetown University Press, 1993) 22–23, 40ff.

PART TWO

The Catholic Social Tradition

Chapter Five

Social Teaching before Vatican II

The conditions of the Industrial Revolution with the emergence of capitalism placed the Church in a new world of human relationships and human problems. The rise of constitutional governments, the unrest of political revolutions, and the instability of the "new economy" forced the Church to search for fresh expressions of justice as evidence of its own mission and service to the world and as part of the life of its members.

The Church had a growing concern over the exploitation and severe working conditions of workers. Before the 1930s there were few worker protections that we take for granted today. While the average male worker had little protection against arbitrary subsistence wages, unsafe working conditions, long hours and job insecurity, the most vulnerable were women and children. There were no child labor laws, worker's compensation, pensions, or minimum wage laws. Because wages did not support even a minimal quality of life, new industrial cities were characterized by unsanitary tenement living, lack of basic educational opportunities, poor nutrition, and violence.

Industrial Revolution

The combination of enormous human suffering resulting from the unsolved issues of industrialization and the rise of socialism, and its more harsh form in communism, provided a complex situation where former Church approaches were no longer adequate. People were numbed by the gap between the promise of progress to be delivered by the machine and the actual conditions of their lives. Life was very difficult. Many urban poor turned to socialism as a defense against the capitalism that impoverished them. Could the Church do anything practical about the real problems of their lives? Were the socialists the only ones with solutions? The Church was on trial before the world.

In the eighteenth century the papacy exercised little influence on Europe's public life.[1] The papacy retained its spiritual position among Catholics, but even its direct control over segments of its internal life was checked by secular powers. Anti-clericalism, the identification of Church with the Old Regime in a climate of revolution, and the fact that intellectual life was centered in secular universities and no longer under the control of the Church, served to marginate the Church in public life. To make matters worse, the Church adopted a position of denunciation of secular trends. Pius IX's *Syllabus of Errors* rejected "scholarly trends" that came into favor with the great expansion of scientific knowledge. A scientific, rather than a metaphysical outlook, was applied to every area of thought, including religion. In the *Syllabus* the Pope made it clear the church would not accommodate prevailing secular thought.

Secular thought did not see the Church as having solutions to modern problems; in fact, it either saw the Church as a problem or relegated to insignificance. This ideological climate, plus the attitude that the state had the right to full control over the structure of the Church within its national boundaries marked the Church in the nineteenth-century with two major issues. First, how was the Church to accommodate the political and social conceptions of new thought systems with the religious ideals of Christianity? Second, how could the Church be involved with the modern state in a manner that respected its integrity and that of the state?

Liberalism and Socialism

The challenge of integrating a religious view of life with the new social order was checked by two major ideologies of the nineteenth century, liberalism and socialism. Both thought systems appeared to contradict traditional values of the Church. Liberalism advocated a

[1] *Church and Society. Catholic Social and Political Thought and Movements 1789–1950,* Joseph N. Moody, ed. (New York: Arts, Inc., 1953) 23.

non-religious or secularist stance that maintained that religion was a private affair. Religion had no place in public life, and its standards had no relevance to politics or economics.

Liberalism had a concurrent theory of laissez-faire economics. This "doctrine" claimed that any interference of the government, labor unions, or social legislation to regulate economic matters was an infringement of private property and the "rights" of the business person.

Along with this economic theory came a social philosophy. A good society consisted of one that afforded the greatest amount of freedom to the greatest number of people. In practice, the greatest number was translated in favor of those who held the greatest power. History shows that the greatest number of people in the world at the time were quite poor. The "survival of the fittest" philosophy of Charles Darwin became a social mindset that explained away the poor and affirmed a rising entrepreneur class. Protestations of the Church were dismissed with this type of "common sense."

Socialism equally rejected religion as offering any light to the problems of the industrial revolution. Religion was part of the problem; it was the "opium of the people." Karl Marx claimed that religion distracted men and women from their historical task to better their own living conditions. Religion, Marx claimed, offered a mystique of suffering that leads to passivity before new problems and legitimated class oppression.

Socialists firmly rejected the Church's emphasis on obedience to authority. They questioned the Church's opposition to revolutionary movements and ridiculed its belief in the next life, calling it a false solace that created a paralysis before the demands of social revolution. Socialism also viewed the value of the human person mainly in the individual's capacity to fuel a new world order, while the Church saw the person as having an inherent dignity.[2] The Church opposed the socialist view of the person as a cog in a greater social process.

Liberalism offered to the new industrial society a climate where the promise of progress, the rights of the individual, boundless faith

---

[2] Socialism did not have a view of the human person as a center of rights. The Church affirmed these rights against the collectivism of socialism. Human rights had their origin in the person, and were not conferred by society, nor were they the consequence of law and custom. Human rights were inherent and inalienable. Thomas Hoppe, "Human Rights," in *The New Dictionary of Catholic Social Thought*, Judith A. Dwyer, ed. (Collegeville: The Liturgical Press, 1994) 454–70.

in human reason, and the worship of technique provided a rival faith to that of the Church.[3] Its utilitarian ethic ignored all values and influences that did not bring immediate economic advance. Socialism, on the other hand, offered to the society the movements of resistance that increasingly satisfied the new political aspirations of those people not profiting from the new capitalist system.

The Church had to respond, not only for obvious pastoral reasons but also to maintain its credibility before the masses. To do this it had to move out of its "siege" mentality. This required that it transcend its own history: the shattering effects of the break up of religious unity by the Reformation, its reactionary defensive style developed during the age of the revolutions. It had to again apply its deeply held religious principles on a new scale to a new situation.

The Church was hesitant to respond to the social question in Europe because of the above past history. In North America the Catholic Church was a minority in a Protestant world. It was fearful of invoking further discrimination by irritating the state by advocating interference in economic matters. The Church was concerned that if it interfered in civil matters, it would set a precedent for the state to interfere in religious matters. From its minority position it was hesitant to lend its support to any movement that advocated "disturbance" of the peace.

Initial Response: Christian Social Movements

The initial response of the Church to the problems of the industrial revolution was traditional. The rich were to give to the poor. Social concern was a matter of charity extended to those beyond one's family circle. Charitable action would restore harmony in society. Only church-based advocacy and private activity would respond to the problems of the Industrial Revolution.

This avoidance of political involvement resulted in a deepening in the public's eyes of the Church's alignment with the Old Regime in Europe. In some ways, the basis of this perception was real. Catholics in Europe who responded to the new needs raised by the Industrial Revolution were generally generous people of the upper class. For in-

---

[3] For how secular ideas function as "faith," see Lee Cormie, "Society, History, Meaning: Perspectives from the Social Sciences," *Proceedings of the Thirty Fourth Annual Convention,* The Catholic Theological Society of America (1979) 31–47.

stance, Albert de Mun in France founded the Committee of Catholic Clubs in 1871 on the idea that the privileged class had an obligation to aid their working class brothers.[4]

These early reformers hoped to restore a medieval economic order, and in some manner reconstruct the craft guilds of the Middle Ages. They wanted to group capital and labor into an independent governmental body in a type of monarchical framework. The ideal was to end class division by making harmonious associations of all the parties who benefited from the economy. They created worker circles to promote industrial legislation and trade unions. However, these groups were to be formed under episcopal authority and were to be based on the acceptance of a type of monarchical framework.

These associations differed from country to country, yet they shared common characteristics. They were too paternalistic and rooted in monarchism and medievalism to meet the needs of working class people who were inspired by newer thinking. Yet, they were the first attempts to involve active participation of the laity in social questions. They focused on unity and solidarity in face of the individualism of liberalism and the divisiveness of socialism. They were non-political in that they tended to cross party lines. Their promotion of legislation was usually nonpartisan. They offered stability, education, and a means of association to workers. Yet, because of their inability to deal with social conflict, or to criticize established authority, in the last analysis, these associations provided support for the status quo and proved to be ill-equipped to be an agent to major socio-political change.

Wilhelm Emmanuel Von Ketteler of Germany (1811–1877) was also a forerunner and inspirer of the German Catholic social movement. He was a major early influence on the Church's response to the social question. In his early years he advocated personal charity as a response to the plight of workers. However, as bishop of Mainz in 1850 he endorsed the central aims of the contemporary labor movement, including government intervention through labor legislation.[5]

The transition that Ketteler made in his own thinking about the social question mirrored that of the Church during this period. In

[4] Moody, ed., *Church and Society*, 146.
[5] Paul Misner, "Wilhelm Emmanuel Von Ketteler," in *The New Dictionary of Catholic Social Thought*, op. cit., 504. See also *The Social Teachings of Wilhelm Emmanuel Von Ketteler*, Rupert J. Ederer, trans. (Washington, D.C.: University Press of America, 1981).

early sermons on problems of property, moral freedom, the family and the goals of human life, Ketteler pointed out that egotism and avarice are not just personal problems but must be fought at all levels in the economic system. He analyzed the philosophies and ideologies that controlled the economy, showing they were unable to respond to the fundamental problems of the workers. Ketteler then turned to the doctrinal principles that could critique these cultural ideas and shed light on a fuller understanding of the human person and society.[6] He was a pioneer in modern Catholic social thought in three ways. He saw the relationship between social organization and its underlying philosophical and ideological presupposition. Today we would call this "social analysis." Second, Ketteler affirmed that Christian conversion went beyond the acquiring of personal virtue. It was meant also to influence society. Third, he insisted that the Christian must address social problems and Christian faith must influence how those problems are addressed.

Many other persons contributed to the Christian social movement as it was developing in Europe and North America. Charles Perin of Belgium, Baron von Vogelsang of Austria, and Giuseppe Toniolo of Torino were among the social scientists who analyzed society from a Christian point of view. These early thinkers, together with clergy who were involved with the labor movement, and lay advocates of social reform, were forerunners in social action before the writing of the first social encyclical in 1891.

While the pontificate of Leo XIII marked the beginning of an official effort to link the social tradition of the Church to the problems of modern industrialism, it did not initiate the movement. In large part the social encyclicals were the consequence of pioneering by social-minded lay and clerical Catholics in many of the countries affected by the new conditions.

Leo XIII

The election of Leo XIII was a turning point in the history of the modern papacy. Most of his immediate predecessors resisted the new forces and changes influencing the social structure of modern Europe.

---

[6] William Murphy, *"Rerum Novarum,"* in *A Century of Catholic Social Thought,* George Weigel and Robert Royal, eds. (Washington, D.C.: Ethics and Public Policy Center, 1991) 10.

It was difficult for these popes to stem the political forces that they questioned because they did not understand them. Leo XIII used a different approach than the negativity and inflexibility of his predecessors. He was more positive, looking for solutions to problems rather than simply denouncing them. He had a grasp of the character and complexity of modern problems since he was an historian, philosopher, and diplomat. More open to modern man and woman and their problems, and more practical in his approach, Leo XIII was willing to engage in open dialogue with the modern world through a series of encyclicals.[7]

The Encyclical as Social Teaching

Social issues received the attention of the papacy from Leo XIII to the present day through encyclicals, letters from the pope on matters of importance. The materials for Catholic social teaching were at hand in the Gospels, Fathers of the Church, and the Scholastic tradition that earlier had applied this tradition to medieval economic conditions. The challenge of the modern encyclicals was to link the values of this tradition to the radically different conditions of the nineteenth century.

A new term, "social justice," formed in Catholic ethics in this process, which dealt with the meaning of justice as it applied to structural questions such as the relationship between capital and labor, the family, the state, equality and inequality, and ownership. Social justice also involved a type of contributive justice.[8] This concept went beyond the usual Thomistic categories of justice.

Traditionally the Church spoke of general or legal justice, and distributive and commutative justice. Social justice however involves the embedding of moral ideals in the laws, customs, institutions, and structures of society as a way to promote the common good. The search for the common good forms a mutual obligation between society and citizens. Society must make it possible for members to participate, and members have the obligation to participate. The U.S. Bishops explain that social justice involves contributive justice in the following

---

[7] Moody, ed., *Church and Society*, 41.

[8] John F. Cronin, S.S., "Forty Years Later: Reflections," in *Readings in Moral Theology No. 5 Official Catholic Social Teaching*, Charles E. Curran and Richard A. McCormick, S.J., eds. (New York: Paulist Press, 1986) 74.

way. "This form of justice can also be called 'contributive,' for it stresses the duty of all who are able to help create the goods, services, and other nonmaterial or spiritual values necessary for the welfare of the whole community."[9]

The introduction of the term social justice into Catholic morality through the social encyclical tradition moved social issues further into the center of the mission of the Church.[10] Public affairs could no longer be regarded as "optional extras" in Catholic life. Yet, it took many years for shifts in spirituality, theology, and ecclesiology to make this transformation occur.[11]

Social Teaching and Doctrine

Social teaching is part of the doctrine of the universal Church. It does not involve new doctrines of faith. It is the result of the common faith of the whole Church as it reflects on its basic beliefs. Social teaching involves attitudes that are sufficiently defined so they form a type of "common sense" for the sincere believer. For instance, the average believer might not know how to solve the problem of world hunger, but that concern about world hunger is a normal outcome of Christian faith and love for others is obvious. Since the attitudes behind social teaching flow from the logic of faith itself, they are matters of conscience in the Catholic community.

How one responds to the challenge of a social conscience varies. On the one hand, racism, sexism, and other forms of social discrimination can be unconscious, and they can appear not to hinder a full Catholic life. However, social teaching upholds that a sincere believer must be open to ongoing conversion away from these cultural deceptions and sinful patterns. On the other hand, in matters of the application of social teaching to policy decision, such as the advocacy of a living wage, the individual is free to determine how this principle is

---

[9] *Economic Justice for All,* no. 71.

[10] For another reading of this period see *Christenenen en Samenleving: Bijdragen tot enn christenlijke sociale ethiek,* J. A. Selling et al., ed. (J. H. Kok Uitgeversmaatschappij-Kampen: 1991). *Aspecten van een christelijke sociale ethiek,* A. Liegeois, J. Selling, L. Anchaert, J. de Tavernier, B. Roebben, J. Verstraeten, eds. (Leuven: Bibliotheek van de Faculteit der Godgeleerdhcid, 1991).

[11] For an overview of some of these changes see Charles Curran, *Catholic Social Teaching, 1891–Present: A Historical, Theological, and Ethical Analysis* (Washington, D.C.: Georgetown University Press, 2002).

best carried out in a specific situation. Some will advocate a higher minimum wage; others may see this as a threat to small business and look for other means to achieve better wages. In other words, what binds in conscience is attention to the principle; the means are often left to the individual's best judgment.

Social teaching is found in places other than the documents of the magisterium, such as encyclicals and letters from bishops or bishops' conferences. It can be expressed in sermons, lectures, movements, and theological reflection. Formally, social teaching is part of the ordinary and universal magisterium of the Church. There is no element in social teaching that belongs to definitions of faith of which no part may be changed. Social teaching contained in the social encyclicals belongs to a class of doctrines that involves faith, but the formulas used need not be taken as unchangeable.

There have been changes in the way the Church has expressed its social teaching. The magisterial teaching on social issues shows continuity in the values and principles it upholds, but there is development and change in the applications of the teaching.[12] Others like Gregory Baum see at times that there is discontinuity in the tradition where the Church shifts its previous position, such as the openness of the Church to aspects of Marxist thought in the 1970s after decades of opposition to the Marxist movement.[13]

The social teaching of any period cannot be isolated from the circumstances that gave rise to it. All social teaching is a response to a concrete historical problem. Surrounding it are all the complexities that form any historical reality. Social teaching also draws on ideas and movements that are outside ecclesial boundaries and expertise: theories of economics, ideas of society, and agenda from secular movements for political reform. Using ideas that are already operative in the society, the Church relates them to Christian principles and uses them to call the Church and the world to social transformation.

---

[12] Donal Dorr, *Option for the Poor: A Hundred Years of Vatican Social Teaching* (Maryknoll, N.Y.: Orbis Books, 1983) ch. 12.

[13] See Thomas Bokenkotter, *Church and Revolution* (New York: Doubleday, 1998); A. McGovern, *Marxism: An American Christian Perspective* (Maryknoll, N.Y.: Orbis Books, 1980); Gregory Baum, *The Priority of Labor: A Commentary on Laborem Exercens* (New York: Paulist Press, 1982); "An Ethical Critique of Capitalism: Contributions of Modern Catholic Social Teaching," in *Readings in Moral Theology Number 10: John Paul II and Moral Theology,* Charles E. Curran and Richard A. McCormick, S.J., eds. (New York: Paulist Press, 1998) 237–54.

Rerum Novarum, The Condition of Labor (1891)

In 1891 Leo XIII promulgated *Rerum Novarum,* the first major so-cial encyclical, which addressed the problem of labor, specifically the need for a living wage. Leo cried out against conditions that were close to slavery in the industrial world. Economic power had become so concentrated that "a very few rich and exceedingly rich men have laid a yoke almost of slavery on the unnumbered masses of non-owning workers" (RN 6). Workers had the right to a living wage, rather than simply the wage that was determined through the law of supply and demand. This prevailing wage proved to be a subsistent one; you worked yet had to live under what was necessary to survive. The lack of means of reprisal left workers with no defense against this oppres-sive system (RN 73). Workers had a right, Leo claimed, to a wage suf-ficient to support not only a worker, "who is thrifty and upright," but also a family (RN 63). Workers had rights to reasonable hours, periods of rest, health provisions, and safe working conditions. There were to be special provisions for women and children, including a minimum age for work (RN 59, 60, 64).

Leo XIII also addressed the mindsets in the culture that fostered "blindness" to these injustices. Against liberalism, he affirmed that religion did have a role in economic life. Against socialism, he ac-knowledged the role of the Church in social affairs and the right of private property. He rejected the belief of laissez-faire economics that the government had no right to intervene in economic affairs. The state had an obligation to promote class legislation, laws that affirm the rights of one class before another. Such laws were necessary when those of unequal power had to negotiate.

Leo XIII advocated voluntary organizations such as trade unions and church bodies devoted to social change (RN 69–72). The latter were designed to discourage militancy by workers and to promote awareness of the reciprocal duties of employees and employers, sup-porting harmony among various classes in the society (RN 35 and 65).

Leo XIII upheld authority. He feared the negative effects of revo-lution on the society and the Church. He widened the moral teaching of the scholastics by applying its principles to a comprehensive vision of society. This depicted the Christian life as affecting society, not just the individual. It was a matter of justice, not merely of charity, to see that the social order does not exploit the poor. Leo began a long proc-ess that incorporated modern social engagement into a life of faith.

While he did not use the term "option for the poor," he laid the groundwork for the kind of church consciousness that could support such an option (RN 5).

Were there weaknesses in Leo's approach? Probably two stand out. Leo was a man of his times who upheld the role of authority to such an extent that his policies were unable to deal with a climate of social conflict. Second, he focused primarily on a better distribution of capitalist wealth, rather than the creation of wealth through capitalism to better provide for the masses.[14] Distribution concerns can be meaningless without the former. The social teaching of Leo's time was less aware of the positive effects of capitalism or the multiple styles of capitalism that we have today. At that time the effects of capitalism were uneven in Europe and the United States. Countries such as England and Germany prospered while others such as Italy were behind in industrialization. In the United States the industrial North was more prosperous than the agricultural South. There were new types of small business, an emerging middle class, and a general improvement in the living standards of some who were not owners. Yet no one could say that workers had a fair share of the profits at that time, and distribution of wealth remained a problem in Western Europe and North America. Leo XIII in *Rerum Novarum* showed the vision and courage necessary to harness the energies and power of the Church to engage in these concerns that shaped the twentieth century.

John A. Ryan

In the United States, John A. Ryan, a Catholic priest from Minnesota, made it his life's work to explain and adapt *Rerum Novarum* to the American situation. Ryan joined the faculty of The Catholic University of America in 1898. He insisted that the social and economic problems facing the nation were at root moral problems. The natural law theory, at the core of Leo XIII's vision, was compatible with both the Catholic moral tradition and the American progressive reform tradition. At the heart of this moral movement was the belief that

---

[14] Richard L. Camp, "The Rights and Duties of Labor and Capital," in *Moral Theology No. 5 Official Catholic Social Teaching*, Charles E. Curran and Richard A. McCormick, S.J., eds. (New York: Paulist Press, 1986) 41.

economic welfare cannot be left just to the impersonal forces of the market. Nor are socialism and its collectivism the answer to modern issues.[15]

Ryan saw the Catholic Church as an actor in the broad social reconstruction that many churches in the United States advocated for the country. Ryan published *The Living Wage: Its Ethical and Economic Aspects* in 1906 and *Distributive Justice* in 1916. His economic thought centered around three core concepts: the worker's right to a living wage, the need for a better distribution of the world's resources, and the right of the state to promote the common good through social legislation.[16]

Ryan joined those in the social gospel movement to advocate for changes in social legislation in the United States. This social program of the Protestant Churches was led by ministers and theologians like Walter Rauschenbusch who were concerned about social conditions. The Catholic and Protestant groups both worked for minimum wage, the eight-hour work day, protection for child and women labor, the right to boycott and picket, unemployment insurance, social security against sickness, and pensions. All these were part of Ryan's 1909 "Program of Social Reform by Legislation." These "dreamers," as considered by some, saw the fruition of their labor in the social legislation of the New Deal Era of the 1930s. Their desired reform took thirty years. Today we still work for these reforms for all segments of the population and workforce.

Pius XI and the Depression Era

Pius XI, in *Quadragesimo Anno,* On Reconstructing the Social Order (1931), reflected that world conditions had changed in the forty-year period since *Rerum Novarum*. Conditions had not changed for the better. Wealth was more concentrated and, along with it, economic and political power. Unemployment had risen. While conditions of workers in Europe had improved in some ways since the time of Leo XIII, vast numbers of workers in the Far East and the Americas re-

---

[15] For an analysis of Ryan's contribution, see Thomas Massaro, S.J., *Catholic Social Teaching and the United States Welfare Reform* (Collegeville: The Liturgical Press, 1998) 22ff.

[16] Jeffrey M. Burns, "John Augustine Ryan," in *The New Dictionary of Catholic Social Thought,* op. cit., 854.

mained extremely poor. Millions were unemployed; the Great Depression was two years old. It left twenty-five million Americans and
Europeans unemployed.[17] The world economic crisis was marked by
famine in Russia, the financial collapse of Germany, the stock market
crash in 1929, and worldwide depression.

Quadragesimo Anno followed the principles of *Rerum Novarum,* yet
interpreted them in the context of the 1930s. It affirmed the role of
labor unions and their effectiveness and lauded the development of
a Catholic social science that had been made available to people
through the study circles, courses, publications, and groups since
Rerum Novarum.[18] The encyclical outlines a "third way" between the
evils of the collectivism of socialism and the individualism of liberal
capitalism (QA 46).

The problem envisioned by the encyclical is that the world is
dominated either by state-controlled institutions or monopoly capitalistic enterprises, where room for individual self-determination has
been eclipsed. Within this context the encyclical affirmed the right of
private property, yet it outlined that all material goods were to be
used in light of the common good (QA 49). Its teaching treats the
role of major institutions such as the state and the importance of
intermediate or subsidiary groups and associations in the social order.
Quadragesimo Anno has the first reference to the concept of social
justice, meaning the reciprocal rights and duties of social groups and
their members in relation to the common good. Social justice is the
obligation of individuals to participate, according to their ability and
position, in group action that is designed to make the institutions of
society conform to the common good in the socio-economic sphere.[19]

Subsidiarity and Corporatism

Quadragesimo Anno is known principally for two main concepts in
social thought: "subsidiarity" and "corporatism" (or "solidarism").
Subsidiarity is a social concept that arose out of the German social

---

[17] Thomas C. Kohler, *"Quadragesimo Anno,"* in *A Century of Catholic Social Thought,*
op. cit., 27.

[18] Marie J. Giblin, *"Quadragesimo Anno,"* in *The New Dictionary of Catholic Social
Thought,* op. cit., 804.

[19] John F. Cronin, *Catholic Social Principles* (Milwaukee: Bruce Publishing, 1950)
112.

movement of Bishop von Ketteler. This principle outlines that the state and all other associations exist for the individual. Societies should not assume what individuals can do, nor should larger societies do what smaller associations can accomplish. The state is responsible to take up those tasks that neither individuals nor smaller societies can perform. While this concept was also used by Leo XIII, in *Quadragesimo Anno* it became an established part of church social teaching as a basic norm for the proper ordering of civil society.[20]

Corporatism was a plan to reorganize the social structure of the economy. A corporatist structure is actually a picture of how the principle of subsidiarity would function in a planned, organized economic society. Corporatism is based upon the assumption than an organized economic society is as natural and as necessary as an organized political society. In the absence of a properly organized political society, the result is anarchy or dictatorship. In the absence of an organized economic society, uncontrolled competition or concentration of ownership and economic control result.

A corporatist social structure is organized not in classes but in vocational groups. All people engaged in a given industry or profession, from worker to management, are in the same group. This type of social organization, which establishes "occupational" groups of trades or professions, aims at overcoming of the division of people into the two camps of workers and employers. It was believed that these people, since they had similar goals through their profession, are naturally united, just as people who live in proximity to one another are united by geography. Through shared interest and common goals the flourishing of the profession or trade results. This would be accomplished in a harmonious atmosphere, rather than in the climate of conflict, as suggested by the socialist, or one of unrelenting competition, as promoted by capitalists. Corporations formed in a corporatist manner were to be the middle way between a liberal and individualist capitalism that exploited the people and an atheistic socialism, which denied spiritual truths and was gaining great power in the world.

Quadragesimo Anno explains these new vocational groupings (QA 81–87) formed through free association. The state was not to control them. Rather, these "industrial councils," as they were called in the United States, were to work collaboratively with the state for the eco-

---

[20] Joseph Komonchak, "Subsidiarity in the Church: The State of the Question," *The Jurist*, vol. 48, (1988) 301–2.

nomic health of the country. What obscured the corporatist visions was its close resemblance to the corporative organization supported by fascism in Italy. Mussolini's fascism differed from Pius XI's corporatism in that in the former, the state formed, maintained and controlled the councils. Authoritarian to fascist-type corporative arrangements in Portugal, Austria, France, Spain, and Brazil all claimed affinity with the Pope's vision. However, in all these situations corporations were organs of state control with political roles.[21] The Pope's vision of corporatism was identified with these programs, mistakenly. After fascism was defeated, this social program could no longer be offered as a serious constructive proposal in the world community. The value of subsidiarity continued in the social teaching tradition, but not under the concrete form of corporatism.

Pius XII, The War Years and the 1950s

In 1939 Eugenio Maria Pacelli was elected pope, and took the name Pius XII. 1939 was the last year of peace before the horrors of World War II were to begin. Pius XII wrote no social encyclical; however, he contributed to social teaching through a series of letters and messages to the world over his twenty-year pontificate. During most of his papacy, the world was so dominated by the political issues of World War II that socio-economic questions were given less attention.[22] Since the time of Pius XI, the world had changed again, because of war, which made the future look uncertain and destroyed many time-held structures.

The "time of realism" that colored the papacy of Pius XII was mirrored in the Protestant community in the movement away from the social gospel thinkers such as Rauschenbusch to the Christian realism of Reinhold Niebuhr. The turn of the century social gospel thinkers reflected a progressive view of society and an overly optimistic view of the human person. Social ills would be overcome, they believed, through the education of the population to better social ideals and the collaborative working together of all members of society. After World War I this progressive view of the human person and society

---

[21] Marie J. Giblin, "Corporatism," in *The New Dictionary of Catholic Social Thought*, op. cit., 246.

[22] Donal Dorr, *Option for the Poor: A Hundred Years of Catholic Social Teaching* (Maryknoll, N.Y.: Orbis Books, 1992) 96.

fell apart and was replaced with the Christian realism of Reinhold Niebuhr. The horrors of war, the experience of the inhumanity of people to one another, led Niebuhr to reclaim a strong doctrine of sin in his evaluation of the modern human condition.[23] Evil in society could only be checked through power as a necessary form of love. Niebuhr's thought became the theological foundation of the post-war cold war policy of the United States, which argued for a deterrent nuclear force to check Soviet aggression.[24]

World War II overshadowed all other concerns in the early days of the pontificate of Pius XII. Throughout the war he tried to remain neutral in the issues that divided the East and the West because there were lives at stake and members of the Church on both sides.[25] In post-war conflicts Pius XII favored the West and their democratic institutions. Despite his awareness of the abuses of capitalism, it remained the only option powerful and viable enough to check the spread of communism. The "third-way" efforts of Pius XI in corporatism had been discredited by this time. Government intervention into capitalistic economies through Keynesian policies had stabilized these systems through the war. Post-war progress of free economies appeared to offer a solution to the poverty of workers and a rise in living standards. Economic liberty provided political liberty and social freedoms. Such factors made it difficult for Pius XII to credibly criticize capitalism, although philosophically he, along with his predecessors, rejected its underlying philosophy.[26]

By 1955 Christian Democratic movements held nearly two-thirds of the seats in the lower houses of parliament in Britain, France, Belgium, Austria, and parts of Germany, France, and North Italy.[27] These movements, Catholic and Protestant, were fed by climates where religious observance was common. Massive youth and family movements gave Christian Democracy and Christian Action a strong position in these countries as well. Christian Democratic movements

---

[23] Reinhold Niebuhr, *The Nature and Destiny of Man. Vols. I and II* (New York: Charles Scribner's Sons, 1934).

[24] Paul Merkley, *Reinhold Niebuhr: A Political Account* (Montreal: McGill-Queen's University Press, 1975) see ch. 14.

[25] W. A. Purdy, *The Church on the Move: The Characters and Policies of Pius XII and John XXIII* (New York: John Day, 1965) 90–91.

[26] Dorr, *Option for the Poor,* 100ff.

[27] Purdy, *The Church on the Move,* 55.

were supported by a strong press, Catholic and Protestant universities, schools, and research and service agencies.[28] Trade unions, social insurance, the welfare state, and mixed economic arrangements enjoyed the favor of the Church and the Catholic parties.

In this climate Pius XII reformulated the teaching on private property.[29] It is a basic human right to have access to whatever material goods are needed for one's full development as a human person. Yet, this right needs to be held in tension with the general right of all people to the use of the goods of the earth. Pius XII spoke primarily against a socialistic appropriation of property. Even other clear and undisputed property rights cannot suppress the individual right to private property. It is the role of the state not to take the property of citizens, but to protect and implement policy reform that ensures this right.

In post-war times new massive social systems were constructed, built upon the international networks created during the war. Pius XII was concerned that the massive systems of the modern world could swallow up the individual person. He was concerned about the growing powerlessness of the individual to take personal responsibility for many aspects of his life. This concern was shared by sociologists such as Max Weber, Emile Durkheim, and George Simmel who questioned the new "bureaucratization of the human spirit."[30]

Perhaps the most controversial aspect of the papacy of Pius XII was his stance toward Nazi Germany and the Holocaust. Popes of the modern era walked a thin line between a non-partisan stance that required from all states simply the freedom to function as Church, to actions of advocacy or partiality, where church power was used to support clear political action, such as the Hungarian Revolt of 1956. Pius XII has been criticized for his partiality for Germany up to and into World War II and for his resulting silence about the Nazi atrocities as well.[31]

Those who support Pius XII claim that the main reason for his partiality for Germany (distinguished from Nazism) was his fear of

---

[28] M. P. Fogarty, *Christian Democracy in Western Europe, 1820–1953* (Westport, Conn.: Greenwood Press, 1974) 8.

[29] Dorr, *Option for the Poor,* 104.

[30] Robert A. Nisbet, *The Sociological Imagination* (New York: Basic Books, 1966) ch. 7.

[31] Purdy, *The Church on the Move,* 255ff.

and opposition to communism. Communism was the primary enemy of both the Church and European civilization.[32] This fear and the responsibility Pius XII felt for preventing reprisals against the Church's members and personnel led to what some see as an undo reserve and silence in spite of knowledge of the atrocities. Others judge that Pius XII acted appropriately given the constraints of the situation. This is an issue about which historians continue to debate.

Social Catholicism of the Pre-Vatican Era

Religious practice is never purely uniform, nor easily defined. Religion always contains within its traditions critical and creative elements; hence, practice is rarely simply the reflection of society. Even within the same religion and the same period of history, religious commitment can express different hopes and expectations depending often on the class or race of the believers and their situation in society. Though it is impossible to come to quick generalizations about an approach to Catholicism shared by all, we will attempt to look for some broad trends that identify ways the Catholic Church responded at this time. We will assume that the social encyclical tradition, in this first period, expressed how the content of faith, spiritual practices, and church membership related to the transformation of modern industrial society. Two trends stand out.

The Church gradually moved from encouraging the upper class to respond to the problems of the industrial revolution through charity to the lower classes to a more broad-based moral message to the working class. All were to take responsibility for the creation of a more just world, and democratic states were to advocate for the human rights of all its citizens.

The Church moved from giving moral legitimacy to a social and political order that guaranteed the *ancient regime* to a gradual acceptance of democratic states. Pope Pius XII in his 1944 Christmas address drew links between political freedom, democracy, and the Christian tradition. Earlier church sentiments viewed democracy as simply one among many equal forms of government, all of which are acceptable to the degree they promote the common good. In later thought the Church gradually saw that democracy was most in keep-

---

[32] Christine E. Gudorf, *Catholic Social Teaching on Liberation Themes* (Washington, D.C.: University Press of America, 1981) 85.

ing with the nature of human freedom and with Christian values around freedom.[33]

Even though the Church reminded states of their responsibilities, social teaching was addressed mainly to the individual. Faith influenced society primarily by the way it transformed the individual to more just relationships. The new hearts of individuals would produce a new society. People were called through faith not only to wrestle with personal sin but also to restructure human life toward greater justice and reconciliation through applying Christian principles to everyday situations.

The relationship of faith to social change was understood in the Vatican I model of the relationship between the natural and the supernatural. The secular involved "natural knowledge" or reason. Faith pertained to a body of revealed, supernatural truths.[34] Between these two orders of knowledge exists a relationship that is negative and extrinsic. The negative relationship exists in that the two orders cannot contradict one another. The extrinsic relationship is grounded in the fact that the same God who reveals the mysteries also endows the human soul with the light of reason. The Church did recognize the natural order and natural causes for social problems. However, in this dualistic framework, the Church gave primary attention to moral and spiritual reform as the goal of faith in its approach to social reform. The implementation of such reform was the special prerogative of the Church. The roots of social disorganization lie in sin and are moral and religious. Without the Church there is no social reform.

The practice of faith fosters social virtues and responsibility in the individual. Of course, there are social overtones and expressions to this growth process. For example, laborers are to work an honest day's work; employers are to pay a fair wage. However, when Catholics acted in the society in a group, Catholic associations are to be the avenue of group action. There were two forms of this action. Catholic Action involved joining a specifically Christian party or social organization or working through established, strictly non-confessional parties or institutions.

---

[33] Heinrich A. Rommen, *The State in Catholic Thought* (St. Louis: Herder, 1955) 480ff. Paul E. Sigmund, "Democracy," in *The New Dictionary of Catholic Social Thought*, op. cit., 275.

[34] William Dych, S.J., "The Dualism in the Faith of the Church," in *Faith That Does Justice*, John C. Haughey, ed. (New York: Paulist Press, 1977) 54ff.

Characteristic of church-sponsored social action is the Catholic Action movement or Sodality Movement of the Christian Family Movement, where each individual was encouraged to engage in greater awareness of social processes through the "see, judge, and act" method. An individual observes and gathers facts on a particular problem, the problem is judged in light of the Gospels and an action is taken. This social inquiry method also was a structural way that the Church reinforced its faith-based view of the human person. The person was free and possessed the capacity to reason. Each man and woman had an eternal destiny and inalienable rights. Indirectly these movements were a protest against any form of totalitarianism and against secularist liberal capitalism as it had developed in Western society.

The movement from Leo XIII to Vatican II was a move away from certain assumptions about the direction of society and the practice of Catholic spirituality toward something new, yet not defined. It was generally held during this period that the problem with society was that secular society had fallen away from the Church.[35] The problem in the citizen's heart was that greed and irreligion had led to overinvestment in secular matters and lack of attention to the spiritual life. Spirituality was a personal response toward a society that was no longer Christian.

While the Church advocated greater social investment, it was supported by a spirituality of withdrawal and separation from the world, which paradoxically was to feed the transformation of society. Social principles were to be taught and then translated into right action. However, the language of the Church's involvement in society was mainly spiritual, and focused on individuals. The work of the Church in society was to aid all in achieving their heavenly destiny. At this point the Church had a commitment to society, but a spirituality of withdrawal from the world.

A just and democratic society provided conditions conducive to the activity of the Church in the world. A society inspired by Christian principles was an ideal broader than the close unity between the Church and social life that existed in the Middle Ages. It recognized in part the autonomy of secular life, or how involvement in earthly affairs related to Christian fidelity. The split between the material order and the supernatural, which characterized Catholic theology

---

[35] David J. O'Brien, *American Catholics and Social Reform: The New Deal Years* (New York: Oxford University Press, 1975) 22ff.

prior to Vatican II, set the stage for the Church's understanding of how the spiritual life and social action intersected.[36] This model depicted the world in terms of the Church, rather than the Church in terms of the world. It strongly separated faith and temporal realities and the roles of the priest and the layperson.

A popular symbol of the times was that Catholics were to walk under the banner of Christ the King. In the United States this meant not only attendance at the sacraments but the social involvement in a round of activities that immersed the Catholic in a social entity that sheltered them from an alien and hostile world.[37] There was compatibility between Americanism and Catholicism. However, Catholics were isolated from reform movements in the wider society.

Separation from broad social movement was fostered by a concern that social action on the part of Catholics would be linked to the clergy and the hierarchy. While there was a role for laity in Catholic Action, these action groups were to be church-based and church-monitored. Catholic Action was participation of the laity in the apostolate of the hierarchy.[38] The Church did sponsor multiple social-welfare agencies and charitable institutions under Catholic auspices. These often extended relationships beyond church boundaries.[39] Yet, most Catholics held that social problems could be solved by personal morality, a Christian upbringing, private charity, and close association with the Church.[40]

Thomas F. O'Dea's *American Catholic Dilemma* spoke of the change needed in the Church at the end of this period.[41] The weakness of the Church at this time came from within, and not just from external factors such as poverty, immigrant populations and anti-Catholic prejudice. This critical climate challenged the Church to look at its formalism, authoritarianism, clericalism, moralism, and defensiveness. Many called for reform. This was a testimony that the Church's

---

[36] For a discussion of the "distinction of the planes," see Gustavo Gutierrez, *A Theology of Liberation* (Maryknoll, N.Y.: Orbis Books, 1997) 43ff.

[37] O'Brien, *American Catholics and Social Reform,* 30.

[38] Purdy, *The Church on the Move,* 176.

[39] Monsignor Robert E. Keegan, "Diocesan Organization in Charity," in *American Catholic Thought on Social Questions,* Aaron I. Abell, ed. (New York: Bobs-Merrill, 1968) 312ff.

[40] Aaron I. Abell, *American Catholicism and Social Action* (Garden City: Doubleday, 1960) ch. 2.

[41] Purdy, *The Church on the Move,* 175.

strength and capacity for self-reflection were more forceful than its elements of decline and disintegration. In spiritual terms, it was a movement of the Holy Spirit. The time was ripe for a renewal in the Church itself, and we will see that this new vision provided fresh incentives for the investment of the Church in the transformation of society.

Chapter Six

Social Teaching of John XXIII and Paul VI

The 1960s

When John XXIII issued *Mater et Magistra* in 1961, it was a time of great change and social upheaval. The devastating impact of the Second World War was still fresh in the minds of many, yet massive social, cultural, political, and economic shifts were about to displace it as a focal experience. After the bombing of Hiroshima, the world was confronted with the reality of atomic weapons. Yet there were signs of hope. The discoveries of the war years began to shape a global system of communication, international science, medicine, and education. Wartime and post-war economic improvements fostered a new consensus in the free world. "Social welfare," or state-sponsored social programs, grew in first world society. Citizens were open to the establishment of new systems of social support in order to prevent the world from ever slipping again into the deprivations of the depression.

New economic outreach transformed the international market. Foreign investments by the United States corporations increased fourfold between 1945–1965. However, along with new investments in foreign lands came awareness of the evils of old and new colonization of Africa, Asia, and Latin America. New desires for freedom arose out of old patterns of economic and political control. Supported by their economic experience during World War II, women were asking for a role in public affairs. A Europe symbolized by the Berlin Wall held a tenuous peace. The cold war between the free world and the communist world was one of markets as well as weapons and military networks. Krushchev was leader of the Kremlim. Castro was actively setting up a new regime in Cuba. There was a Catholic president in the White House. It was an unprecedented time of optimism, forward-looking planning, and enthusiasm for the future.

John XXIII

John XXIII turned the face of the Church toward the world. John shared in the optimistic outlook of his day. This optimism was displayed primarily in his embrace of the world.[1] John was positive not just about the world in general. He was hopeful that the world before him, the modern world, would be a new era for the human family.[2] The conquest of space, the kind of society that was emerging from rapid economic growth amazed him. He hoped that the benefits that had already reached many in modern society would soon touch those not yet released from their poverty by improvements accomplished in industrialized societies.

In convening Vatican II, John XXIII called for a renewal of the doctrines of the Church in consistence with the contemporary world, or a spirit of *aggiornamento*. This did not mean he wanted church teaching to simply adapt to cultural beliefs or to take on the plausibility structures of modern thinking. Rather, he believed that in real exchange with modern culture, deeply held beliefs in the Church would take new form, and their inherent power in the gospel would assume a new energy and force in the world. The world was not a place where the Church was to give correction; the world was a dialogue partner with whom new solutions would be found to the problems of humanity. John XXIII's embrace of the world meant his support of the public, political, and social engagement of the Church and its members.

John's two major social encyclicals, *Mater et Magistra:* Christianity and Social Progress (1961) and *Pacem et Terris:* Peace on Earth (1963), displayed a spirituality of embrace of the world. John was not afraid that commitment to the world and its values would cause people to neglect their spiritual vision or life. Rather, he affirmed that an interior

---

[1] Peter and Margaret Hebblethwaite, *John XXIII: Pope of the Century* (New York: Continuum, 2000). E.E.Y. Hales, *Pope John and His Revolution* (New York: Image Books, 1966).

[2] Donal Dorr, *Option for the Poor* (Maryknoll, N.Y.: Orbis Books, 1992) 117.

unity could exist between religious faith and action in the temporal sphere.

The 1960s were a time when the "establishment" of power and authority in many sectors of society was being questioned. In this context John XXIII addressed the question of authority. He spoke of human authority as coming from God. But he distinguished between authority and the office holder. Human authority is subject to a higher authority, attention to what is morally right and to the common good (PT 47, 84). This position opened the door to the moral possibility of questioning authority as an aspect of Christian living. Such a conception would have been almost impossible in the time of Leo XIII, whose fear of civil disorder closed most doors to any censure of authority. Rather John's spirit allowed a more critical evaluation of those in authority. His position legitimized some dissent in society as an expression of Christian commitment.

John's optimism fed his belief that people could cooperate on the international level. In the context of an escalating arms race and cold war, he gave humankind a favorable evaluation. Christian realists, like Reinhold Niebuhr, in contrast, held that people in groups tended to engage in more evil than they might alone. The larger the group, in fact, the more it is able to defy any social restraints.[3] Sin, for Niebuhr, is more than a conscious rejection of the common good; sin involves living under a deception.[4] Since a group maintains its self respect by hiding the truth of its shared life from itself, the group is more susceptible to pretension than the individual.[5]

This attention to the negative potential in human beings led Niebuhr to believe that it was only through force and counter force that the shadow side of human nature could be held in check. Evil has a social dimension that is institutionalized nationally in a type of group pride. Niebuhr felt that self interest has to be taken into account as a continuing fact of human life, especially on the international level. His theology did support the cold war "balance of terror" and fear of a nuclear holocaust as an unfortunate reality of maintaining a

---

[3] Reinhold Niebuhr, *Moral Man and Immoral Society* (New York: Charles Scribner's Sons, 1932) 48.

[4] Reinhold Niebuhr, *An Interpretation of Christian Ethics* (New York: Harper and Brothers, 1935) 70.

[5] Reinhold Niebuhr, *Reflections on the End of an Era* (New York: Charles Scribner's Sons, 1934) 73.

"real peace."[6] In his words, "The domination of one life by another is avoided most successfully by an equilibrium of power and vitalities, so that weakness does not invite enslavement by the strong."[7]

John's fostering of international systems therefore was an important antidote to the tension of the cold war build up. He did not deny the realities that were maintained by the school of Christian realism. However, his emphasis was more on the collaborative potential of the new world order.

Developmentalism

On the whole, John's optimism followed the prevailing optimism of his age. Key to this thinking was the theory of development. During the Kennedy era people were so pleased with the post-World War II successes in the U.S. economy that they believed that the eradication of poverty was just around the corner. People thought that economic growth, increasing the size of the economic pie, was a key to the solution of poverty. The same "development" experienced in flourishing post-war economies could be accomplished by countries across the globe that were poor if they departed from their traditional modes of organizing their economy and adopted modern industrial techniques. This translated into the belief that if third-world countries abandoned their agricultural societies and industrialized, their expanded gross national product and subsequent improved status in international trade would relieve their national poverty.

A nation's poverty, according to this theory, was more a matter of economic choice or its solution a lack of political priority than a technological or institutional necessity.[8] However, what was not evident at the time, or what was not addressed by those who put forth these theories, were some very important "facts" of first-world development.

Through the Marshall Plan after World War II, the United States and other major powers gained access to trade relationships in Africa and South America, who held "colonial" ties to major European countries in exchange for aid to Europe for post-war reconstruction.

---

[6] Paul Merkley, *Reinhold Niebuhr: A Political Account* (Montreal: McGill University Press, 1975) 195–96.

[7] Niebuhr, *An Interpretation of Christian Ethics,* 245.

[8] A classic theorist of development, W. W. Rostow, *The Stages of Economic Growth* (London: Cambridge University Press, 1971).

A major factor in the new post-war growth in industrialized nations was the removal and use of natural resources from the poorer nations. As we moved into these countries and built factories and refineries, the industrialization that we were promoting did not serve the needs of their economy. Rather, these countries were to make products that in turn were to be shipped to and sold in first-world countries. The "new economy" of development theory developed "centers" or richer economies and "periphery" or dependent economies. Poorer countries could not set economic goals. They were dependent on first-world investment and susceptible then to a new type of economic control. Even those who had money in these economies tended to invest according to this pattern instead of following a different vision of national interest.

As this development era continued, poorer countries borrowed money from international banks and their systems in order to stay in this international economy. In order to manufacture products, they had to import expensive machinery that they purchased from the first world. They also had to import the technological knowledge to run it, fix it, and improve it. The ability for poorer countries to orient their industry to the creation of goods that could be purchased by the average citizen was totally impaired by the fact that their total resources, balance of trade, and brain power were monopolized in a dependency relationship with the first world. The result was that, in the ten years of the development era, poverty in poor countries increased rather than decreased.

Limits to Growth and the Welfare State

John XXIII's rather romantic view of capitalism, shared by those who held a development mentality, overlooked some important facts. First, just because an economy expands, it does not follow that distribution of wealth in the economy will necessarily change. This is also true across the globe. It was at this time that people began to take note that 20 percent of the world's population was using 80 percent of the world's resources. Second, people did not consider seriously enough that third-world countries experienced limits to growth that were not faced by first-world countries. For instance, first-world economic development was stimulated by the third-world's natural resources. The third-world countries could not repeat this process. Third, people caught in the development mentality did not realize that an indefinite period of rapid economic growth can no longer be presumed. It was only later that a group fostering a "limits to growth" mentality entered the mainstream economic discussion.[9]

The Welfare State in more prosperous countries responded to this awareness of the "limits to growth" on a national scale. The Welfare State, or the tendency of the state to provide an ever expanding array of social services, actually began with the various ways governments intervened in the economy prior to World War II. It was built on a consensus after the war among workers that they would never again face the deprivations of the depression years.

The Welfare State is built on the premise that economic growth will not necessarily provide for the poor. Rather, a free-enterprise system has an inherent tendency toward imbalance and concentration of wealth. In England, for example, the Welfare State was connected with a tax system sufficiently tough to redistribute wealth in a significant way.[10] In the United States, the Welfare State never had this same economic bite. However, anywhere in the Western world where it was put in, it represented a compromise—a way of combining social compassion with the efficiency and respect for the initiative of the free-enterprise system. John supported the Welfare State and saw it as a constructive tool to mitigate the deficiencies and cope with the causalities of the economic system (MM 167–68).

From the way things looked to John XXIII, there was no real need to call for a radical reconstruction of society. Progressive economic and social movements were in place in society to create the conditions that could respond to the Church's classical social concerns of the need for full employment, to overcome scarcity (MM 20) and promote an equitable society (MM 109). John XXIII noted that modern society was marked by "technical and scientific progress, greater productive efficiency, and a higher standard of living among citizens" (MM 59). However, the post-war society also posed new problems for the Church's social mission. We find in John XXIII and his successor Paul VI a gradual realization that all was not well with the modern world.

---

[9] This discussion has been advanced in the 1990s as ethicists and environmentalists reject the development indicators of "growth," as growth in the GNP, as adequate measures of a sustainable future for the globe. See Larry Rasmussen, *Earth Community, Earth Ethics* (Maryknoll, N.Y.: Orbis Books, 1997).

[10] Dorr, *Option for the Poor,* 125.

Post-War Economy

The emphasis on economic growth after World War II required that the post-war economy be built upon an ever-expanding per capita consumption level. Thus was born the "high consumption" society. This type of society has profound implications far beyond the economy itself.

In a high growth society producers have to entice consumers to spend at least at the same rate from an ever expanding personal income. Through advertising, product differentiation, or the creation of real or imagined differences in essentially the same type of product, and physical and stylistic obsolescence, consumers were convinced that they needed to buy new products and discard the old. On the level of pastoral practice, we see consumerism as a personal vice; however, in this light it is also a socially constructed reality. Concepts of virtue and vice are reversed in this new economy. Consumption is turned into a virtue; and thrift—which had been one of the cardinal American virtues and part of the Depression ethic—had to be demoted to at best a minor virtue. People were encouraged to spend the higher wages they were earning.

At the same time old myths regarding the poor were maintained in society. The absence of thrift, along with laziness remained as the favored explanation for individual poverty. Yet to insure that the poor participated even marginally in the economy, government-sponsored economic security programs grew. The continuous expansion of new products resulted in a sharp increase in natural resource use and an increase in environmental pollution. Talk of "clean air" entered the American vocabulary. Potential resource shortages were dismissed with the argument that science and technology would provide timely substitutes, and pollution was acknowledged as the price of progress.

In this consumer society government was called upon to play an ever more active role. To fuel this consumer economy the United States had to tap the world's resources. As a result, foreign investments by United States corporations increased fourfold between 1945 and 1965.[11] To protect these investments and to maintain a democratic front before communism, the United States had to maintain a worldwide military network. This military expansion was possible because the U.S. was not strapped with war reconstruction as other capitalist

---

[11] For this overview I am relying on Charles K. Wilber and Kenneth P. Jameson, *An Inquiry into the Poverty of Economics* (Notre Dame, Ind.: University of Notre Dame Press, 1983) esp. 1–19.

countries. The military was a huge budgetary output; however, the cost of the military was balanced by the industry that it created. In the next decade, this was referred to simply as a military-industrial complex.

During the pontificate of John XXIII, we had the "golden age" of American capitalist democracy and comparable growth across the free world. In addition to successful government intervention in the economy, this period saw the launching of the Peace Corps and the War on Poverty. It was the era of the New Frontier and the Great Society. Per-capita income and consumption expanded dramatically. Full employment and stable prices were achieved. People believed that all that was needed was a fine-tuning of the economy in order to banish forever the twin evils of inflation and unemployment. The eradication of poverty was just around the corner. This was the time when John wrote his encyclicals. Both reflected this optimism, while *Pacem in Terris* addressed the concerns of a cold war that was the by-product of the increased military build-up.

When John XXIII reflected on how things had changed since Pius XII, he did not have to look far. Things had changed not only in the internal situation of each individual country but also in the mutual relations of the countries across the globe (MM 46). John noted the discovery of atomic energy, its use for military and peaceful ends, medical and chemical research, automation of industry and services, modernization of agriculture, increased social mobility, and developments in radio and television. John saw that people were laying aside colonial systems. Political participation was increasing. The world was growing more globally interdependent and some "supranational" national organization was becoming more and more important.

In order to respond to these developments and to affirm the right of individual initiative, John XXIII reaffirmed the principle of subsidiarity. This principle of Catholic social teaching directs that a problem should be solved at the lowest level of an organization that can address it effectively. Massive governmental structures should not usurp the right for individuals and small communities to define their futures. Yet, the post-war world order also demanded new forms of coordination and cooperation.

New Social Relationships

A characteristic of John XXIII's social thought is his emphasis on socialization, or "the multiplication of social relationships" (MM 59,

62, 63). John differed from the conservative movements of the century that defended the "traditional" independence of the individual
against the encroachments of society in the form of the state. Rather
John viewed this rugged individualism as rooted in nineteenth-
century thought, not the freedom supported in the Church's social
tradition. A cultural climate of individualism had weakened traditional social relationships and the obligations attached to them. On
the one hand, the cultural quest for freedom created a greater individual independence; on the other hand, it made it easier to live free
from social constraints. What fed a greater scope for initiative also
allowed a new opportunism and exploitation of the poor. When the
poor tried to protect themselves against exploitation, the rich justified their actions as needed for freedom and scope for initiative.

John XXIII recognized there was need for new forms of social
institutions and restraints. Society was more than a stage on which
individuals fulfilled themselves. Rather society itself needed to be
tended and shaped. This demanded planning and control. Those who
enjoyed the benefits of the nineteenth-century approach resisted the
implications of this approach and the programs that resulted. Tax
assessment, credit facilities, price support and regulation, and even
state ownership of some industries were seen as within the legitimate
role of the state. While John XXIII affirmed the principle of subsidiarity, he also recognized that the common good required far more
state "interference" than was needed in the past. Men and women
had to join together in new associations, such as health care and
insurance programs, to meet their needs in modern society. *Mater et
Magistra* mandates this extra involvement on both the national and
international level. John's stance cautioned against an ideological use
of Catholic social teaching on private property and the right of
personal initiative as a cover and legitimization for resistance to the
changes needed to promote social justice.[12]

Pacem in Terris

John XXIII's *Pacem in Terris* outlines fresh avenues of social justice
in light of major changes across the globe. A growing awareness of
equality, resistance to patterns of racism, calls for decolonization, and
new demands for the status and role of women reflected that humankind itself was in a new phase of its development, which would call

[12] Dorr, *Option for the Poor,* 132–42.

for new forms of political organization (PT 44–45). John recognized there was no political organization that could attend to a common good beyond that of nation states or an alliance of states. Structurally this meant the world needed a universal public authority capable of acting toward a universal common good (PT 137). Its role would be the protection of basic human rights (PT 9–27). John's recognition of freedom and human rights as the foundation of the social order was an important step in the Church's modern social teaching.[13] It re-interpreted traditional natural law, notions of the common good, and the order willed by God around an integrating concept of the dignity of the human person.[14]

In *Pacem in Terris* John insists that key to the peace of this new world order is attention to issues of deterrence and disarmament and recognition of the brain and economic drain the arms race is causing the world (PT 109). A policy of complete disarmament based on better relations between nations would focus on trust rather than fear. In his characteristic optimism John XXIII believed this program "can be brought to pass" (PT 113). John changed the whole frame-work for discussion of the use of violence in an atomic era. He insisted that "in this atomic era, it is irrational any longer to think of war as an apt means to vindicate violated rights" (PT 127). Vatican II called this shift a whole new attitude toward war (GS 80).[15]

Vatican II

Between the teaching of John XXIII and Paul VI is the teaching of Vatican II. Since an ecumenical council is a meeting of the leadership of the whole Church, the process of the council itself, beyond the documents it produced, had a profound effect on social teaching.[16]

---

[13] See David Hollenbach, S.J., *Claims in Conflict: Retrieving and Renewing the Catholic Human Rights Tradition* (New York: Paulist Press, 1979); *The Common Good and Christian Ethics* (Cambridge: Cambridge University Press, 2002).

[14] Kenneth P. J. Hallahan, *"Pacem in Terris,"* in *The New Dictionary of Catholic Social Thought,* op. cit., 706.

[15] See Thomas J. Gumbleton, "Peacemaking as a Way of Life," in *One Hundred Years of Catholic Social Thought*, John A. Coleman, ed. (Maryknoll, N.Y.: Orbis Books, 1991) 305.

[16] For reflection on women at the council, see Carmel Elizabeth McEnroy R.S.M., *Guests in Their Own House: The Women of Vatican II* (New York: Crossroads/ Herder and Herder, 1996).

This can be seen in three ways. First, the council produced documents on issues that were not directly related to social justice, but involved theological understandings that ultimately bore upon social practice. The relationship of the Church to the world, a vision of the human person, concepts of nature and grace, authority and religious freedom, all impacted a new vision of Catholic life that influenced how the Church's social mission was understood. Second, at the council the participants developed a new consensus on social matters that had not previously existed. As bishops and cardinals from Europe and North America listened to the issues of the bishops from Asia, Africa and Latin America, the meaning of global problems moved from the theoretical to the pastoral. They became pastors listening to other pastors about the problems of their people. Early concerns of the council focused on the tensions between the liberal and conservative Church in Europe and North America. However, by the latter sessions of the council, concern shifted to justice in the world. The council ended with a new consensus that gave social teaching "more weight," since its issues were better understood in the body of the leadership. This conviction regarding social affairs carried over into the implementation of the social message of the council into the dioceses of the world.

Third, the council produced *Gaudium et Spes*, the document on the Church in the Modern World, which sought to address the pressing cultural, social, economic, and political questions of the day. This document was the longest of the council documents and was debated and re-drafted throughout the council's four sessions. The significance of *Gaudium et Spes* is that for the first time a formal statement by an ecumenical council addressed the world beyond the Church in all its pluralism and complexity. Previous councils addressed themselves solely to the internal doctrinal and disciplinary affairs of the Church, as did all other documents of Vatican II.[17] *Gaudium et Spes* was both doctrinal, in the sense that it articulated fundamental dogmatic principles on the nature and destiny of men and women, and pastoral, because it sought to apply those principles to the circumstances of the modern world.

---

[17] Mary Eberstadt, *"Gaudium et Spes,"* in *A Century of Catholic Social Thought*, George Weigel and Robert Royal, eds. (Washington, D.C.: Ethics and Public Policy Center, 1991) 82.

Gaudium et Spes notes the sweeping social changes that have affected all aspects of human society (GS 5). All must strive to read the "signs of the times." Men and women are to use their human freedom responsibly to shape this world according to those values that safeguard human dignity. This responsibility is exercised through conscience. Here the council goes beyond a simple following of law to a call to be creative and discerning in moral responsibility for the world.

The document advances social teaching in four ways. First, it tempers the extraordinary optimism of John XXIII. It demonstrates the beginnings of a realism that Paul VI will develop. It does so, not by toning down John XXIII's Christian hope and high ideals, but by adopting a more dialectical approach. The ideal is contrasted with reality, a reality marred by social evil. For example, the bishops recognize that people are often "spurred toward evil by the social circumstances in which they live" (GS 25). Here is the acknowledgement of social or structural sin. They condemn inequality (GS 29, 66) and call for social change (GS 26, 42, 66, 85, 86).[18]

Second, when the document speaks of peace that is built on justice, justice is not simply the putting right of political grievances. Just relationships extend to the whole economic order. The council went against the opinion, common among statesmen in more "developed" countries, that a more peaceful world can be brought about without too much tampering with the present inequitable world order. The council documents make clear there are not two distinct international questions, one about peace and one about economics. The two are the same question.

Third, when the document deals with the question of an option for the poor, it goes beyond the concept of poor individuals. It speaks of poor countries. Those in extreme need are not isolated individuals who have slipped through an adequate social system, but whole peoples living an entirely different reality than the wealthy (GS 63).

Fourth, *Gaudium et Spes* begins thinking on the question of a new international economic order, a question that is taken up by Paul VI in more detail. The document calls attention to an incipient doubt over the logic of the development era by calling for a reassessment of economic and social structures. It notes the injustice in international trade and the unequal powers of trading partners (GS 83, 85). Before

---

[18] See Lois Ann Lorentzen, *"Gaudium et Spes,"* in *The New Dictionary of Catholic Social Thought,* op. cit., 416.

the realities of the internationalization of labor, it notes that human labor is not a commodity. Human labor is "superior to the other elements of economic life. For the latter will have only the nature of tools" (GS 67).

The council affirmed the common purpose of all created things (GS 69). This forms a backdrop to its teaching on private property. In Latin America it was common to have *latifundia* or large estates. The question arose whether it was ever right to expropriate and divide up this land, a key question of land-reform ethics at the time. What would justify the confiscation of such properties? The mere fact there are so many poor people in these countries is not sufficient reason for confiscation of lands. The key point to discern is whether the landowners are making proper use of their land. The direct connection between the possession of huge land-holding and the blatant exploitation of the local population was in the mind of the council fathers, yet it had to be balanced with the right to private property. Dorr finds in the council fathers' openness to expropriation the willingness to accept that in many actual cases the balance tips in favor of the poor and powerless. In the concrete, the right to private property has to yield to the cry of the poor—and therefore expropriation becomes justifiable.[19]

Another important issue of *Gaudium et Spes* is its framing of the teaching on the obligation to help the poor. Traditionally, the Fathers and Doctors of the Church taught that people are obliged to come to the relief of the poor, and to do so not merely out of their superfluous goods. Leo had taught that people are obliged to give to the poor out of what remains over when they have provided for their own needs and for what is appropriate to their station in life. In practice, this gave rise to the attempt to measure what amount of wealth is appropriate to the status of different classes of people. The remainder was deemed "superfluous." This kind of calculation allowed the rich to assume they had no obligation to give to the poor until the normal status symbols of their class had been acquired. Vatican II went back to a more ancient tradition, before Aquinas, upon whom Leo had based his teaching. They relied on Basil, Augustine, Gregory the Great, Bonaventure, and Albert the Great. The obligation to help the poor was basic to the Christian life, and was not just based on superfluous goods.

---

[19] Dorr, *Option for the Poor,* 159.

Gaudium et Spes represents a notable change of emphasis on property and its rights. There is a shift away from the rights due to property owners. One does not merely have to meet the basic needs of those in dire want but also must ensure that power and wealth are distributed fairly. To do this there was need for major changes in the economic structures of the world.

Paul VI and the 1970s

The economic consensus of the development era began to show its cracks by the 1970s. Between 1973–1975 there was the longest and deepest recession/depression in the United States and many places in the world since the 1930s. By the 1970s it was evident that the gap between the rich and poor was far from narrowing; it was growing wider. Paul VI's encyclical *Populorum Progressio:* On the Development of the Peoples (1967) offered a new analysis of the relationship between the rich and the poor. It addressed the relationships of rich and poor nations, rather than rich and poor individuals or classes. The social question was no longer just national; it was worldwide.

The war in Vietnam, revolt of the young on campuses, inflation, food and oil shortages, and recession in the United States and in much of the free world provided a changed atmosphere to the optimism of John XXIII. However, new institutional developments in the economy had the most significant impact on the changed reality of the 1970s. Multinational corporations using transfer pricing could now buy and sell from their own subsidiaries and thus establish prices that had little connection to their true market price. When a single corporate headquarters is buyer and seller of goods, the concept of competition shifts in meaning. Materials made in a poorer country were often undervalued in this system, with companies seeking third-world destinations since they had to pay less tax to produce their goods.

Cross-subsidization led to extension of control on the part of a few corporations over many other facets of economic life. Cross-subsidization is the use of power and resources developed in one profit center to start or expand another. A large company could undersell another in one part of the country from the profits accrued in another. After a smaller company was taken over, they could then raise prices. This practice led to one company extending control into related industries. For example, energy companies could control not only oil but electric and coal resources as well. The result was that 60 percent of the resources of a country was run by a few hundred firms, and the rest was made up of smaller firms dependent on the others for survival.[20]

The extent of these new developments, some in use on smaller scales for years, made it difficult for economists to plan well or to predict the interventions that would stabilize the economy. The impotence of governments to control multi-national corporations and the rise of economic blocks such as OPEC shattered the consensus built during the development era. Its optimism was checked by the simultaneous appearance of massive unemployment and double-digit inflation.

Paul VI, instead of praising development efforts in the third world, pointed to the ambiguous character of neo-colonial interventions. He bluntly raised the question, why are whole countries poor? He saw three reasons for the economic domination of first-world countries at the international level and their power both politically and economically at the national level of other countries. The first cause is the evil effects left by colonialism. Not only were foreign powers destructively intervening in third-world countries but also within them a small privileged national elite held a monopoly of wealth and power. The second cause of such widespread poverty was a "new colonialism" caused by first-world investment in the third-world and the reciprocal political, cultural, and economic control that resulted.

The third cause was the imbalance of power between nations, an imbalance that gave rise to injustice in trade relations between them. On an international level the system of trade insures that "poor nations become poorer while the rich ones become still richer" (P.P. 57). Paul asserted that the rule of "free trade," taken alone, is no longer able to govern international relations. Instead, he calls for a structure to promote real competition among trading partners. A support system is needed on the global level that is analogous to those on national levels that support weaker sectors of the economy. A similar system needs to be introduced between rich and poor countries. This proposal for a planned approach on a world scale, aimed at the protection of the weak and the stabilization of markets, is very close to the

---

[20] Wilber and Jameson, *The Poverty of Economics,* 3, 34, 176–77.

demands made a few years later for "A New International Economic Order" by the United Nations.

Paul VI stressed that in the past the Church's involvement to foster human progress was done mainly through local and individual undertakings, but now these are not enough. Rather in this new situation the Church must offer a conception of integral human development, a development of the whole person and of all persons and peoples, as a guide toward social action (P.P. 14–21). A central point in Paul's concept of human development is that individuals and peoples should be enabled to have the prime responsibility for their own development (P.P. 15, 25, 27). The importance of basic education and literacy is the key that enables people to assume responsibility for themselves, their lives, and their world.

However, development is not only a concern of the poor. Since development is a new name for peace, concern over development belongs to all. To enable this new vision of integral human development, Paul calls for a change in the attitudes of the non-poor as well as a change in structures. One approach alone in insufficient.

While there are no purely "Catholic" answers to social and economic problems, the Church needs to unite with all people of good will, government authorities, and people of learning to work toward solutions to world problems (P.P. 81–86). A new consensus needs to be formed, and in Paul's mind, the first-world powers have a key role in its development.

Paul recognizes that change in attitudes is insufficient without a change in structures. Particularly there was need for a world government, some authority that can monitor international trade and the ensuing cultural, political, and social relationships that flow from this position (P.P. 78). The close link between the economic order and the political order demanded that new agreements be established across a broad spectrum of issues from price controls to support for new industries. Coordination of these efforts needed to happen through new international structures.

Perhaps the most controversial issue during Paul's pontificate was widespread revolutionary activity in third-world countries and the Church's role in it. Was engaging in revolution an act of discipleship? Did the traditional teaching on revolution hold in these troubled times, that is, that revolutions should be avoided and they cause more harm than good? Paul noted that the Church has to be realistic about revolution, and so do those in positions of control. When flagrant and long-standing violations of human rights are ignored, the path of violent revolution ensues.[21] These are situations where injustice cries to heaven (P.P. 31). Paul does not legitimate revolution in a blanket manner. He saw it as a real threat when the legitimate needs of the poor are ignored. Paul reminded the Church and the world that revolution produces new injustices, and recovery is long and difficult. However, unless the present situation is faced with courage and injustices addressed, the choice between the real evil in the present and the projected cost of greater misery in the future gets tipped in favor of revolution. He reminds the world, "When whole populations destitute of necessities live in a state of dependence barring them from all initiative and responsibility, and all opportunity to advance culturally and share in social and political life, recourse to violence, as a means to right these wrongs to human dignity, is a grave temptation" (P.P. 30).

Octogesimo Adveniens

On May 14, 1971, Pope Paul VI sent an apostolic letter to Maurice Cardinal Roy of Quebec, chair of the Pontifical Commission of Justice and Peace. Titled *A Call to Action (Octogesimo Adveniens),* the letter marked by the eightieth anniversary of Leo XIII's *Rerum Novarum.* Between Paul's earlier *Populorum Progressio* (1967) and his new work, the synod of bishops produced in November 1971 *Justice in the World (Justitio in Mundo)* in which the bishops underscored the centrality and indispensability of the work of justice in the preaching and living out of the Gospel and in the Church's mission.[22]

Octogesimo Adveniens inaugurated another major shift in the methodology of Catholic Social Teaching. Departing from previous papal policy, Paul VI stated the difficulty in uttering a unified message from Rome about social problems all over the world and to put forth a solution that has universal validity (OA 4, 42). Paul reexamines the tendency in the past, on the part of Rome, to hand down solutions to specific social questions. Catholic Social Teaching relied on a method that assumed one can readily deduce applications of principles to

[21] Alfred T. Hennelly, S.J., *"Populorum Progressio,"* in *The New Dictionary of Catholic Social Thought,* op. cit., 766.

[22] Ronald Hamel, "Justice in the World," in *The New Dictionary of Catholic Social Thought,* op. cit., 496.

changing circumstances. The effectiveness of this approach is re-examined in face of growing realities of social complexities.[23] Each continental reality was so different that it became increasingly diffi-cult to say something true that equally applied in the same way to all. Differences of region, culture, and socio-political systems increase the need for personal discernment in decisions regarding social justice. Paul thought it was the task of the Christian community to analyze their own country's situation and to discern the vast options for ur-gently needed changes (OA 4). Politically, it left room for a measure of pluralism in relation to options about political activity.

In this encyclical Paul addressed the political realities of inter-national relationships. In contrast to emphasis on economic issues alone, Paul acknowledged that most social problems are at bottom political problems. Many popes proposed political solutions to eco-nomic and social problems, but Paul recognized clearly that designing and bringing into effect such solutions brings one into the sphere of political activity. This position is very significant for a shift in Catho-lic spirituality. It indicates that political activity can be an expression of Christian discipleship.

Development or Liberation?

While Paul never used "liberation" language, his approach to the need for equality and participation in order to promote human dig-nity laid the groundwork for this concept developed in depth by the Latin American church (OA 22). The concept of liberation is a far more dynamic lens to view the world's problems than the develop-ment mentality used in the 1960s. When development is taken as the focal point through which analysis is done, there is a tendency to see difficulties such as poverty, apathy, and poor distribution of resources as problems that have not yet been solved. This clouds the real rela-tionship between the rich and the poor.

Paul VI recognized that some nations or groups are poor, not just because they have failed to climb the development ladder but be-cause they have been prevented by others from doing so. Large segments of populations are excluded from active participation in shaping the social, economic, and political structures that provide the

---

[23] Philip S. Land, "The Social Theology of Pope Paul VI," *America*, May 12, 1979, 394.

context for their lives. This is true not only within countries but also between countries. This lack of political participation, and power, creates a social marginalization manifested in poverty and degrading dependency. This is to be overcome, not through increased public assistance or private charity, but through the participation of those who are marginalized in the reshaping of systems and structures of their societies.[24] Decisions for change are inept without the political power to enforce them. For Paul VI, "the need is felt to pass from economics to politics" (OA 46). The taking up of responsibility, called for by John XXIII, must now extend to the political sphere.

Paul's turn to the political echoes liberation sentiments in that both share a perspective in which political action is necessary for change (OA 46). Oppression caused by being marginated from political power needs to be shaken off. Oppressed peoples and social classes aspire to change, which puts them at odds with wealthy nations and oppressive classes (OA 45). Paul admits that the conflictual aspect of the economic, social, and political processes needed to change and calls for the Church to stand on the side of the poor in these situations (OA 15).

Paul VI shares in the liberation sentiment that history is not just the passing of time, but the sphere in which men and women assume conscious responsibility for their destiny (OA 37). People create history and in this process create themselves and their communities. They do this "in the course of a historical and psychological process in which constraint and freedom as well as the weight of sin and the breath of the Spirit alternate and struggle for the upper hand" (OA 37). The gradual exercise of true freedom leads to the creation of new men and women and to a qualitatively different society.

At the deepest level, liberation is that which is brought to us by Christ. Paul echoes the christological dimension of the human struggle for liberation. Christ, the Savior, liberates men and women from sin, which is the ultimate root of all disruption of friendship and of all injustice and oppression. The Christian's hope rests in knowing that the Lord is already working with us in the world and continuing the "redemption which was accomplished on the Cross and which burst forth in victory on the morning of the Resurrection" (OA 48). This hope also springs from knowing other men and women are at work in

---

[24] Bernard F. Evans, *"Octogesima Adveniens,"* in *The New Dictionary of Catholic Social Thought,* op. cit., 692.

the world on issues of justice and peace. Christ makes all free and enables each person to live in communion. This forms the basis for all human community.

These aspects of the liberation process that are shared by Paul VI are not successive phases but rather three aspects of a complex process that finds its deepest sense and its fullest realization in the saving work of Christ. Response to this work of Christ through political options requires faith, and since response is done in concrete situations, one must recognize a legitimate variety of possible options. "The same Christian faith can lead to different commitments" (OA 50). Different strategies can affect a common concern for justice. However, as Christians began to enter into the murky waters of political activity, and in political situations far removed from the Christian parties and parallel Catholic society of mid-century Europe, the question arose. Does this plurality of options permit Catholics to cooperate with movements or organizations advocating positions opposed to church teaching?

Paul VI and Marxism

Christians cannot adhere to any ideological system that contradicts their faith or their belief in the dignity and destiny of the human person (OA 31). In this respect Paul VI criticizes both liberalism and socialism (OA 32–36). On some continents, however, the political parties making strides and offering programs for national change and development were Marxist. The question arose, how far could Christians enter into the activities of these parties, and at what point must they part company because of their incompatibility with Christian belief?

Paul makes the distinction between the use of Marxist analysis and following Marxist philosophy. To use Marxist analysis in social analysis means to ask some of the same questions of a situation as Marx did in his writings. Questions such as how does money or control over resources affect what ideas are circulated, undermined, or suppressed in a society reflect Marxist analysis. This type of questioning has also made its way from Marxist philosophy into mainstream social thought. Most good social analysts would ask this question.

To follow Marxist philosophy means to think about life as Marx did. The Church has condemned Marxist philosophy because it holds that human beings are simply part of a historical process wherein the underclass will gradually, through conflict, overcome the upper class and a classless society will be formed. The Church has condemned this worldview because it views the human person not as free, but rather as a cog in a historical process whose outcome is already set.

Paul VI cautions against accepting a Marxist type of analysis of society without adverting to how it is related to the Marxist view of the world or ideology. It is illusionary "to accept the elements of Marxist analysis without recognizing their relationships with ideology" (OA 34). It is also dangerous to enter into class struggle unconscious of the "kind of totalitarian and violent society to which this process leads" (Ibid.). Christians were not forbidden to join with Marxists movements, but they were to do so with their eyes open.

Christians were called to discern how any system served societal transformation, but were cautioned not to accept any system uncritically and as offering a total worldview. Liberalism also held "an erroneous affirmation of the autonomy of the individual" (OA 35). Christians were not to confuse a liberal ideological position with the meaning of Christian freedom.

Social Catholicism in the 1960s and 1970s

The 1970s marked a reading of the "signs of the times" called for by John XXIII. However, this reading was more critical than affirmative. The complexity of the world system made the handing down of solutions to social problems from Rome more problematic. The 1970s opened a new door to the recognition of pluralism in the Church and a call for local discernment of the call for justice within a particular situation. This more contextual and diverse approach to social problems also stimulated a spiritual renewal characterized by option for the poor and willingness to engage in political activity for the cause of justice. It forged a link between the Church and the sciences needed to read society: sociology, psychology, political science, and economics.

In the 1970s the Church thought less deductively about social policy, trying to glean solutions to social problems from principles alone. A more inductive approach was introduced, which accepted that if one is to discover universal principles about social morality, then one must start from the variety of cultural and geographical situations in which moral issues arise. This call for discernment and reading the signs of the times encouraged continental churches to begin a formal reflection on the meaning of faith in relationship to the question of justice and the call to political activity in their context. It set the stage for the rise of two new theological movements in the Church, political theology in Europe and liberation theology in Latin America, and its counterparts in Black, Hispanic, Feminist, Asian, and African theological reflection. All shared the common starting point of reflecting on the meaning of Christian faith from a concrete place, with specific concern for justice, in modern society. The Social Catholicism of this period cannot be assessed without attention to these significant movements.

Chapter Seven

Political Theology

The Catholic Social Tradition, since the Industrial Revolution, reflects the struggle of the Church to adapt to the modern world and
yet avoid an uncritical adoption of the ideals of the Enlightenment.
To adjust to this new world, the Church sought to integrate "history"
and "society" into its form of theological thinking. History means
more than the passing of time; rather, it reflects how human freedom
affects the real conditions of human flourishing and suffering. Society
is not a given; rather, it is something we construct as a shared social
condition in which we live and as a vehicle through which we become
fully human. Political and liberation theology take both seriously,
allowing "history" and "society" to become central categories in their
interpretation of the Christian life. Both theologies have had profound impact on the way the Church thinks about its social mission
and formulates its spirituality of social involvement.

Political Theology

Political theology arose in Germany in the 1960s. It reflects the
post-war awareness in Europe that after Auschwitz theology could no
longer be done in a purely speculative fashion. Theology had to address the real suffering done in history. Political theology prefigured
the sense of the "new evangelization" called for in the post Vatican II
Church, evangelization that brought the meaning of the Gospel to
the great struggles of human living. It endeavored to reflect the sentiment of *Gaudium et Spes* that the hopes and fears of the peoples of

the world were of grave concern to the Church. Catholic theologian Johann Baptist Metz and evangelicals Dorothee Solle and Jurgen Moltmann are major theologians of this movement. Political theology contributes to our understanding of social teaching as a vision of the modern context of faith and theological links between the meaning of faith, society and the nature of political action. We will look at its expression primarily in Roman Catholic thought.

Changed Context of Modern Society

"God is dead" was a familiar cry of the 1960s in theological circles. This was not a designation of atheism, but an attempt to express a post-war experience of the struggle to believe. God was experienced as absent from the world. This sentiment arose as a response to the suffering and inhumanity of the war, but it also was fed by a growing secularized atmosphere in the modern industrial society begun by the Enlightenment.

The Western European Enlightenment shifted consciousness away from the religiously unified world of the Middle Ages to a situation where God was no longer a working hypothesis for morality, politics, and science. Technology, rational thinking, and control of nature replaced a divinized world where God's presence was known from the cosmos, human existence, or from history. The human person found only himself or herself in the world, not God. Reality no longer appeared as numinous or mysterious. Reality was simply the sphere where human beings experienced themselves alive and facing the world day by day. The Enlightenment shattered the unity of religion and society and reduced Christianity to a single phenomenon among others in a pluralistic world.[1]

Theological Responses to the Enlightenment

One response to this Enlightenment world was existential and personalistic theology. In order to accommodate Christian faith in a secularized society, existentialist theology accepts the separation of the public dimensions of life from the private. Religion is relegated to the personal sphere, leaving the social dimension of Christianity to a

---

[1] Michael Paul Gallagher, *Clashing Symbols: An Introduction to Faith and Culture* (London: Darton, Longman, Todd: 1997) ch. 6.

secondary importance. The result is that the Christian message is privatized, and the practice of faith consists mainly of individual decisions, private virtues, and the focus on I-Thou encounters with God.

Political theologians claim that existentialist approaches are inadequate for modern faith because they do not meet the challenge to express the relationship between faith and societal living under the conditions of modern life. To link faith and society, theology must be "deprivatized," and it must lead the believer to see the relevance of the Christian message beyond the personal realm and must express the meaning of the Gospel in relationship to the real issues of life in society. Political theology, in this sense, gets it name. Political is contrasted with the private and individual, with the acknowledgement that to express one's faith socially in modern society, social involvement necessarily includes political action.[2]

Political theology sees itself as a fundamental theology, that is, one that defends, justifies or gives an account of the authenticity of religion, the task of "apologetics."[3] Since modern unbelief often arises from the scandal of social evil, and goodness appears powerless before massive human suffering, religion must address suffering and evil to be viewed as real. Political theologians are aware that not everyone responds to problems in modern society with faith. Some simply deny suffering and reject the need for God at all. In place of God they believe in rational society or technological power. Political theology criticizes this approach. Society is no substitution for God, and technology and reason do not resolve all of life's questions. Religion is just one option among many in Enlightenment thought, an antidote or balm to problems. But closer examination reveals that this type of religion is humanly created and simply fills a social need without embracing a religious posture. In an elective universe where humans can fill all needs without a deity, the prototype Enlightenment world, such a humanly constructed "religion" is an illusion. This inaccurate view of religion is fostered by Enlightenment attitudes.

Political theologians hold that the Enlightenment culture defined the Church as unnecessary and promoted a weak Church, one which

---

[2] Francis P. Fiorenza, "Political Theology and Liberation Theology: an inquiry into their Fundamental Meaning," in *Liberation, Freedom and Revolution,* T. McFadden, ed. (New York: Seabury Press, 1975) 9.

[3] Johann Baptist Metz, *Faith in History and Society* (New York: Seabury Press, 1980) 7.

is convenient, and culturally correct. Such a Church is incapable of representing the Gospel or challenging its members. The Enlightenment world-view promised humankind health, wealth and happiness through the powers of rational humanity and the innovations of technology. It did not address the reality of human suffering or encourage acknowledgement of the many who never shared in its promise of progress. Who needs a Church or religion that makes demands when people are urged to embrace only one side of life, the sweet without the bitter?

It is not hard to recognize that modern people experience the spiritual emptiness that such an evasion of life produces.[4] A religion that simply mimics the prevailing cultural biases cannot serve the spiritual needs of the people. A religion that makes no demands, cannot console. A religion that does not foster faith cannot provide means for transformation. For political theologians the mindset of modern culture itself is a false consciousness, one that obscures rather than points to God's reality and its significance for human happiness. Political theology sees cultural criticism as essential for theological reflection.

Political Theology Critically Responds

What is needed today is the "enlightenment of the Enlightenment," according to political theologians. The Enlightenment called on men and women to use their reason to improve their lives. However, the political or public reason in the Enlightenment was directed to what already existed. It was not a call to create new social conditions. The Enlightenment did call men and woman to act morally. However, the morality espoused had more to do with individuals acting with honor in a society of exchange than a moral praxis that would correct the weaknesses of society. The human person who the Enlightenment focused upon was not every human being, rather it was the person who had already achieved power in the society, the new middle class.[5]

What is evident to political theologians is the majority of people in the world have not "come of age." They are not middle-class persons,

[4] For a similar cultural criticism of modern society, see Christopher Lasch, *The True and Only Heaven: Progress and Its Critics* (New York: W. W. Norton, 1991).
[5] Metz, *Faith in History and Society*, 53. See also 43.

the only persons recognized by the rhetoric of the Enlightenment. These people suffered, were forgotten, and marginalized, and today are the underclass of the world. Political theologians want to reorder theology so that the human person is properly identified and not equated with the middle class alone. They intend each human person, and all human beings, free from these inadequate methods of interpretation can be recognized and seen as the object of God's love.

How does one link faith, history, and society in a way that God's transcendence in modern society is recognized? Political theologians see religion as key to the future of society. Throughout history men and women have acquired an identity as a subject, a unique human person, and become the subject of their own history through their practice of religion. Religious awareness gave them a basis of self-worth beyond that rendered by their situation or society. Besides grounding human dignity, religion also recognizes the truth of God's transcendence. True religion affirms God's identity beyond any cultural definitions or dismissals of God's reality. For political theology religion and religious practice are key to the future of society because the truth of God's transcendence protects human beings from being reduced to any system of thought or definition. Without religion human dignity is often eclipsed or forgotten. Religion recognizes that essential to human personhood is the capacity to grow in freedom in history and society, or in the language of the encyclicals, to grow in integral human development.

How do political theologians articulate a vision of the Christian faith that relates to modern society and yet steps outside the limitations of the worldview of a particular situation? In other words how do political theologians stand free from the cultural biases in which they too are immersed? They do so through incorporating themes, of freedom, memory of suffering, the future, and narrative into their theological reflection. Attention to these theological realities makes it more difficult to "settle" into a mere cultural expression of religion. By inquiring into these themes we hope to catch some major movements of this important theological development.

Human Freedom

Among the most central concepts in contemporary theology is freedom. Since modern living highlights the capacity and right to be free as never before in history, human freedom is a central and important

area for theological reflection. Yet political theologians consider freedom with three nuances that distinguish them. All three are criticisms
of common theological emphases. First, human freedom is considered
in broader terms than categories of personal self-awareness. Second,
notions of God are avoided that are abstract and depict God as
absent and removed from the concerns of daily living. Third, political
theology does not oppose a private spiritual life and social involvement; rather, it sees them as compatible.

When freedom is thought of only in private terms, God removed
from everyday life and problems of evil in society, and spirituality is
limited to interpersonal relationships and the practice of personal
virtue, there is a distortion of religion. Metz claims the result is a
"bourgeois theology" that actually conceals rather than illumines the
real path of Christian freedom and conversion. This distortion
widens the gap between what Christianity preaches and claims and
what Christians actually live and surrender to in modern society.[6] It
makes it easier to compartmentalize one's living and one's religion.
The above is the religion of the middle class. It appears to espouse
belief in conversion; however, its religious vision rests more in the un-
questioned status of the middle class in the world, and its religious
practice establishes not the reign of God but middle class self-interests
and future.[7] Any adequate theology must correct this problem.

Human freedom rests not in an act of self awareness, but in a confrontation with the truth of oneself that occurs only through action.
Political theology claims that real self awareness comes through action.
The "light" of self awareness that occurs in this process cannot be
known apart from being done. The process of doing, in turn, defines
human action in freedom. As men and women reflect on their actions, they never really know through their conscience alone the total
quality of their action. Conscience rather immerses men and women
more deliberately into life itself and the mystery of their own freedom and ultimately to union with God. For political theologians conscience is not a possession of self-knowledge of personal freedom, but
rather that which leads one in a movement forward into action into

---

[6] Johann Baptist Metz, "Political Theology," in *Encyclopedia of Theology: The
Concise Sacramentum Mundi,* Karl Rahner, ed. (New York: Seabury Press, 1975)
1239.

[7] Johann Baptist Metz, *The Emergent Church,* Peter Mann, trans. (New York:
Crossroad, 1986) 5.

the darkness and mystery of freedom. In Metz's words, ". . . he has the light of truth not when he looks back to comprehend himself but only when he forgets himself in the rapture of each new deed."[8] In some spiritual traditions this is called the "rapture of action." In political theology this relationship between social involvement, self understanding, and union with God is the basis of the mystical/political identity of the human person.

It is not just any doing or activity that leads to true freedom.[9] It is action that imitates the love of Jesus in the concrete realities of one's social situation. Jesus Christ is the one who frees us to know ourselves, to experience our freedom in a way we could not by ourselves.[10] Following Christ is not limited to just knowing about him or having an intellectual grasp that he brings salvation to our lives. Rather, following Christ concretely in action is essential to knowing him.[11] One knows the liberation, which has been given to them in Christ, when one acts out of it. In modern times the following of Christ is a search in the darkness. It is an affirmation of values of human worth and dignity before obstacles, frustrations, and set backs. For political theology men and women only follow Christ as disciples in an obscurity or searching of freedom in which they come to know not only Jesus but also their true selves.

Because of the great suffering in modern society, the following of Jesus can only be done in hope, in the midst of the concrete realities of the present day. It isn't done simply within oneself, through personal reflection, but in a co-world with others where the freedom of the "other" affects the possibility of concretely living out one's own ultimate freedom. The following of Christ is done in community and society.

The reform of the Church and the transformation of society thus are integral to Christian living. Ultimately, faith links us to the memory of Jesus, and faith brings the event of Jesus Christ into the reality of our own lives and into the society in which we live. In contrast to a

[8] Johann Baptist Metz, "Freedom as a Threshold Problem Between Philosophy and Theology," *Philosophy Today*, 10 (Winter, 1966) 271.

[9] The concept of "doing" to which political theologians refer is also called praxis. See Roger Haight, S.J., "Praxis," in *The New Dictionary of Catholic Social Thought*, op. cit., 776–77.

[10] Metz, *Faith in History and Society*, 54.

[11] Johann Baptist Metz, *Followers of Christ* (New York: Paulist Press, 1977) 40. See also *Faith in History and Society*, 51–54.

view of the Christian life where society is seen as a place of Christian activity, where one applies what one learns privately or spiritually, political theology sees society as an essential medium for the discovery of theological truth and the meaning of human freedom.

Political theology does not deny the individual's relationship to God or the traditional function of personal conscience. However, central to its theological reflection are the promises of the reign of God in the New Testament, freedom, justice, peace, and reconciliation. These represent not just private realities, but public ones as well. In other words, they emphasize that these realities of the Kingdom cannot be entirely identified with the longing for peace and freedom in the individual. These promises make the individual free in that they commit them to critique their absence in society and work toward their creation. Political theology does not seek to return the world to a less secularized society, but rather to create within secularized society the realities of the Kingdom.

Memory of Suffering

The Enlightenment looks at history in terms of evolution and progress. Thus, the Enlightenment culture holds in memory only what has succeeded, forgetting what has been destroyed. Political theology calls for another approach to the past, which can elicit a different focus on the future.

The real history of humankind shows that not everyone "developed" or progressed by the changes in modern society. As Germany acknowledged the events of the Holocaust, it was aware that the "modern age" was more than a series of progressive accomplishments, but also involved a history of domination and subjugation. A "moral" remembrance of history means history's disasters can not be evaded. Political theology was extremely important in post-war Germany when denial of the facts of the Holocaust occurred. It provided the corrective that memory has to include the memory of suffering. To engage in such a truthful yet painful memory requires faith.

Memory of Jesus' own passion and death gives the Christian the strength not to pick and choose in his or her remembering and to avoid what does not fulfill a cultural or personal vision of progress and development. Through memory of the passion, death, and resurrection of Jesus in the praxis of freedom, the suffering inherent to human life in history becomes transparent.[12] As Christians work to overcome this suffering, they know Jesus in a new way.

Christian memory links us to the future because it gives rise to the eschatological hope made possible in Jesus Christ. Hope in turn assists us to make practical the truth of the passion, death, and resurrection of Jesus in the world, not by turning a deaf ear to the problems of our society but by transforming the conditions of those who suffer. Christian memory mediates between the already and the not yet of the eschatological salvation made possible in Jesus Christ because it anticipates the future as a future of those who are oppressed, without hope and doomed to fail. It is a dangerous memory and a liberating memory because it reminds us not of some open future, but precisely of this future and the future of these peoples. It compels Christians to change themselves so that they can take this future into account. Finally, it is the memory that protects the true identity of the human person in the world who slips through the legitimating qualities of the middle class. It is precisely these "other" human beings whose identity is lost in contemporary consciousness.

Memory is more than reminiscing about the "good old days" or a memory of individual happiness. Memory, in political theology, has a future content. It is a "dangerous memory" because it "threatens the present and calls it into question because it remembers a future that is still outstanding."[13] For political theology, memory of the suffering and death of Jesus does not lead to cultural optimism alone. It does not foster belief in "progress" or natural progression or a leap to the "new man" of the Enlightenment who believes life proceeds from suffering, but that the future follows a script already known.[14] Rather memory is a reflection on concrete human suffering that is the point at which the proclamation of the new and essentially human way of life that is announced in the resurrection of Jesus Christ can begin. This memory does more than mirror existing social relationships; it remembers those who have been lost, who have suffered in history. This memory is open to a new future.

---

[12] "Praxis" here refers to the doing related to knowing as described above.

[13] Metz, *Faith in History and Society,* 200.

[14] Ibid., 112. This would be known through evolutionary or socialist modes of thought, class struggle, or theories of development. Metz would hold that an eschatological approach would cut through these theories and ask whose development, whose progress, and whose process? See 101, 111.

Future

Political theology uses the concept of the future as a key term of theological reflection. It does this in three ways, and again all three are critical. First, a Christian understanding of the future criticizes other philosophical orientations to history. Second, political theologians criticize views of the future in which it is defined simply as "not yet" rather than radically "new." Third, they avoid linking the future with a view of nature that gives it a pre-determined goal.

The future is difficult to detect in popular philosophy, either traditional Scholasticism, transcendentalism, personalism or existentialism, according to political theologians. The future is seen as an extension of the present, what is "always" there. What is "not yet" or the "new" cannot be considered in these approaches. The "new" requires the kind of "doing mind" that is indigenous to human freedom. Action and reflection done in hope creates something "never-have-been." This for political theologians is closer to the future of the eschatological hope of the Gospel and the way for its message to take root in modern society.

Political theology is concerned about society's influence on people's thinking or human reason.[15] People often consider themselves "radical" or "progressive" thinkers, but they are often so conditioned by the "common sense" of their society that they never break through into a new future, which addresses the concerns of the oppressed. Yet how we think about the future is important. When we follow the prevailing thought of our day, we generally forget the poor and those who suffer. The future is simply the "not yet" of our projected future, which does not address their needs. This cultural view of the future does not take into account that God's kingdom "breaks through" and often upsets our tidy systems. The future therefore needs to be approached through a critical reason, which accepts that the future promised by God cannot in any way be adequately conceived under the conditions of the present.[16]

[15] For further analysis of Metz's theology, see Matthew L. Lamb, *Solidarity with Victims: Toward a Theology of Social Transformation* (New York: Crossroad, 1982), James Matthew Ashley, *Interruptions: Mysticism, Politics, and Theology in the Work of Johann Baptist Metz* (Notre Dame, Ind.: University of Notre Dame Press, 1998), Rebecca S. Chopp, *The Praxis of Suffering: An Interpretation of Liberation and Political Theologies* (Maryknoll, N.Y.: Orbis Books, 1986).

[16] Metz, "Political Theology," 1240.

Our view of the future is related to our view of history. As long as history is thought of primarily as past and present, it can be thought of as a reality that has taken place or is taking place now and can become "common sense" or static in our imaginations. The future in such a system of thought is something already imagined, but "not yet." The future has a goal that is pre-determined.[17]

However, for political theology, history is the history of freedom. It is the history of the human effort in struggle and obscurity to act freely in spite of the lack of neat systems of understanding of what is ahead. It is a history of suffering. True history only comes to light in view of God's promise centered in God's transcendence.[18] Sometimes it is only over a long period of time that we understand the sense of an event or a direction that is emerging in society. The true future gets its unity, not because it arises out of our schemes but because it rests in God's transcendence. It does not arise out of human potential alone, but out of a partnership with God in which our freedom is summoned to its historical potential. This future is capable of freeing something new, centered in a truth that must be done rather than just known.

Memory links one to the past, the present, and the future and involves one in a dynamic doctrinal tradition. One might think that doctrine centers one in a past and is not open to the type of future described above. Nothing could be further from the truth in political theology. Memory of freedom is also a memory of tradition. Political theology's focus on the future is not a call to dissociate oneself from the tradition; rather, one comes to Christian identity within it.

Political theologians assume that contained within the development of dogma is the tension between prevailing consciousness and true freedom that underlies the critical approach dogma upholds. Memory is not vague and without substance; rather, it involves a dogmatic faith tied to a certain content.[19] Tradition and dogma are not mental escapes for the Christian; rather, they call them beyond personal experience into the reality of the other and they promote action. Contained within dogma is the dangerous memory of the freedom of Christ that promotes Christians to imitate Jesus both in

---

[17] Metz, *Faith in History and Society,"* 163.

[18] Johann Baptist Metz, "The Responsibility of Hope," *Philosophy Today*, 10 (Winter, 1966) 282.

[19] Metz, *Faith in History and Society,* 201, 204.

action and critical consciousness within society. For political theologians dogmatic faith and imitation of Christ are "indissolubly connected to each other" through memory.

Narrative

Dangerous memory is transmitted in a narrative way rather than in a speculative manner. Since contemporary culture treats the tradition simply as history, as something of the past to be intellectually grasped, political theologians use the concept of narrative to go beyond this approach. Dangerous memory communicates what cognitive categories cannot communicate.[20] Memory recounts the conflict and contradiction in life. It is a story of the suffering experience of those who are treated as non-persons, a story of violence and oppression, injustice and inequality, guilt, finiteness, and death. Narration of these stories links history to the reality of salvation where this conflict and contradiction is reconciled in Jesus Christ.[21] Through narrative the story of salvation is tied to real situations, and the story of real situations is linked to salvation and not torn from its truth as a history touched by salvation rather than simply a disaster.

Narrative gives history, as a history of suffering, a transformative character and frees history to be a new future. It connects our story, and the story of those who suffer and have suffered, to the story of the passion and death of Jesus Christ.[22] It presents to Christian freedom the reality of the distance between what is and what ought to be in such a manner that can only be overcome through faith, solidarity with victims, and action for justice. To oppose the meaninglessness created by suffering becomes indispensable to the Christian life. Narrative thus takes us beyond the mere acceptance of suffering, or the focus on our own suffering, and brings us into the suffering of the

[20] Ibid., 206.

[21] It is obvious that the eucharistic liturgy is the main ecclesial tradition for both expressing and empowering faith as imitation of Christ in solidarity with the living and the dead. Metz argues in later work, "Do this in remembrance of me," constitutes the key way in which Christianity has preserved its distinctive form of memory. See Johann Baptist Metz, *A Passion for God: The Mystical-Political Dimension of Christianity* (New York: Paulist Press, 1998) 131.

[22] For a study of the link between memory in political theology and the Eucharist, see Bruce T. Morrill, *Anamnesis as Dangerous Memory: Political and Liturgical Theology in Dialogue* (Collegeville: The Liturgical Press, 2000).

"other." Narrative acknowledges that some have been overcome, and through this memory of suffering it stimulates solidarity with victims.

In the spiritual tradition "passio" refers often to the acceptance of suffering or a type of passivity before suffering linked to memory of Jesus' suffering and death on the cross. But here, through the narration of "passio" in the lives of real victims, and uniting it to the memory of the passion, death, and resurrection of Jesus, the Christian is lead to action. The memory is not a mere psychological one, but one Christians also accomplish.[23] The Christian, reconciled through Jesus Christ participates in salvation in history through action for justice seeking a new future for victims. Narrative, as story, connects us with the incarnational heart of the Christian faith.

Political Theology and Social Teaching

Political theology and social teaching share the concern of living the call to justice in the Gospel vis-à-vis modern society. While different forms of expression, both are modern assertions of the inherent connection between faith and justice in the Christian life. Political theology, however, assists Catholic social thought in addressing particular theological problems of linking faith and justice in the Christian life.

First, political theology demonstrates that theological thinking is rooted in a context. Theology is not something done outside history, or a time and place. Encounter with a culture free gospel is impossible.[24] However, this "root" in culture has a downside. Political theology reminds the Church that theology too has to examine itself to see whether it simply reflects the world-view of the prevailing world order, using God-language to legitimate the status quo, or whether it can critically reveal God's transcendence as calling into question all systems of injustice and the theories that support them. A main obligation of all theology is self-criticism in regard to its implications for just living. Resistance to the status quo is not only a form of Christian discipleship but also it is an essential ingredient in theological reflection.

[23] Metz, *Faith in History and Society,* 90.
[24] Michael Paul Gallagher, *Crashing Symbols: An Introduction to Faith and Culture* (London: Darton, Longman and Todd, 1997) 103.

In this sense political theology is rooted in the prophetic tradition, and it contributes to the prophetic element of Catholic Social Thought. However, political theology also reminds the Church that it does not simply look at the world from the outside as an object to be understood. The Church, when it engages in social teaching, views the world from within and is already impacted by the world it seeks to transform.

Political theology also highlights a new relationship between theory and practice in theology. Instead of abstract social principles being applied to particular situations, political theology suggests that only through immersion in a social situation will one even understand what social principles mean. Political theology reverses the traditional theory-praxis relationship in Catholic Social Thought. Insofar as social thought was conceived as an independent and a-historical theory that could simply provide a guide for faith and action in a particular situation, political theology claims that this approach is inadequate. Theory about Christian life in society is a changing articulation of ethical aims that arise from faith, revelation, and practice and lead to practice. Political theology holds that the perennial nature of Catholic social thought, attested to by the tradition, has its core structure in the sociopolitical content of the Christian Gospel itself. The trial between Jesus and the social authorities of his time is a constant trial between his eschatological message of the kingdom of God and our sociopolitical reality.[25] Political theologians include practice as a source of theology along with other sources for reflection such as revelation, philosophy, and the tradition.

Faith is not something prior to sociopolitical action in the sense that Christians have a faith and apply it to action for justice. Political theologians find in the moral and social practice of Christians the truth of the faith itself, and not simply its preservation, is at stake. Political theology holds, perhaps stronger than other schools of thought, that "witness" to faith is constitutive of faith itself.[26] Faith in practice is the door to knowing Jesus. Only through imitation of Jesus do Christians really know him.

We find though a mirror of this approach in the posture assumed by the Synod of Bishops in 1971. Social teaching and action for

---

[25] Kroh, "Political Theology," 749.

[26] It is a debate in and about political theology as to the full relationship between orthopraxis and orthodoxy.

justice are not simply an activity of the Church, but part of the constitutive nature of the Church itself. We find this theme in the Synod Document of Justice in the World when it states: "Action on behalf of justice and participation in the transformation of the world fully appear to us as a constitutive dimension of the preaching of the Gospel, or, in other words, of the Church's mission for the redemption of the human race and its liberation from every oppressive situation" (JW 6).

Finally, political theology contributes to social teaching its vision of the following of Christ. To imitate Christ is individual and societal, religious, and political. Christians witness to God's transcendence by not doing "business as usual" in society. Memory of God provides the constancy and basis of standards of human rights, justice, solidarity, peace and freedom, not any universal theory. This memory and the action, which flows from it and sustains it, provide the stability and heart to engage in a cycle of committed action. It enables both the articulation of tentative theories that hold out ethical goals and projects and the committed action of solidarity.

Political theology is less an "ethic of society" and more an "ethic of change."[27] An ethic of society in Christian circles is a vision of ideal order and an articulation of universal principles that guide the formation of healthy society. This is not a useless approach. However, political theology emphasizes more the tentativeness of Paul VI when he calls for a more inductive rather than deductive approach to social teaching. This was a call to action, summoning men and women to action and political involvement for justice. Paul VI claimed that "it is not our ambition, nor is it our mission to utter a unified message and to put forward a solution which has universal validity." The complexity of modern society called for a new approach. Paul VI called on Christian communities to analyze with objectivity the situation that is proper to their own country and to act on it (OA 4).

Neither social teaching nor political theology considers theory useless. Use of the social sciences and attention to their independence as a source of ethical reasoning is a trademark of political theologians. However, these theories are tools for discernment, tools that require critical reflection and discernment as to their usefulness in a particular situation.

---

[27] Ibid., 750. This also arises from its association with the Frankfort School of Philosophy.

Political theology respects that the context of Christian living is no longer the creation of a "new Christendom," but rather a transformative witness to justice in a climate of secularization. Christians cannot find their faith nurtured only by previous patterns, but they must believe differently. Faith in our times is always faith before unbelief, the characteristic of the secular mind. Faith is justified before contemporary unbelief, not through an apologetic of words but through the naked existential decision of the individual to include in faith's practice its essential historical and social character. Political theology does not aim to create a new version of Christianity, but rather to retrieve its transforming power. In that sense it shares with social teaching a desire to question the public imagination and be open to the truth that lies hidden by prevailing systems of thinking. It shares with its counterpart, liberation theology, the desire to form Christians able to transform their society and become more fully human in the process, but not to create a new Christendom.

Chapter Eight

Liberation Theology

Liberation theology arose out of the desire in Latin America to do sustained theological reflection on the meaning of the Christian message in a situation of oppression and conflict. In the 1960s, the Latin American Church became more conscious of the causes of the poverty and misery of the majority of its population. In turn it began to recognize a new way of living the faith from those who were committed to the poor and their liberation.[1]

This new way of living the Gospel needed articulation. People sensed the import of the Christian message for societal transformation, but it needed to be expressed and better understood. Liberation theology, therefore, is not a new rendering of the Christian message or an alternative version of Christianity. It is a theology that seeks to bring the message of the Gospel to a concrete struggle for human liberation and to express the Gospel in its essential liberating core.

Latin American liberation theology is not the only form or approach to liberation theology.[2] Various liberation theologies grew up across the globe at this time. They responded to poverty, racism, cultural marginalization, or patriarchy. However, Latin American liberation

---

[1] Roberto Oliveros, "History of the Theology of Liberation," in *Mysterium Liberationis*, Ignacio Ellacuria, S.J., and Jon Sobrino, S.J., eds. (Maryknoll, N.Y.: Orbis Books, 1993) 3–32.

[2] For instance, black theology of liberation appeared in the United States at almost the same time. See Gustavo Gutierrez, "Liberation Theology," in *The New Dictionary of Catholic Social Thought,* op. cit., 548–53. In the next chapter we will look at other forms of liberation theology.

theology was the most developed of these theologies. It strongly influenced the Church and Latin American society after Vatican II and was a major influence on the Church in understanding its social mission and the relationship of faith to justice and spirituality across the world. In order to touch upon some major themes of liberation theology and catch its spirit, we will first recall the meaning of theology itself, and then ask why did the Latin Americans feel they needed to express a theology? Why were they not satisfied simply with a social program for political reform?

Theology as a Response of Faith

The heart of theology for liberation theologians is a critical reflection on praxis, the struggle against oppression. It is in this reflection the liberation theologians seek to uncover and explain Jesus' revelation of the values of God's heart and to re-express their reason for believing in these circumstances. If faith is a stance of the whole person before God characterized by trust, hope, love and commitment, Christian faith is a response to "revelation," to God's initiative recognized to be present and operative, as Mystery, in human experience and history and fully expressed in Jesus Christ. Theology is the intellectual effort to use human reason to attend to this divine self-communication, to learn important truths about God and the created world and the relationship between them.[3]

Liberation theologians asked the question, how do we articulate the mystery of God and God's relationship to us as the Latin American people struggle against massive poverty and unjust structures? God was not dead in Latin America. Faith was alive and strong even amid overwhelming poverty. However, the faith of many Latin Americans was experienced in a situation that was not calm, peaceful, and functional, but rather oppressive and unjust. God was not primarily experienced in the developmental patterns of the life cycle because life was cut short through violence and poverty. The main societal pattern that provided the cultural backdrop for reflection on the experience

---

[3] For a clarification of theology and its history in order to place liberation theology among its contemporary and historical counterparts, see William J. Hill, O.P., "Theology," and Wayne L. Fehr, "History of Theology," in *The New Dictionary of Theology*, Joseph A. Komonchak, Mary Collins, and Dermot Lane, eds. (Collegeville: The Liturgical Press, 1987) 1011–35.

of faith was not secularization, as it was in Europe. It was poverty and a gridlock of societal structures that made hope for a progressive and gradual improvement of life remote and politically unfeasible. Normal routes of societal change possible in more developed countries were closed for the most part to Latin Americans. Change for them could only come through more radical means.

Situation of the Latin American Church

Latin American theology reflects a post-Vatican II theological trend to begin theological reflection with human experience, rather than consideration of major church doctrines.[4] By the 60s the Latin American Church confronted a situation of massive poverty and structural paralysis. Only the Cuban revolution was an exception in a hemispheric pattern of powerlessness before the poverty, poor education, and hopelessness of the Latin American people. In many Latin American countries post colonialism left 95 percent of the land in the hands of 5 percent of the population. Many countries were ruled by military dictators and their roving armies. Latin America was also highly Catholic, with close to 90 percent of the population claiming to be members of the Catholic Church. This made the Church the main and perhaps the only institution capable of confronting these powerful and authoritarian regimes who used violence to control the people.

When Catholic theologians looked into the tradition to find resources to face this situation and the need for national development, and to challenge the status quo, they found the prevailing theology and understandings of Catholic morality, lacking. What was needed, in the words of the theologian Juan Luis Segundo was a new key, a "political key" to read and understand the significance of Jesus in such a situation of oppression and conflict. Segundo and other Latin Americans did not think that a political approach was the only rendering of the Christian message. However, it was a necessary and truthful one in a situation of conflict and massive structural oppression.[5]

[4] Jon Sobrino, *Christology at the Crossroads: A Latin American Approach,* John Drury, trans. (Maryknoll, N.Y.: Orbis Books, 1978).

[5] Juan Luis Segundo, *The Historical Jesus of the Synoptics,* John Drury, trans. (Maryknoll, N.Y.: Orbis Books, 1985) 104; see also 71–85, 178–88. Segundo maintained that the political key is one among others. If it is to be helpful in unlocking Jesus' significance for people struggling against the powers of evil today

Liberation theology arose not just from a new type of theological activity but from a shift in pastoral focus in the Latin American Church. The Catholic Church in Latin America was established through colonization. Catholicism came to Latin America at the time of Columbus as an integral part of the Spanish and Portuguese conquest of the Western Hemisphere. Spanish and Portuguese missionaries set about evangelizing Latin America in the sixteenth century. They worked in close relationship with their respective monarchs. The result was a deep relationship between "cross and crown" that became characteristic of the Church in Latin American culture. The subsequent ruthless exploitation of the indigenous people by their colonizers was generally not opposed by the Church. Often church leadership was imported from Europe and dependent on good relationships with that power structure. Thus the bringing of the Catholic faith to Latin America is a story mixed with sin and grace because of the subsequent oppression of the indigenous peoples and their religions. The fact remained that by the 1950s the Church in Latin America still identified its pastoral focus with the descendents of the colonizers, not with the majority of the people who were poor and disenfranchised.

Conditions by the 1960s had become so bad that a decision had to be made to change this direction and commit the powers and energies of the Church to the cause of the poor. This move toward social commitment was not uniform; however, by 1968 the conference of Latin American Bishops in Medellin set the Church in a new direction. In this ecclesial action, the Latin American Church defined itself anew. Latin American theologians reflected that the action of the Church at Medellin made a statement. No longer would the Latin American Church allow itself to be given an identity by Europe and North America seeking to explain Latin American reality to it through categories used to define social issues in their own societies. This act of self definition had its theological counterpart, liberation theology.[6]

(and against discouragement at evil's success), the political key must be completed and balanced by the anthropological key of Paul (Romans 1–8) and by interpretive keys coming from the signs of our own times. See Frances Stefano, *The Absolute Value of Human Action in the Theology of Juan Luis Segundo* (New York: University Press of America, 1992) xxi. It is important to note that the word "political" refers to Jesus' "single-minded concern for delivering people from the evils which kept their humanity in check" (Stefano, n. 39, xxviii, Segundo 87–102).

[6] For more on the situation of Latin America, see Penny Lernoux, *Cry of the People* (New York: Penguin Books, 1982).

Characteristics of Liberation Theology

The starting point of Latin American theology is not the history of theological ideas, philosophical movements, or cultural change but rather the situation of Latin Americans in a climate of underdevelopment and oppression.

Latin Americans reflected on this concrete situation, not just through social analysis, looking for its causes, but through faith. Their faith told them that their poverty was not God's will; in fact the reality of their misery was due to profound social injustice. The injustice that controlled their land was contrary to the promises of the Kingdom, and it was against God's will for every human being to enter into the life of the Kingdom and to know the joy, hope, and love of God. Poverty in this sense was a starting point for theological reflection. Material poverty was distinguished from the spiritual poverty of the Gospels. It was not good that people were deprived of the means for life. Material poverty, not chosen but thrust upon people, was contrary to the Gospels. It was "anti-evangelical."[7]

The person upon whom Latin Americans reflected was not the integral developing person of first world reflection, but the non-person of Latin America. The majority of people in Latin America were considered non-persons in that the societal structures did not recognize them. They were marginated, stripped of legal status, and exploited. The poor in Latin America were also symbolic of the world's poor, who were non-persons according to the world economy. During the 70s some held that 50 percent of the world's population were extraneous to the world's economic system. They were too under-educated to be workers in an increasingly technological labor market and too poor to buy anything profitable to produce.

The existence of the non-person was a challenge to both the economic, social, political and cultural world, and our religious world. If 50 percent of the people of the globe do not matter or count in our world system, it is a dehumanizing system and is not morally legitimate. If Christian freedom upholds that all people have their intrinsic dignity and a right to human fulfillment, what does Christian freedom mean when so many in the world have little chance to the options

---

[7] *Puebla 1159.* See *Puebla and Beyond,* John Eagelson and Philip Scharper, eds. (Maryknoll, N.Y.: Orbis Books, 1979) 267. All future references are from this source.

that express this freedom in concrete terms: i.e., the right to food, clothing, shelter, education, self expression, and a future free from want for basic needs?

The task and role of liberation theology is primarily to denounce this situation as contrary to God's will and to announce God's liberating message to the poor, not in general or in some vague thematic manner but precisely in terms of the Latin American situation. This meant that liberation theologians had to examine Christian theology itself and separate themselves from aspects of it that appeared to justify this state of affairs.

In terms of our earlier discussion of faith and ideology, theologians had to criticize theological formulations, ideology in this sense, which misconstrued God's relationship to the concrete situation of poverty in Latin America. We might be familiar with some of these. For instance, we may have heard it said to the poor, "You are poor now, but God will give you happiness in heaven." At first glance this seems to be a religious insight into limited situations in human life. But taken in another way, it can legitimate a situation of poverty. Its hidden message can be, accept your poverty because God wills it. Do not expect a change in your situation in this life, do not demand it, and do not strive for it. Ultimately, from the perspective of those of us not suffering poverty, it sends the message, "Do not bother us, our life style or the state of things that works for us."

Latin American theologians criticized this type of theological formulation for three reasons: First, because it used theology to promote class interests of those who were profiting from an unjust situation. Second, because it was not faithful to the meaning of revelation. Material poverty is not the will of God. Third, since Latin America is the only part of the third world that is primarily Christian, religious ideas such as the above could be used to paralyze people toward change since these ideas easily become part of the popular culture. Attention to theology and the vision of life it communicated became important in bringing those in a Christian culture to change.

The Poor

Liberation theology went one step beyond criticism of formulations of Christian theology that appeared to hide God's real relationship to the Latin American people. It said the poor were the privileged carriers of the Gospel.[8] Latin Americans recognize that there are various types of oppression, such as racial, sexual, cultural, and age discrimination. However, they give material poverty a primary focus in their theological synthesis. They view those who are socio-economically poor not just as individuals but as a class in society. They adapt this position from Marxism, using Marxism as an analytical tool to gain clarity in understanding the real situation of the poor in their social system. Because they do not want poverty to be confused with the voluntary poverty in Christian practice, or the spiritual poverty in the tradition, they give socio-economic poverty a privileged place in their analysis of who are the poor in Latin America. Their use of class analysis also assists them to name the relationship between classes in Latin American society as conflictual. The interests of these classes are not reconcilable, in other words, they are inherently opposed.[9]

These theologians went beyond an analysis of who are the poor to bring faith to bear on this situation. The poor are not just as a class of society, but people who are fighting against their situation, and people of faith crying out to God (Puebla, 1137). In the poor is the image of Jesus who himself was marginated in his society and eventually put to death for his opposition to the status quo. The poor therefore are the recipients of the promise of the Kingdom. It is here that the profound theological character of liberation theology's attention to the poor is made clear.

Commitment to the poor is not just a moral response of a good person who sees an unjust situation and responds. Commitment to the poor is an act of union with God. To be concerned with the poor

[8] This is grounded in the fundamental texts of the Beatitudes and the Last Judgment. "The Christian faith affirms—and this is a dogma of faith that cannot be contradicted under penalty of gravely mutilating that faith—that it is in the poor that the greatest real presence of the historical Jesus is found and therefore the greatest capacity for salvation (or liberation). The fundamental texts of the Beatitudes and of the Last Judgment, among others, leave this point settled with total clarity; many other things are affirmed as dogma with much less biblical support." Ignacio Ellacuria, "Utopia and Prophecy in Latin America," in *Mysterium Liberationis,* op. cit., 303.

[9] Clodovis Boff, "Epistemology and Method of Liberation Theology," in *Mysterium Liberationis,* op. cit., 75–80. Later in liberation theology, thought moved from this concept of "class struggle" to the issue of violence. The poor as living in a culture of death and violence, seeking life over death emerged, as a central focus in liberation thought.

is to share in a dimension of the mystery of God. To live in union with God is to enter into this same concern for the poor. To make this choice of freedom is not only to commit one to the poor but to realize oneself in freedom. This is a grace and not done simply through moral determination. When the disciple makes this option for the poor, he or she responds to God's salvific call.[10]

Liberation theologians do not deny God's universal call to all classes to live in faith, hope, and love and to share the joy of God's life. However, they feel that emphasis on the poor makes true the meaning of this universal call. In human imagination it is easy to interpret universality to mean myself, and others like me in my class. But response to God is response to the "Other," the other in God's mystery, not the God of my self-creation. Response to God as "other" is also lived out in response to the "other" in my neighbor. Since that which keeps my neighbor poor goes beyond our interpersonal relationship, my response to my neighbor must also be societal and political, seeking to transform the structures that maintain this system of oppression.

Liberation theologians emphasize that God's promise of freedom and liberation is first to the poor. God's promise of salvation is not portrayed in a trickle down fashion, given "universally" and then "even" to the poor. The God Jesus proclaimed was a God who willed love and liberation for the poor. The poor are preferred not because they are necessarily better than others from a moral or religious standpoint but because God is God.[11] God's heart goes first to the one who suffers.

The word "liberation" in this sense is a profound religious symbol, synonymous with salvation and God's loving intent toward us that frees us from sin, calls us to our full humanization, and missions us to build the Kingdom of God. Liberation is the term used to interpret the central mystery of Christian grace and salvation given to all.[12] In Latin America this option for the poor has terrific consequences. It places the Christian and the Church at odds with the status quo and places them on a path of commitment, conversion, and suffering. It invites them to share in the paschal mystery of Christ.

---

[10] Liberation theologians would see the option for the poor as an aspect of what is called in moral theology the "fundamental option."

[11] Gustavo Gutierrez, "Option for the Poor," in *Mysterium Liberationis,* op. cit., 241.

[12] Roger Haight, *An Alternative Vision* (New York: Paulist Press, 1985) 46.

The Poor and the Hermeneutic Circle

Latin American theologians share with political theologians a suspicion that current systems of thought, even theologies, tend to serve the status quo and not the cause of the poor. For this reason commitment to the cause of the poor becomes a necessary pre-condition for having access to theological truth. There is a suspicion in liberation theology that not only social science but traditional theology, interpretation of Scripture, and church practice reinforce the existing state of affairs.

The conviction grew among Latin American theologians that in order to gain freedom from the blindness in society to the needs of the poor and the distortion in the prevailing theory that supports the status quo, one has to begin with a commitment to the poor and some immersion in their social situation. Experiencing life from the perspective of the poor can invite one to conversion and offer a new viewpoint in which to examine a situation.[13] This immersion can lead to reflection on one's experience with "ideological suspicion," or an unfavorable judgment about the ideology or way of thinking that justifies and thereby keeps in place the oppressive practice. At a practical level this might be the awareness that life is not what one was told. For instance, the cultural belief that the poor are to blame for their situation generally would be corrected after one had direct experience with the poor.

At a theoretical level this suspicion can be aimed at the social scientific analysis or theology. For instance, Latin Americans became aware of the discrepancy between the promises of the development era in the 50s and 60s and the existing underdevelopment in their land, marked by higher degrees of poverty than before. Suspicion of development thinking led Latin Americans to do their own analysis and to develop the theory of dependency. This theory at the time more adequately described the political-economic reality in Latin America.

"Ideological suspicion" can also be applied to a theological concept or the interpretation of the Bible. Here theology is seen as an ongoing interpretation of the meaning of faith, rather than a set of

---

[13] It is important to note that this is not automatic. Someone can serve the poor and never change their prejudices. Rather placing themselves in a new situation offers them the opportunity for a conversion of mind and heart.

unchangeable truths, no aspect of which can be altered.[14] Liberation theology expresses the "ideological suspicion" that the inherent liberative meaning of a doctrine can be clouded by the way it is interpreted. For example, Jesus can be presented in an abstract way, simply "from above," with emphasis on his divinity to such an extent that his historical life and its liberative meaning are hidden. Jesus' suffering on the cross can be used to reinforce fatalism among the Latin American people, interpreted to link their suffering with God's will for their lives. In liberation theology, therefore, each doctrine is analyzed and interpreted in terms of its meaning for a discipleship marked by commitment to the poor. There is today a liberation perspective on all the major doctrines of the Church. This is the result of the work of liberation theologians who approach theology not just as a body of sacred truths. Rather they see theology as an interpretation of revelation that has to be constantly reinterpretated according to the signs of the times and the needs of the poor. Juan Luis Segundo calls this process of interpretation, or "hermeneutical circle," "the continuing change in our interpretation of the Bible which is dictated by the continuing changes in our present-day reality, both individual and societal."[15]

The general movement in a hermeneutic process is the following. First, someone would move from insertion into a life situation with the poor, to reflection on the experience with faith. There then would be a critical examination of the prevailing interpretation of the doctrines or biblical texts that are used to understand the situation, or the social theory generally used to reinterpret how institutions function in the situation. The third step is to reflect on how the experience might serve to reformulate or reexpress the doctrine or teaching in a manner that uncovers its meaning. In the case of Scripture, this would result in new principles for interpretation of the Bible. The final step in the hermeneutical circle is a new statement or formulation, revised social theory, or interpretation of the biblical text that is

---

[14] Liberation theologians generally would not consider that their work replaces central doctrines of the church or creates a "new theology." Rather they seek to "mine" the meaning of the Christian mysteries for the situation in Latin America and offer their interpretation to the universal Church in the manner in which it also illumines the meaning of the Christian life of all at this time in history.

[15] Juan Luis Segundo, *Liberation of Theology* (Maryknoll, N.Y.: Orbis Books, 1976) 74.

aimed at animating new investment and praxis for the cause of the poor.[16]

On a practical level this might look like the following. Someone does service among the poor and begins to question what they were taught about the poor. They think of the text "who is my neighbor" in a new way. When they began their service, they understood helping their neighbor as giving direct service. Now, however, they begin to question their responsibility beyond giving aid and then returning to a comfortable lifestyle with no more questions. They study the systems that affect the conditions in which these poor are living. They realize being "neighbor" means more than giving just a helping hand. When they try to advocate change and meet resistance and are told to go back to "helping their neighbor" by giving direct aid, they realize that the status quo is served by such theology. They add onto their own understanding of "neighbor" the responsibility to examine the systems that keep people poor and change them.

Liberation theologians thus link their work with and for the poor to the intellectual search of theology, faith seeking understanding. They hold that the work for the poor makes it possible for them to do better theology. Theology is a second act, done at sundown, after concrete work for justice has been done. For liberation theologians the decision to commit to the poor arises not simply from moral impulse; it is an act of faith. This "faith in doing" or praxis gives one a different access to the truth than intellectual pursuit alone. To take the perspective of the poor, or to serve them, in some way, gives one a spiritual perspective to be open to God's revelation. It gives one a "new spirit" or new way of doing theology. The world of the poor becomes the privileged locus of the presence and revelation of God.[17] One reads the Bible or does theology with new eyes, listening for texts or interpretations of the doctrines of the Church that speak to the poor and God's promise to be with them in the process of transforming their world.

Theology is about the mystery of God and the God-human relationship. Liberation theology seeks to name God and the people's experience of God in Latin America. Part of this process is to point

---

[16] See Thomas L. Schubeck, S.J., *Liberation Ethics: Sources, Models and Norms* (Minneapolis: Fortress Press, 1993) 66–68.

[17] Pablo Richard, "Theology in the Theology of Liberation," in *Mysterium Liberationis*, op. cit., 151.

out how God's name has been distorted and used to legitimate oppression. When liberation theologians try to name God and make the experience of God explicit, they distinguish between their articulation of God and false images. They seek to destroy images of a routine God who is too facile and manipulated by the powerful concerns of mainstream society. For instance, liberation theologians would criticize a cult of the crucified Jesus in Latin America that would leave Christians with a sense of fatalism before suffering, and powerless before the problems in their society.

For liberation theologians indicate that the idols of society, and the religious language used to enshrine them and defend them, need to be deconstructed. To name God is to acknowledge the presence and face of God among the most oppressed. It is to define God as with the poor and their struggle for justice. It is not enough in Latin America to say, "I believe in God." Liberation theologians ask, what God do you believe in, a God of life or a God of death? Are you willing to abandon a definition of God in whose name others are oppressed or destroyed? Liberation theologians hold there is an "unceasing interplay" between the concrete life and the word of God (EN 29). This interplay leads one back to concrete practice, prayer, gratitude and deeper companionship with God. It also is the source of a new articulation of faith and life as expressed in liberation terms.

The "truth" in liberation theology is a constant search for a truth that supports truly human attitudes and liberative action, for it is in this action that God's Kingdom is revealed. For this reason, orthopraxis, doing the truth, is linked to orthodoxy in the liberation synthesis.[18] Theology is always a second act, the first being "faith, which expresses itself through love" (Gal 5:6).

Church and Conscientization

At the heart of liberation theology is the reinterpretation of the Christian faith as a radical engagement of the Church in the world. Liberation theology holds that proclamation of the Gospel calls men

---

[18] For a critique of the notion "preferential option for the poor," see Stephen Pope, "Proper and Improper Partiality and the Preferential Option for the Poor," *Theological Studies* 54 (1993) 242–71. For a critical examination of the relationship between orthopraxis and doing theology, see Bernard J. Verkamp, "On Doing the Truth: Orthopraxis and the Theologian," *Theological Studies* 49 (1988) 3–24.

and women into an *ecclesia:* it gathers them into a community. God's love is universal, so all are called. However, this universality involves God's preference for the poor. The Church is to witness to the God who creates, liberates, and redeems history and who has a preferential love for the poor. The Church is to make visible, the invisible: it is to be a sacrament of God's love and action in history.

The liberation willed by God for all people has three levels: liberation from all in society that oppresses; liberation within each human life from that which is experienced as evil, and liberation from sin. The Church is called to minister its essential religious mission, by engaging also in the transformation of all that promotes injustice or reduces the possibility of full human development.

A problem that faced the Church in Latin America is the oppressed themselves needed to become fully involved in bringing about their own liberation.[19] But for this to happen the poor need a type of evangelization in which the truth of the Gospel is brought to bear on their situation in a manner that enables them. Liberation theology emphasizes the poor with spirit, rather than the passive poor, those who suffer their destitution with resignation and do not notice the injustice done to them. The poor have Jesus' special care and presence, regardless of their attitude toward their poverty. However, it is the mission of the Church to assist the poor to become active in their own liberation.

Some liberation theologians incorporate the work of Paulo Freire into their vision of the mission of the Church. Freire's pedagogical principles were aimed at education as conscientization. Education was more than being taught about the world, which in Latin America

[19] Juan Luis Segundo sees two different models of liberation theology depending on the importance given to the role of the poor as direct subjects of both liberation and evangelization. He asserts that early liberation theology had as its goal the "deideologizing our customary interpretation of Christian faith . . . as a necessary task in order to get the whole church to carry to our people an understanding of our faith both more faithful to Jesus' gospel and more capable of contributing to the humanization of all people and social classes on our continent." This involved helping middle-class people come to a mature understanding of their faith. The goal was to offset the use of Christian theology to promote a type of fatalism and a cult of suffering. Later, theologians became more involved with the poor and saw themselves as being evangelized by them. Segundo claims there are inherent tensions in these two approaches in liberation theology, especially surrounding its capacity for critical thinking in its second manifestation. Juan Luis Segundo, "The Shift within Latin American Theology," in *Signs of the Times*, Alfred T. Hennelly, ed. (Maryknoll, N.Y.: Orbis Books, 1993) 67–80.

could mean being taught that the status quo was the nature of things. The process of conscientization involves a concurrent growth in self awareness and a critical awareness of social reality.[20] There are three stages in the process of conscientization: the first is the empirical investigation of the stages of consciousness, for example, a person can see a situation but fail to understand it causes. His or her understanding might be magical and fail to grasp causality or naïve and see causality as unchangeable. A second stage is the self-awakening and critical process that helps persons grow in awareness of themselves as subjects of their lives. A third stage involves a dialogical method of discovering contradictions in their situation, posing them as problems and then trying to change them.[21]

Since participation of the oppressed is hindered by oppressive social structures, the historical mission of the Church is to activate all the mechanisms that promote liberation.[22] The Church is called to use its resources and social power to be an active agent of social transformation. This historical mission of the Church, in the Latin American understanding, becomes the primary way it fulfills its transcendent identity as a sacrament of the saving mystery of God.

Base Communities

Liberation thought approaches the Church as small communities of Christians, or as "base communities." These ecclesial communities are to foster an adult faith and a mature spirituality that is capable of a committed discipleship, and able to make the sacrifices involved in social transformation.[23] Liberation theologians move away from the

[20] Paulo Freire, *Cultural Action for Freedom* (Cambridge: *Harvard Education Review*, 1970) 27. Freire defines conscientization as "the process in which men, not as recipients, but as knowing subjects, achieve a deepening awareness both of the socio-cultural reality which shapes their lives and of their capacity to transform that reality."

[21] Paulo Freire, *Educating for Critical Consciousness* (London: Sheed and Ward, 1973).

[22] Gaspar Martinez, *Confronting the Mystery of God* (New York: Continuum, 2001) 126. Here he provides a short description of the role of the Church in the developing thought of Gustavo Gutierrez.

[23] Juan Luis Segundo, *The Community Called the Church* (Maryknoll, N.Y.: Orbis Books, 1973) *Masas y minorias en la dialectica divina de la liberacion* (Buenos Aires: La Aurora, 1973).

thought of the Church as a "mass," where membership comes through family heritage or culture. They are less interested in trying to get all people to be members of the Church. Instead, they see the Church as a committed minority. They seek a Church where faith is a conscious personal decision, the maturity of which is demonstrated in its commitment to the poor.

This movement toward mature discipleship began in the middle-class church in Latin America and then was extended to the poor who religiously were more bound to practices of popular religion. Liberation theologians understood their function in this case to be organic intellectuals of the common people, unifying and structuring people's understanding of their faith, as well as grounding and defending practices coming from this faith.[24]

The "base community" model of the church developed in Latin America as a church "from below." Basic Christian communities include a wide variety of small, loosely structured religious groups involved in projects ranging from Bible study to political action. However, they arose from a move to radicalize the Christian life, making each member of the church truly active. Base communities are lay oriented and in the most part lay run. They were designed to help each person become a responsible self in society and the Church.[25] Base communities can be found among all classes of people in Latin America. However, in this style of church, its ministerial role is one of accompaniment of the people of God, especially the poor, "on the way." Liberation theologians see solidarity with the poor not only as the real situation of the church in Latin America, but as a call to the universal Church to do the same.

Shifting of Moral Norms

Latin American theologians did not develop a new moral theology, but they did bring a new emphasis to moral reflection in the church. The strong place of commitment to the poor in liberation thought shifted understanding of what it meant to live a moral life in Latin America. Some Latin Americans felt that their moral obligations were fulfilled if they kept the Ten Commandments, the laws of the Church,

---

[24] Segundo, "The Shift within Latin American Theology," 74.
[25] Marcello de C. Azevedo, "Basic Ecclesial Communities," in *Mysterium Liberationis,* op. cit., 636–53.

and had good intentions. However, in a situation where the nation required serious social transformation, liberation theologians questioned whether this view of morality was "enough." Did it capture the moral "ought" of the times?

The theologian Jon Sobrino focused his reflections on the following of Jesus, or the meaning of discipleship in this new context. At core, Christian morality is union with Christ, and the practice of the behavior that is consonant with that vision. Looking at the historical life of Jesus was the way to answer the question, what was the Christian supposed to do?[26] The central preaching of Jesus was that of the Kingdom of God. Hence to follow Jesus is to seek the Kingdom he proclaimed. Sobrino argues that one cannot know Jesus unless she or he follows Jesus.

A closer examination of the historical Jesus reveals that if one wants to follow him in establishing the Kingdom, one must make an option for the poor. This means that one's concept of the "good" can not be a static one, in other words, one cannot assume knowledge of right and wrong in a complete way. Instead, one's sense of moral obligation would constantly be revised and enlarged through the actual following of Jesus in immersion in the concerns of the poor. This praxis of following Jesus involves trying to be effective and not just having good intentions. While the moral worth of one's actions are not judged merely on their success, the disciple has to be willing to (1) immerse themselves into the situation of the poor, to undergo some experience of poverty, (2) to analyze the situation in terms of the structural causes of poverty, to use social analysis and a prudent use of the social sciences, and (3) to engage in a type of planning and response that would be the best and most efficacious action to close the gap between what ought to be and what is in a particular situation.

The moral call to foster the coming of the Kingdom holds a central place in the liberation vision of Christian morality. Liberation theology understands that no amount of human action is going to bring about the Kingdom. In an irreplaceable way, the Kingdom is God's to bring about at the end of time. However, our actions in time are significant in preparing the conditions where the Kingdom can come.

Since the condition in Latin America most in need of the coming of the Kingdom is that of material poverty, the lack of necessary goods that degrades human beings, response to material poverty is

---

[26] Sobrino, *Christology at the Crossroads,* 108–39.

the centerpiece of liberation ethics. Material poverty is seen in the Scriptures as "a scandalous condition inimical to human dignity and therefore contrary to the will of God."[27] Response to material poverty has, therefore, a priority in mediating a sense of moral obligation in the life of the Christian. It is not that liberation theologians did not believe in the Ten Commandments, the laws of the Church, development of the virtues, or other measures of conventional morality. It is that these alone are no longer adequate in mediating the total moral call to Christians in a Latin American situation.

In Luke's Beatitudes, the poor are blessed because in Christ, "the elimination of the exploitation and poverty that prevent the poor from being fully human has begun. . . . Poverty is an evil and therefore incompatible with the Kingdom of God, which has come in its fullness into history and embraces the totality of human existence."[28] The Christian is called to take on a type of spiritual poverty, as a commitment to solidarity and protest.[29]

Liberation theology is realistic about the human efforts and projects that ultimately mediate the coming of the Kingdom. The utopian vision of liberation theology is mediated by the Kingdom of God. However, human utopias, while never identical with the Kingdom, mediate a vision of a better society.[30] When Christians create concrete projects to transform situations of injustice, these are always partial, done in situations of limitation, and at times are defeated. A liberating praxis of discipleship expresses Jesus' saving mystery by taking seriously the terrible pain of the oppressed masses. It works to unmask the explanations given to explain away theses sufferings. Finally,

[27] Gutierrez, *A Theology of Liberation,* 291.

[28] Ibid., 74.

[29] Ibid., 299.

[30] Utopia and Christian hope can be distinguished. Utopia stresses a this-worldly, immanent, and concrete vision of something that does not yet exist, but could and should exist. Christian hope points to the absolute future, the divine mystery, our own final end, revealed now in sacramental form, but will be unveiled and fulfilled beyond death. The interrelationship between the two are that planning for a more human future, and working toward it "are regarded by Christianity as part of the task demanded of man by his divinely willed nature, a task to which man is obliged and in which he fulfills his real religious duty, viz. the openness of freedom in believing hope for the absolute future." Karl Rahner, "Marxist Utopia and the Christian Future of Man," in *Theological Investigations,* VI. (London: Darton, Longman and Todd, 1969) 64.

it lives in solidarity by taking authentic responsibility for historical transformation.[31]

The Cross

In modern times, the Latin American church is a church of the martyrs. The cross and its meaning are central to its theological discussion. In the early days of liberation theology, theologians criticized the individualist and fatalist theology of the cross that existed in Latin America. Such a vision of the cross led people to glorify suffering rather than seek to overcome it. This paralyzed efforts to engage in transformation of society. Theologians noted that the dominant systems of society were left untouched by the scandal of the cross.

The focus on the cross in the piety of the individual left its social meaning untapped. As important as was the asceticism of the cross or a personal piety of necessary renunciations, the social import of the cross was ignored. To use the cross for finding meaning in one's own suffering is an existential theology of the cross. While these common approaches carried a psychological or therapeutic function, they were not enough.

Liberation theologians criticized these approaches to the cross, even though they carried partial understandings, because they were "incapable of announcing universal salvation and the call to solidarity proclaimed in the cross of Jesus."[32] A liberation vision of the cross involves solidarity with those who suffer, the struggle against unnecessary suffering and sin, especially as it is structurally reinforced, and the willingness to suffer because one follows Jesus who suffered unto death. One can engage in a following of Christ in society that leads to suffering because inherent to the Christian cross is hope in the resurrection.[33] The liberation view of the cross does not stop at the cross; it is also rooted in the resurrection. Christians share in Jesus' resurrection now, in the sacraments and through every act of welcoming Christ's victorious grace through an imitation of him in solidarity with the poor.

---

[31] Javier Jimenez Limon, "Suffering, Death, Cross and Martyrdom," in *Mysterium Liberationis,* op. cit., 702–15.

[32] Ibid., 704.

[33] Joao Baptista Libanio, "Hope, Utopia, Resurrection," in *Mysterium Liberationis,* op. cit., 725.

Ecclesial Conferences of Medellin (1968), Puebla (1979) and Santo Domingo (1993)

The Latin American Church implemented the directives of Vatican II to gather for regional conferences at which they could address the concerns of their continent. The first conference was at Medellin in 1968, the second at Puebla in 1979, and the third at Santo Domingo in 1993. These conferences were not meetings of liberation theologians but of bishops. While all bishops did not share the perspective of liberation theologians, it is possible to see the direction of these ecclesial conferences, and the liberation theology movement, as two hands of the Church in Latin America taking hold of the needs of a continent caught up in a process of profound social transformation.[34]

Paul VI, the first Pope to visit Latin America, opened the conference at Medellin. The bishops' primary goal was to implement Vatican II to the needs of their own continent. Known as leaders of a religiously conservative Church, the bishops at Medellin however did not take the option of generating vague thematic documents. Rather they focused on the socio-economic conditions of their continent, and their pastoral ramifications, as the concrete situation where they as pastors were called to collaborate with God.

At Medellin, the Latin American bishops did not just apply the teachings of Vatican II to Latin America. They offered their own interpretation of the "signs of the times," calling the Church to promote social change and real justice in Latin American society. They recognized the aspirations of the poor, and clearly indicated that the Church must stand with the poor as their advocate.[35] To do this the pastoral energy of church institutions had to be redirected, the causes of poverty understood, and effective action planned that would lead to a new social order. They knew that such action would bring trials and persecution to the Church. But in spite of this risk, they knew that the Church had to stand with the poor in order to be a credible evangelical force in the midst of the Latin American situation.

At Medellin the terms option for the poor, liberation, institutionalized violence, and "social" sin were either referred to or implied in

---

[34] For a history of the movement from Medellin to Santo Domingo, see Edward L. Cleary, O.P., "The Journey to Santo Domingo," in *Santo Domingo and Beyond.* Alfred T. Hennelly, S.J., ed. (Maryknoll, N.Y.: Orbis Books, 1993) 3–23.

[35] Curt Cadorette, M.M., "Medellin," in *The New Dictionary of Catholic Social Thought,* op. cit., 590–94.

ecclesial statements. The bishops actually advanced social teaching by using these concepts to express the spirit and call of the Catholic social tradition in their situation. The bishops at Medellin recognized the sinful influence of structures as situations of "institutional violence" against the poor in their country (Medellin 2.16). Structures not only induce individuals to sin but discourage and seek to defeat the human spirit from seeking its full humanity. Those who are dependent on a structure for life sustenance or cultural support experience instead, through the very way the structure organizes and distributes goods and services, an affront to their basic human rights. Medellin pointed to unjust structures in which the sins of lack of solidarity are crystallized (Medellin 1.2).

The bishops recognized that the Church too was influenced by this situation of sin to the degree that it allowed existing social and political structures to leave it untouched by the situation of the people. As Helder Camara, one of the architects of Medellin, described it, "The Spirit of God was with us pushing us to discover, in our continent, the most painful of colonialisms: privileged internal groups who maintain personal wealth at the expense of the misery of their countrymen."[36] This dramatic change on the part of the Church of Latin America meant the renunciation of centuries of state patronage and the transformation of the Church into a servant of the poor.[37]

A decade later, the bishops met again at Puebla, Mexico. Pope John Paul II made his first papal journey to Mexico to open the Puebla Conference in 1979. The major concern of the bishops at Puebla was not whether to say something new, but whether they would reaffirm the decisions and directions of Medellin.[38]

The option for the poor made at Medellin was a public option of the institutional Church. This meant that communities within the Church made a similar option on behalf of the institution to which they belonged, thus redirecting many of the pastoral energies of the Church. In the ten-year period many priests, religious, and lay people were persecuted by the military regimes, and the power structure they supported because of their option for the poor. Many were

---

[36] Helder Camara, "CELAM: History is Implacable," *Cross Currents* (Spring 1978) 55–58.

[37] See *The Church and Culture since Vatican II,* Joseph Gremillion, ed. (Notre Dame, Ind.: The University of Notre Dame Press, 1985).

[38] See Dorr, *Option for the Poor,* 260–71.

tortured and killed. The Church had named structural injustice and denounced poverty caused by injustice and sin. They had awakened ordinary people to recognize the injustice done to them and take action, and they had stood in solidarity with the poor for their liberation and humanization. They had done this to the point of recognizing that in extreme cases the strong presumption in the church against revolution had to be overcome (Medellin 2.19).[39]

The core teaching of Puebla is a reaffirmation of the option for the poor made at Medellin (Puebla 1134–65). It teaches that sin as a "rupturing force" arises from the hearts of human beings and leaves its mark on the structures they create (Puebla 281). Puebla deepened the teaching of Medellin on the concept of social sin. Structural sin reflects and incarnates the sinful condition of humanity and the sinful choices of individuals. Structures do not sin, people do. No structure can force an individual to sin, but it can make it easier to sin than to be just (*Reconciliation* 16).[40] A social structure is sinful insofar as by the way it organizes the distribution of goods, services, or power, it violates human dignity in a manner that could be avoided, or it facilitates and supports individual acts of selfishness.[41] Puebla did not back away from the Church's commitment to the poor after a decade of suffering and conflict. This decision illustrated, "that 'option for the poor' stands out as the strongest and most characteristic option of Puebla and of the Church of Latin America in its evangelizing mission."[42]

Option for the poor and social commitment was at the core of an integrated vision of the Church and the Christian life in Latin America. It was more than a political option or a strategy for social change. The Church in Latin America was not just a political organization, but a community of faith responding to the Word of God. The Eucharist and focus on the transforming Word of God was at the heart of the thousands of *comunidades eclesiales de base*. These communities were served by apostolic teams formed in and by the Church. These smaller

---

[39] For a description of how the teaching of *Medellin* nuances the teaching against revolution in *Populorum Progressio,* see Dorr, *Option for the Poor,* 210–11.

[40] John Paul II, apostolic exhortation *Reconciliation and Penance* (Washington, D.C.: United States Catholic Conference, 1984).

[41] See Mark O'Keefe, *What Are They Saying About Social Sin?* (New York: Paulist Press, 1990).

[42] Archbishop Marcos McGrath, C.S.C., "The Puebla Final Document: Introduction and Commentary," in *Puebla and Beyond*, John Eagleson and Philip Scharper, eds. (Maryknoll, N.Y.: Orbis Books, 1979) 109.

communities interacted in the secular society and were linked together by the broader Church. It was this complex of witnesses that was the Church who had made a "preferential option for the poor" at Puebla.

By the time of Puebla, formal tensions around liberation theology were surfacing in the Church. Liberation theologians strongly present at Medellin were systematically excluded from the roster of experts and advisers of the Puebla Conference.[43] The bishops who crafted the Puebla Document were divided over liberation theology and the institutional reforms within the Church that were consequences of its preferential option for the poor. After Puebla, inquiries and attacks on liberation theology, summarized in a Vatican document in 1984, left concerns, doubts, and fears whether the hope of reforming the Church from within along liberation lines would actually happen in Latin America. Support for liberation theology from across the world and clarification of key concepts led to a more positive response to liberation theology in 1986.[44] John Paul II wrote to the Brazilian bishops, stating that liberation theology was "useful and necessary." This action helped to assure those ambivalent about liberation theology to accept its language as expressive of the Church's pastoral role in Latin America.[45]

By the time the bishops gathered again in Santo Domingo, Dominican Republic, in 1993 there had been serious shifts in the Latin American reality. Military dictatorships had lost their grip on several Latin American countries, but the process of torture and disappearance had left the people in a mixed state of fear, insecurity, and denial.[46] Democracy was established but often was weak and susceptible to cor-

---

[43] Curt Cadorette, M.M., "Puebla," in *The New Dictionary of Catholic Social Thought*, op. cit., 797–801. Cleary, "The Journey to Santo Domingo," 16.

[44] Congregation for the Doctrine of the Faith, "Instruction on Certain Aspects of the 'Theology of Liberation'" (August 6, 1984) and "Instruction on Christian Freedom and Liberation" (March 22, 1986) in Alfred Hennelly, ed., *Liberation Theology: A Documentary History* (Maryknoll, N.Y.: Orbis Books, 1990) 393–414 and 461–97.

[45] "Letter to Brazilian Episcopal Conference" (April 9, 1986) in Hennelly, ibid., 448–506. For a fair treatment of the criticism of liberation theology, see Arthur F. McGovern, *Liberation Theology and Its Critics* (Maryknoll, N.Y.: Orbis Books, 1989).

[46] For more recent Latin American history, see Edward L. Cleary and Hannah Stewart-Gambino, eds., *Conflict and Competition: The Latin American Church in a Changing Environment* (Boulder: Lynne Rienner, 1992).

ruption. The Church had a tradition in which it supported democracy. It was strong in opposing authoritarian regimes, yet the Church questioned how to foster realistic development of democratic structures.

Economically some in Latin America gained affluence, while others, still the majority, declined. Problems resulting from international debt, inflation, the changing world capitalist system after 1989, and restrictions placed internally on Latin American economies by international money lenders left Latin Americans still on the margins of the new world order. Neo-liberal policies deepened the impoverishment of the people.

Latin America also experienced new pastoral problems arising from religious competition, not necessarily from mainline Protestant churches but from smaller fundamentalist groups called *sectas*.[47] The continuing problem of cultural Catholics, blending of traditional spiritual practices and new theology, and the need for integration of lay movements and formation of a growing clergy were part of the "new evangelization" needing articulation, programs, and leadership. It also shared in the problems of Western society, ecological deterioration, the challenge of the postmodern mindset, and the eclipse of transcendence.

Commentators on Santo Domingo characterized the Church's stance amid these conflicts as "cautious." The Church challenged the first-world perception that since the fall of socialism, the world was going reasonably well. It pointed to the growth rather than the decline of poverty in the last decade as signs the world was getting worse for the majority.[48] It recognized women, indigenous people, and blacks in a manner more explicit than Medellin and Puebla.[49] It named programs and directions for evangelization and development at all levels of the Latin American Church: youth, family, parish, small communities, diocese, social movements and those between the church and society.

Some found the language of Santo Domingo theologically conservative and even regressive. They interpreted the stress on the "see, judge, act" model of Catholic social response in its document more

---

[47] Cleary, "The Journey to Santo Domingo," 9.

[48] Jon Sobrino, "The Winds in Santo Domingo," in Hennelly, *Santo Domingo and Beyond,* 173.

[49] Maria Pilar Aquino, "Santo Domingo through the Eyes of Women," in Hennelly, ibid., 212–25. See also Stephen P. Judd, M.M., "From Lamentation to Project: The Emergence of an Indigenous Theological Movement in Latin America," 226–36.

than on the liberation emphasis on praxis first and then theory, a signal of a return to a former vision of the relationship between faith and society. However, the call of Santo Domingo to evangelize the culture of Latin America, to continue to stand with the "other," to build the identity of the Latin American Church in its context and to integrate its stance in the wider life of the Church, provided a direction for the future, even though this direction might be more subdued than earlier conferences.

Social Doctrine

At Puebla, John Paul II referred to the social teaching of the Church, as "social doctrine" (Puebla III.7). Some questioned whether this signaled a return to a former approach to the Church's social teaching, as a set of universal and timeless principles from which one could deduct conclusions in all circumstances. If this were true, it would be a departure from the practice of Vatican II, claims Marie-Dominique Chenu. In *Gaudium et Spes* we find that the phrases "the social teaching of the Gospel" and "the Christian doctrine about society" were substituted for the term "social doctrine."[50] Dorr suggests that John Paul II uses the term, not in its former sense, but to communicate that a position of the Church on a social matter is something that arises from its fundamental nature and not something open to compromise.

Use of the term social doctrine also separates John Paul II's thinking from a school of thought in Latin America, which dismissed the relevance of social teaching in the Latin American context. Caught between ideologies of socialism or capitalism, some Christians in Latin America attempted a "third way" that was to be an embodied form of Christian democracy in Latin America. This vision depended upon Catholic social doctrine. However, this ceased politically to be a realistic option by the 1970s. Some thinkers associated Catholic Social Doctrine with this third way and when the political relevance of these parties waned, they dismissed the relevancy of social doctrine with it, urging the only option was for the Church to identify with the political left.

---

[50] Dorr, *Option for the Poor,* 267–70. Marie-Dominique Chenu, *La 'doctrine sociale' de l'Église comme idéologie* (Paris: Cerf, 1979) 87–88.

John Paul II's use of the term social doctrine suggests that he saw the role of the Church as more complex than identification with a third way or solely with the political right or left in Latin America. Social doctrine taught that Christians, and the Church as a whole, were to discern concrete historical action in each circumstance that aided the full humanity of the people in the location. John Paul II held that the normal way Christians opt for the human person is through making difficult choices between systems, laws, policies, and programs as they appear in concrete circumstances. There is no "low rent" option where one simply can follow an ideology or system of politics unconditionally. Debate, however, between inductive and deductive approaches to Catholic Social Teaching, fed also by the liberation emphasis on social involvement as prior to theorizing about social reality, frame an ongoing tension in approaches to Catholic Social Thought.

Liberation Theology and Social Teaching

Liberation theology, as it has been integrated into the pastoral direction of the Church in Latin America, has incorporated a preferential option for the poor into its understanding of one's fundamental moral option toward the Other. The Latin American church has named an option for the poor as an essential element of a Christian moral attitude toward God, self, others, and the world. This expands the notion of Christian charity to commitment to change the structures that shape interpersonal relationships. It connects the notion of autonomy of the person, central to Vatican II renewal in moral theology, to its essential link to the building of community. Christian freedom cannot be regarded as only individualistic, but must include an essential call to solidarity with the Other, in this case, the poor.

Liberation theology has integrated the role of ethical indignation as moral awakening. It has moved away from a vision of ethics where the "good" is only a known quality, to stress that insight into the good grows with the process of conversion. It shares with social teaching the perspective that the presence of social evil gives rise to a new ethical imperative. It highlights how church membership should lead us beyond the concerns of our family, class, and neighbors toward a wider circle of concern. It specifies how the Christian life is a movement out of self to the other, especially in circumstances of civil, economic, and social discord. It points to how investment in transforming the world should give us new evaluational principles and interpretative stand-ards to judge the meaning of Christian practice and the good life.

Liberation theology done within the context of the Latin Ameri-can Church specifies what happens when a local church takes up Paul VI's challenge for local discernment and the importance of justice in the life of the Christian specified by *Justice in the World.* Social, politi-cal, economic, and international problems exist in all the countries of the world. However, in Latin America they were taken up with such intensity that other countries had to question themselves, a topic we will explore in the next chapter. The use of social analysis became part of doing pastoral planning for change and engaging the Church in the task of social transformation. The need to study and critique one's own culture in order to stand freer from its prejudices and blindness was integrated into Christian spirituality. Liberation theol-ogy heightened awareness in the Church of the role of context and perspective for defining and living an evangelical life in our times and engaging in evangelization.

Liberation theologians contributed to social teaching and the social tradition as a whole, a heightened focus on the relationship between spirituality and ethics. They made clear that commitment to justice has the reciprocal function of making one more sensitive to the essen-tial aspects of faith. While the tradition has always linked committed deeds and believing, liberation theology has called the whole Church to ask itself what it truly believes. Is God a God of life or death? Is our fundamental faith in God or mammon? Does God reveal in the signs of our times, especially in the face of the poor of the world, or has revelation ceased?

The base community movement in the Church in Latin America has stimulated the formation of analogous but not identical groups across the world. Groups have been created within the Church to pro-vide a setting where a more mature and personalized sense of Chris-tian discipleship can occur. Communities that are too vast or too structured have been unable to provide both the communal setting and integrative focus of faith and living needed for movement toward an adult spirituality. To remedy this, smaller groups have been engaged in consciousness raising, biblical and theological study and renewal, prayer, and social action. Liberation theology has helped clarify in the Church that a heightened sense of personal responsibility, supported by a small community, is not for self alone. Existing communities, such as parishes, retreat houses, religious communities, and dioceses through reflection on liberation theology have been assisted in linking the service of faith and the promotion of justice, not just as ministries but as the integrating focus of their identity as communities.

Liberation theology has entered the social tradition of the Church at three levels. At a first level liberation theology has retrieved from the biblical tradition stories, images and interpretations of Jesus that illumine the struggle for justice in Latin America today. This profound biblical interpretation has influenced the Church as a whole. At a second level, a more empirical one, liberation theology has provided a reinterpretation of all the major doctrines of the Church in light of their significance for the transformation of the structures that perpetuate poverty in our world. It has offered perhaps the most extensive reflection on poverty and its causes that we have known in the Church.

At a third level, the mystical political, liberation theology has challenged Christians and the Church to rethink the interpretation of its relationship to God, as developed in first-world cultures and presented in third-world situations. It has called this interpretation into question as to its penchant for defending access to God on intellectual lines alone without a doing faith in service of the other and a searching faith for the God who revelation supports stands with the poor. It has reexamined the language of spirituality as to its potential for animating a call to conversion that is demanded by the circumstances of the century. It has criticized a spirituality of poverty that is aimed at personal asceticism alone without recourse to the meaning of renunciation for others. It has stretched the Church's imagination to see response to the world's poor as a driving force in its own identity and renewal. It has illumined the face of the goodness of God as standing with the poor and criticized a self-satisfied conscience. It has challenged the Christian to depend on God, revealed in the midst of social problems that confront us, rather than, as the Pharisee in the Gospel, to feel satisfied with an ethical code formed apart from ongoing relationship to God, the community of the Church, and the needs of others in the world of poverty and need.[51]

---

[51] For further reading see *Born of the Poor: The Latin American Church since Medellín,* Edward L. Cleary, O.P., ed. (London: University of Notre Dame Press, 1990); Ricardo Antoncich, *Christians in the Face of Injustice: A Latin American Reading of Catholic Social Teaching* (Maryknoll, N.Y.: Orbis Books, 1987); Carlos Ronquillo, C.Ss.R., *Moral Theology from the Perspective of the Poor: An Inquiry into the Contributions*

Both liberation theology and the social encyclicals are historical documents formed in concrete circumstances. Both try to respond to those circumstances in a Christian way. Both deal with ethical problems without offering technical solutions to them. Both appeal to the human conscience before God, urging it to assume responsibility for building a just world.

The social encyclicals are written by the magisterium of the Church to help understand the contemporary mode of reality of the world and the human person in it. They are to help analyze and stimulate the drawing up of projects with a view to the possibility of a fuller humanization of this world.[52] They do not however limit themselves to recalling general principles. In the words of Paul VI, social teaching develops "through reflection applied to the changing situations of this world, under the driving force of the Gospel as the source of renewal when its message is accepted in its totality and with all its demands. It also develops with the sensitivity proper to the Church which is characterized by a disinterested will to serve and by attention to the poorest" (OA 42).

Certainly liberation theology has partnered with the social encyclicals in serving the concrete ordering of society, which is part of the Church's evangelizing mission of proclaiming the good news to the poor. It has fostered that love through which the Church tells the poor that exploitation and injustice will cease to exist, because in some partial yet concrete way, the Church has sought to transform the world and the culture of our day. This commitment of love has fostered the ongoing reflection on the call of the Christian life in society today. In this sense the modern social tradition of the Church cannot be fully understood without the powerful contribution of the liberation theology movement.

---

of Liberation Theology to Moral Theology (Rome: Pontificia Universitas Lateranensis: Academia Alfonsiana: 1996).

[52] Josef Fuchs, S.J., "Natural Law," in *The New Dictionary of Catholic Social Thought*, op. cit., 673.

Chapter Nine

Social Catholicism after Vatican II

The urgency and enthusiasm Vatican II opened in the Catholic community was felt across the world. Each continent sought to relate their faith to their context and to re-express in that context the meaning of their Christianity. The celebration of the liturgy in the vernacular imaged a deeper movement of inculturation of the faith. Attention to context grew as an important element in theological reflection, and insights into the Christian mystery and its significance for life began to be voiced outside the usual boundaries of Northern Europe.

At the Vatican council the Church learned that it was not just Western and Eastern but also Asian, Latin American, and African.[1] This insight, coupled with a growing awareness of global social changes demanded new response from the Church. Thinking in terms of context, or "turning to history" became not only a theological option, but a pastoral necessity. Expressions of Christian identity and mission were voiced, first distinguished by regions—Latin American, African, Asian, European—and then by social groups as the poor, women, blacks, Hispanics, and indigenous peoples.

Location was expressed not only by place but by how one's position in society marked by race, class, and gender was a starting point for consideration of relationship to God and the meaning of God's revelation, held in Scripture and tradition. The Church became aware that human beings, while essentially sharing a common identity and

---

[1] Dorr, *Option for the Poor* (Maryknoll, N.Y.: Orbis Books, 1992) 151.

dignity, also had personal and unique experiences of God, self and world conditioned by their social place. The document Church in the Modern World recognizes the common dignity of all people beneath the difference and the mission of the Church to these diverse people in new contexts (GS 41–44). After Vatican II, it became apparent that none of these social or geographical identities could be understood in isolation. Contexts and identities are multiple and overlapping. The realities of class, caste, race, gender, and ethnicity, and local, regional and global economy and polity are intertwined.

Context of the Church in the United States

The moral awakening in Latin America was mirrored in other parts of the world, as the Church was confronted with social problems globally and in its own context.[2] The United States, after Vatican II, unlike Latin America, experienced post-war prosperity. Yet, the war in Vietnam, racial and ethnic conflict, women seeking a new share of equality and civil rights, a waning confidence in public institutions, the gap between general rise in living standards and the invisible poor who had not been included in the growth of the American economy, troubled America.[3] Stephen Carter says it clearly. Americans look at the 1950s and early 1960s as the golden age of American society. TV programs like "Father Knows Best" mirror a world where traditional values, order and propriety set the stage for a non-conflicted social life built on common agreement of general standards of living. Everyone knew his or her "place" in this world. But behind the public façade of this "golden age," those whose lives did not fit this image, suffered.[4] Domestic abuse was transparent, patterns of bigotry and racism were accepted as "the way things are," poverty was blamed on the victim, women were oppressed by gender and marginalized from

[2] See J. Bryan Hehir, "The Church and the Political Order: the Role of the Catholic Bishops in the United States," in *Readings in Moral Theology, No. 12: The Catholic Church, Morality and Politics,* Charles E. Curran and Leslie Griffin, eds. (New York: Paulist Press, 2001) 175–90.

[3] For reflection on loss of faith in public institutions, see Kenneth R. Himes, O.F.M., "The Crisis of American Democracy: A Catholic Perspective," in *American Catholic Social Teaching,* Thomas J. Massaro, Thomas A. Shannon, eds. (Collegeville: The Liturgical Press, 2002) 184–203.

[4] Stephen Carter, *Civility: Manners, Morals, and the Etiquette of Democracy* (New York: Harper Collins, 1998).

public advancement, anyone not white and middle class was an out-sider. The "good old days" were not as good as we thought.

When the North American bishops returned from the Vatican II, they needed to implement its directives in a public atmosphere different from Europe. After World War II, theologian John Courtney Murray put a theoretical framework on the Catholic experience in the United States, and its separation of Church and state.[5] Distinguishing between the temporal and the spiritual matters, Murray acknowledged that even though spiritual power has its own dignity, its role is not to control the temporal power of the state. Rather through the conscience of the individual believer acting as a citizen, the church legitimately touches the actions of government.[6]

Murray held that the Catholic entered civil society with the heritage of a long wisdom of political and social thought that affirmed human reason and provided a basis for pluralism, civic order, and harmony. Far from forming bad citizens, Catholicism taught as true doctrines of human dignity, justice, and freedom that were central to the American experiment.[7] The Church and its members shared in public life with others not on the basis of distinctive Catholic tenets of political life but on the basis of commonly shared values and principles, which for Catholics were also solidly grounded in faith. The American separation of Church and state was not a separation of Church and society.[8] The Church can and should defend its right to be church; its involvement in society always arises out of its essential religious mission. In turn, the Christian life is not simply a matter of personal piety, it has a public dimension

A common adage in American society was "one should not mix religion and politics." People often used this to uphold a separation of Church and state. However, it grew to mean a separation of Christian

[5] John Courtney Murray, *We Hold These Truths: Reflections on the American Proposition* (New York: Sheed and Ward, 1960, and 1988). See also "The Problem of Religious Freedom," *Theological Studies* (1964) 503–75.

[6] See Robert W. McElroy, *The Search for an American Public Theology: The Contribution of John Courtney Murray* (New York: Paulist Press, 1989) and "John Courtney Murray," in *The Dictionary of Catholic Social Thought,* op. cit., 650–53.

[7] David O'Brien, "American Catholics and American Society," in *Catholics and Nuclear War,* Philip J. Murnion, ed. (London: Geoffrey Chapman, 1983) 16–29.

[8] For a Canadian example of a similar but distinctive church-society interaction, see Walter Block, *The Canadian Bishops on Economics and Theology* (Vancouver: The Fraser Institute, Center for the Study of Economics and Religion, 1983).

living and political life. This type of common-place thinking, coupled with the beginning of a distrust of political institutions, formed a recipe for maintaining little connection between Christian faith and social living during the postwar Church in America.

There were notable exceptions to this manner of thinking. Dorothy Day and the Catholic Worker movement, Thomas Merton who linked spirituality and social criticism, and other forms of social Catholicism before and during World War II existed. David O'Brien remarks that Catholic social consciousness tended to respond to a crisis, but was not sufficiently integrated into Catholic life to have much influence on public debate in the more affluent years after the war.[9] However, after Vatican II, steps were taken to move social awareness from the margins of Catholic life into its mainstream. The common prejudice in American society, shared by many Catholics, was slowly eroded.

Models of Church Involvement

Since Vatican II, Catholics and other Christians have made strides in the integration of faith and citizenship in American society in a variety of ways. Brian Hehir offers a framework for understanding the multi-dimensional way the Church responded to civil affairs and how Catholics brought their faith into the public arena.[10] The concrete ways the church and its members express the link between faith and citizenship in American society: movements, pastoral plans, formation of mission statements of Catholic institutions, Catholic spiritual activities, liturgical theology linking faith and justice, catechetics, bishops' statements, demonstrations, advocacy, direct service, letter-writing, parish and diocesan commissions on social justice, can be grouped under three headings.

The first is an educational-cultural model. This model focuses on the Church's role to shape the "religio-cultural conception of society." It seeks to form the "ethos" of society, or public sensibility about values

[9] Joseph P. Chinnici, O.F.M., *Living Stones: The History and Structures of Catholic Spiritual Life in the United States* (New York: Macmillan Publishing Company, 1989). See ch. 16 on Dorothy Day; ch. 18 on Thomas Merton. See also "Social Catholicism," in David O'Brien, *Public Catholicism* (New York: Macmillan, 1989) 158–94.

[10] J. Brian Hehir, "The Right and Competence of the Church in the American Case," in *One Hundred Years of Catholic Social Thought,* John A. Coleman, S.J., ed. (Maryknoll, N.Y.: Orbis Books, 1991) 66–70.

of a good life, in contrast to "ethics," delineation of more specific proposals. This first model of involvement emphasizes actions of the Church that communicate and develop a Catholic moral vision, values, sense of the common good, and a critical reflection on culture. The major agents of this model are the Church's attempts to form values through family life, schools, parish and community involvement a set of "transcendent data," which in turn should have bearing on the conscience of the citizen. Hehir describes the method of this model as "from the conscience of the citizenry to the choice for policy." Such formation is an aspect of the teaching ministry of the Church. This process takes a long time, and its efficacy can be measured only in the long term.

A second model is the legislative-policy model. Here the Church engages in the public life of society, entering into the civic process by which policy and legislation are formed. It uses "both teaching and advocacy, espousing both principles and policy positions." This approach is an example of the regional discernment called forth by Paul VI and the Catholic tradition of linking principles and their apparent applications in concrete policy choice. This model is reflected in the statements of the American bishops that occurred after the council, as well as the political lobbies, legislative action networks, and legal action associations sponsored by various Catholic Conferences.

As groups of Catholics join with others with the intention of shaping public policy, they act within this model, although they often cannot "speak for the Church," per se. Such groups can represent a variety of positions along the political spectrum, and Catholics can belong to political groups who take opposing views on a policy matter.[11] The Church functions in this model according to the processes in American civil society. The Church can be morally convinced of the rightness or wrongness of a particular policy direction. Yet, Hehir notes that neither it, nor any group of its members, "has the intrinsic power to command universal assent in church or society."[12]

A third model is the prophetic-witness model. Here the Church as a whole or a community from within, acts as a clear counterpoint, to existing societal vision and policies. When anti-war protestors go to prison, when priests, religious, and lay people risked arrest marching

---

[11] When the matter involves a specific public teaching of the Church, this discussion needs to be nuanced to treat all values at stake.

[12] Hehir, "The Right and Competence of the Church," 68.

against the racist Jim Crow laws in the South in the 60s, or protesting American military training camps in Central America, these are prophetic actions. The difference between this model, and the gradual and transformative approaches of the first two, is its lack of compromise. In addition, its strategies are aimed at highlighting a radical opposition to the present state of affairs.

Christians in the Protestant tradition share in all three responses in their respective churches. The sectarian-prophetic tradition of the Protestant church is expressed in the theology of John Howard Yoder and Stanley Hauerwas. The civil rights movement in the United States can not be understood without the prophetic actions of Southern Baptist leader Martin Luther King, Jr. and the black church.[13]

These three languages of Catholic social response after Vatican II have one common denominator. They assume that the faith of the Catholic, while informed by powerful symbols of belief in Scripture, tradition, and the life of the Church, expresses itself in forms that are public and accessible to those who do not share Catholic belief.[14] In the move from ethos to ethics, faith does have a bearing. It opens the community and the individual to new and wider understandings of meaning based on the significance of the entrance of Jesus Christ into history, and the meaning this brings to a particular issue.[15] However, the ongoing understanding of this relationship between faith and societal ethics enters the consciousness of the Christian in multiple forms. All expressions become "public facts," accessible to all, if not agreed with by all, through the concrete form they take in society.

Church Formed by the World

The Church after Vatican II was formed by the social circumstances in which it found itself.[16] As the Latin American Church was

---

[13] Gayraud S. Wilmore, *Black Religion and Black Radicalism: An Interpretation of the Religious History of African Americans,* 3rd ed. (Maryknoll, N.Y.: Orbis Books, 1998).

[14] For the way the Church discovers and communicates socially significant meanings of Christian symbols and traditions, see Michael J. Himes and Kenneth R. Himes, O.F.M., *The Fullness of Faith: The Public Significance of Theology* (New York: Paulist Press, 1993) 4, 13.

[15] See Vincent MacNamara, "Christian Moral Life," in *The New Dictionary of Catholic Social Thought,* op. cit., 634–50.

[16] Lewis S. Mudge, *The Church as Moral Community: Ecclesiology and Ethics in Ecumenical Debate* (New York: Continuum, 1998).

transformed by acknowledging the material poverty of the masses, the Catholic Church in the United States faced a changing domestic scene, and the challenge of the post-war place of the United States in the world. Catholics had grown from twenty-one million to forty-two million between 1940 and 1960. After World War II, the G.I. Bill made higher education in the reach of thousands of veterans. This created a more educated laity, and served as a leveler in the American Catholic Church. The Catholic community was more confident and became a significant part of American society, if not one of the communities who were well-off.[17] The election of John F. Kennedy, the first Catholic president, symbolized a new moment in Catholic identity in the United States. Family income rose, and American Catholics enjoyed the post war boom in the American economy.

Because Catholics moved into the mainstream in American society, their identity was no longer formed in the Catholic ghettoes and parallel style of society marked by the 1950s. Catholic identity had to be continually negotiated and re-expressed. Openness to the world, rather than segregation from it marked this process. What it meant to be a Catholic could no longer just be given; it had to be negotiated with influences beyond the boundaries of the Catholic Church and their subsequent integration into Catholic life and practice.[18] Black and Hispanic members of the Catholic Church were still very segregated in the Church immediately after the council. The societal injustice this mirrored in the Church demanded change in a Catholic identity that was weak in the area of interracial understanding. While massive social change in the United States was a catalyst to growth in the Church, the fact that the world became a global society also had a profound effect. The migrations of the peoples of the globe changed the face of American parish life.

The world after the council was on the move; however, this is not the first vast migration of people. Between 1750 and 1930, fifty million Europeans migrated, one-fifth of the European population. Recorded emigration had never happened on that scale, as the population increased more than fourteen times over.[19] The Catholic Church

---

[17] James Hennessey, *American Catholics* (New York: Oxford University Press, 1982) 283.

[18] See Frans Jozef van Beeck, S.J., *Catholic Identity After Vatican II: Three Types of Faith in One Church* (Chicago: Loyola University Press, 1985).

[19] Rasmussen, *Earth Community, Earth Ethics* (Maryknoll, N.Y.: Orbis Books, 1996) 45.

in the United States was formed by this immigration.[20] Postwar America reflected this immigrant population growing in stature in mainstream society. Today over a hundred million people live outside the country in which they were born, twenty-three million are refugees. Miserable conditions in the third world and hope of better incomes in the first world continue to propel population movements that the world has never seen.

The Catholic Church was called to a new day at many levels after Vatican II. Global and domestic challenges and rapid cultural change were "signs of the times" that shook its foundations. Incorporating new people's into its reality, as well as being open to members who had long been in its ranks, but without voice, faced the Church with concrete experiences of "the other," which shaped its social expression.

Globalization

The postwar world was connected in new ways by improved technologies of transportation and communication and by an increasingly global and interdependent economy. Problems, especially economic ones, could no longer be adequately understood within the framework of the nation-state alone. The internationalization of labor, the fact that labor can be pulled from outside geographical boundaries, and companies move easily from one country to another, changed the way unemployment was analyzed. Unions no longer controlled the only available labor and had to revamp their bargaining strategies. Families experienced these changed labor conditions as down-sizing required transfers to new locations or the search for jobs.

Globalization was not just a concept for analysis, but something that changed the way people looked at the world. Globalization today is understood as the increasingly interconnected character of the political, economic, and social life of the peoples on this planet. Better communications, the migration of peoples, often stimulated by war, ease of travel, new opportunities for study and business, and international media coverage brought Catholics face to face with new peoples and cultures.

---

[20] See Dolores Liptak, R.S.M., *Immigrants and Their Church* (New York: Macmillan, 1989).

Robert Schreiter refers to the growing link between the local level and the global level as the "new catholicity."[21] The Church has always stood for the creation of community, but the new question was how to create community amid the pluralism of the world. After Vatican II, the North American Church, as the Latin Americans, had to look at its own thinking, and see whether its own concepts and behavior facilitated the mission of the Church in this new world, or not.

Robert Schreiter argues that key to understanding the Catholic experience in this new world is one's view of culture.[22] There is an integrated and a globalized view of culture, each upholding an important aspect of modern life. An integrated approach to culture views it as patterned systems in which all the parts create a unified whole. The strength of this approach is the sense of meaning communicated, identity formed, and unity and harmony fostered.

Globalized approaches to culture reflect the tensions and pressures of a mobile world. Culture is something to be constructed, and it involves struggle between members of different groups to be recognized and heard. Inequality of power is recognized, and the common "narrative" of the dominant group is disrupted, in order to show that the way the dominant way of life is explained is really not the case for everyone. Culture in this latter sense seeks to create a "space" between self and the "other" where both can find a place. This alternative sense of culture arises as recognition grows of differences within a local culture and the impact of global realities on everyday living.

People in a globalized culture have many identities, as they belong to more than one community. Each community to which they belong gives them an identity and meaning, and at times these various identities clash. In a globalized culture symbols are received from outside one's daily reality that impact an understanding of the world. Vast agencies of communication transport patterns and symbols across the world that are integrated or resisted differently in each local situation. Sometimes cultural symbols coming from the outside are alienating or superficial and do not create meaning for people in a local area. For example, TV programs from the U.S.A. do not model family life in Ethiopia, where malnutrition rather than shopping malls is a common denominator. Yet through the way modern media stimulates

---

[21] Robert J. Schreiter, *The New Catholicity: Theology between the Global and the Local* (Maryknoll, N.Y.: Orbis Books, 1997).

[22] Ibid., 46–61.

the imagination, someone can live in another world and take on another's reality, at least in fantasy. The world watching the war in Iraq reflects this phenomenon. Images of starving people impact the first-world living room, even though many do not know how to integrate this reality in a meaningful way into their lives.

Symbols and patterns that circulate the globe in this manner are "cultural flows" rather than cultures, since they are insufficient to create a culture, and are not received uniformly. Instead, they are accepted or rejected in local areas, and reconfigured according to local identities. Cultural flows can be superficial. For example, the export of American music, TV, T-shirts, and McDonald's across the world does little to communicate the more important aspects of American life. Americans can adapt spiritual practices from Asian religions, without entering into the total cultural matrix that gives them meaning.

The positive value of more important types of cultural flows is they can also circulate ideas and sentiments that have limited power in one culture, but in a global context provide meaning to the experience of many. Notions of human rights, women's equality, liberation, peace, and ecological responsibility are "cultural flows" that circulate the world today and have impact on the world and the church community. Many find in them images of what is alienating in their own lives and culture and define the transformations necessary to steer the world on a more constructive course.

Both visions of culture can help us understand social Catholicism after Vatican II. Integrated notions of culture show the need for new voices in theology, black, feminist, Hispanic, Asian, and African. Christianity expressed in the idioms of Northern Europe did not express the Gospel adequately in light of these distinct cultural and social identities. Integrated notions of culture highlight the role of social teaching itself, as providing within Catholic culture a vision of how to work for the peace and justice that underlies all unity and harmony.

Globalized models of culture allow the naming of the conflicted and complex reality in which the Church strived to grow, even at a local level. Globalized visions of culture take into account problems of power, oppression, moving from one place to another, fashioning new identities out of negotiating multiple identities, and the quest for survival for those marginated in mainstream society. They assist the church community to recognize the life experience of its members, and those in the wider society, who are not members of the "dominant group" in order to grasp how God works in the world.

Awareness of the interplay between the global and the local points to new ways the Holy Spirit builds a "new Church" and a "new unity" in changing times. Cultural flows challenge prevailing global systems as to their impact on people or question how national views of the world form the Church and help or hinder its mission. The movements associated with cultural flows not only give civil and political outlets for educational, cultural, legislative, and prophetic actions of the church community but also provide a framework where the Church contributes its Catholic social tradition to the common problems of humanity.

The tension that exists between the global and the local called the Church to listen to the voices that have not been integrated into its life. Here the "new voices" of blacks, women, Hispanics, Asians, and Africans join with the liberation voices in Latin America and Europe to not only facilitate the identity of their respective communities, but to form a new world Church. Both views of culture symbolize challenges faced by the Church and its members. On the one hand, the Church experienced its own unity and that of the world is incomplete as long as we have failed to integrate the world of its many peoples into the common world of one global society. On the other hand, it learned that to listen to the voices of the poor when their reality remains that of the discordant voice of the "other" requires the Church and its members to stand in the darkness, rely on God, and to be open to new direction.

Decades after Vatican II one can look back to see how ideas flow quickly in human society and the Church, but ideas are received and institutions are transformed slowly and often with pain and struggle. Social Catholicism after Vatican II is a blend of new ideas and awareness in the community and institutional and communal actions that required new commitments and understandings of faith, spirituality, and the Church. We will now examine two prototypes of this change; new voices in theology and the major statements of the American bishops on war and peace and economic justice, noting also documents on racism and women.

New Voices in Theology: Black Theology

At the same time Gustavo Gutierrez wrote *A Theology of Liberation,* James Cone in the United States wrote *A Black Theology of Liberation.*[23]

---

[23] James Cone, *A Black Theology of Liberation* (Philadelphia: J.B. Lippincott, 1970).

Black theology was given impetus by the civil rights movement and the rise of the black power movement in the 60s. The starting point for black theology is the naming of the humiliation and suffering caused by racism. Black theologians point out that interpretation of the Bible, Christian theology, and practice has been used in the past to justify the subordination inherent to racism. The critical goal of black theology is to show racism as incompatible with the Christian message, and to purify the tradition of a misuse of Christian doctrine and practice to perpetuate racism.[24] Its positive goal is to name for the black Christian the truth of the liberating love of God, to connect God's promise to bring about the Kingdom to task of overcoming systems of domination, and to link Christian worship, work, and witness to the building of a true Christian community, one that is purified of its racist heritage.

Black women theologians developed black theology to include the social, religious, and cultural experience of black women as sources for theological reflection. They adopted the term "womanist" to distinguish this theology from that of male black theology and from the growing corpus of feminist theology written initially by white Euro-American women.[25]

Black theology was assisted by a sustained social scientific analysis of the meaning and function of institutional racism in the United States that accelerated from the 60s onward. This comprehensive articulation of the depth of racism in American culture and its links with poverty, sexism, class exploitation, and imperialism, put black theologians in dialogue with other theologians speaking from positions in society where injustices are traceable to political economy and culture. The goal of this dialogue, using the medium of theology, is to provide support for members of their own ethnic group as well as lead to transformation of the greater U.S. society.[26] It serves the whole

[24] For an overview of the history and meaning of Black Theology, see M. Shawn Copeland, "Black Theology," in *The Dictionary of Catholic Social Thought,* op. cit., 91–96.

[25] See Diana L. Hayes, *And Still We Rise* (New York: Paulist Press, 1996) 135–60. Anne M. Clifford, *Introducing Feminist Theology* (Maryknoll, N.Y.: Orbis Books, 2001) 116–20.

[26] An example is *The Ties that Bind: African American and Hispanic American/ Latino/a Theologies in Dialogue,* Anthony B. Pinn and Benjamin Valentin, eds. (New York: Continuum, 2001).

Christian community in its critical function of ridding church life and practice of its racist overtones.

Most important for Catholics was the expression of black awareness within the Catholic Church. In 1968, Martin Luther King, Jr. was assassinated in Memphis. The black community erupted in anger, frustration, and despair. In April that year, the Black Catholic Clergy Caucus met in Detroit and stated, "The Catholic Church in the United States, primarily a white racist institution, has addressed itself primarily to white society and is definitely a part of that society."[27] This was a wake up call for the American church. Black historian Cyprian Davis writes, ". . . it is remarkable that the church as an institution opened itself with a minimum of resistance to the needs of its black members in most areas."[28] In 1971, the National Office of Black Catholics was opened. Priests, religious and laity set up national organizations and pushed for equal rights in the church.[29] Jay P. Dolan comments, "For the first time in over a century, black priests were appointed to the hierarchy."[30]

Institutional racism in the Catholic Church is far from over. However there have been strides made in the Church. This growth and movement in black theology that supported it points to the fact that a moral awakening in the Church does not always come purely from within, but from without, and recognition of the "signs of the times." The civil rights movement called the Church to be a better Church, and made it a clearer witness to the Gospel. It helped the church to recognize its own members and to make institutional changes that could foster their rightful and fuller incorporation in the church.

[27] Cyprian Davis, O.S.B., *The History of Black Catholics in the United States* (New York: Crossroad, 1991) 258.

[28] Ibid., 259.

[29] Joseph M. Davis, S.M., and Cyprian Rowe, F.M.S., "The Development of the National Office of Black Catholics," *U.S. Catholic Historian* 7 (1988) 265–89; as quoted in Cyprian Davis, O.S.B., "God of our Weary Years: Black Catholics in American Catholic History," in *Taking Down Our Harps: Black Catholics in the United States,* Diana L. Hayes and Cyprian Davis, O.S.B., eds. (Maryknoll, N.Y.: Orbis Books, 1988) 46.

[30] Jay P. Dolan, *The American Catholic Experience: A History from Colonial Times to the Present* (New York: Doubleday, 1985) 447. For a description of the effect of this public dimension of the Black Catholic church on Black Catholic theology see M. Shawn Copeland, "Method in Emerging Black Catholic Theology," in *Taking Down Our Harps,* op. cit., 120–44.

Today there are approximately 1.5 million black Catholics in the United States. Since the 1960s there have been other institutional signs of movement toward a greater inclusion of black Catholics in the Catholic Church in the United States. In 1979, the American hierarchy addressed the issue of racism in a pastoral letter, "Brothers and Sisters to Us." In 1984 ten black bishops issued a pastoral letter on evangelization and African American Catholics, "What We Have Seen and Heard."[31] In 1987 the first black Catholic congress in the twentieth century was held in Washington, D.C.; in the fall that year Pope John Paul II gave a special audience to black Catholic leaders in New Orleans. In the same year the Black Secretariat in the service of the National Council of Catholic Bishops was established.[32] Today leadership of the National Conference of Catholic Bishops of the United States, the Catholic Theological Association of America, and other major Catholic institutions is being given by black Catholics.

The gifts of black Catholics and their spiritual tradition to the wider Catholic Church in America are many.[33] Their heritage is community centered and steeped in a rich biblical tradition. They have a liturgical expression that is of both mind and heart and a this-worldly awareness of God in daily life fostered by a long history of black religion formed out of struggle.[34] Their awareness too has had a global dimension. Black theologians have been united in heart and in dialogue with the experience of their black brothers and sisters in South Africa, and their confrontation with apartheid.[35]

Hispanic/Latino Theology

Popular thinking views Hispanics as newcomers to the United States. The truth is Hispanic history begins two centuries before the Declaration of Independence in 1776. From the end of the fifteenth

---

[31] *Brothers and Sisters to Us.* See *American Catholic Social Teaching,* op. cit., no. 13. *What We Have Seen and Heard,* ibid., no. 15.

[32] Davis, *The History of Black Catholics in the United States,* 260.

[33] See *Theological Studies* (December 2000) vol. 61. no. 4. This issue is devoted to "The Catholic Reception of Black Theology."

[34] Jamie T. Phelps, O.P., "Black Spirituality," in *Taking Down Our Harps,* 179–98.

[35] See, for example, A. Boesak, *Farewell to Innocence* (Maryknoll, N.Y.: Orbis Books, 1977) and Kairos Theologians, *The Kairos Document: A Theological Comment on the Political Crisis in South Africa. Challenge to the Church* (Johannesburg: Skotaville, 1986).

century, with the arrival of European explorers to the Americas, what we know today as the United States, Central and South America, Mexico, and large segments of the Caribbean developed through contact and conquest that destroyed populations and gave rise to populations of people with unique ties to the Americas.

Hispanic history in the Americas begins with the Spanish exploration and colonization of the North and South American continents. While 1492 is noted as the "discovery of America" by Christopher Columbus, those who already resided in these lands experienced it as also the beginning of their condemnation to enslavement, humiliation, sickness, and massive death. Theologian Virgil Elizondo remarks, "For the natives of the Americas, 1492 was quite the opposite. It was the beginning of the invasion of gun-bearing gods-turned-monsters from unknown lands against which their own weapons and tactics of war seemed totally impotent."[36]

Today African American and Latino/a cultures and identities are the result of a "fusion" of Euro/American, Iberian, American Indian, and African cultures. The theological term Latino/a or Hispanic theology is used to refer to theological reflection that arises from groups who are descendents of Spanish speaking or Latin ancestry. Mexican/American and or Chicano, Puerto Rican, Cuban, Dominican, Central American, South American, and Spanish people living in the United States, although coming from different historical trajectories, would all be considered under this single experience. Today over thirty million U.S. citizens are from this heritage, 11 percent of the population. For our purposes, we will focus on Hispanic theology as it emerged in the United States, especially from the Mexican-American community within the Catholic Church.

The Chicano movement in the 1960s addressed the exploitation and oppression of Hispanics in the country and began a socio-analytical account of their unique and shared exploitation with blacks, along with its economic, social, political and cultural results. The Church was implicated in the critique since it was historically the Church of the colonizers and by its silence gave tacit approval of the ongoing suppression of the Mexican American people. When the Chicano movement

---

[36] Virgil Elizondo, *Guadalupe: Mother of the New Creation* (Maryknoll, N.Y.: Orbis Books, 1997) xiii. For an understanding of this period of history, see Leonardo Boff and Virgil Elizondo, eds., *1492–1992: The Voice of the Victims*, Concilium, vol. 1990/6 (London: SCM Press, 1990).

developed it the 1960s, it seemed for some that the only way to be liberated from this history was to discard the Church. Hispanic theologians began an alternative path to examine the meaning of the new identity that had been formed in the Church and society through this difficult history and to express the faith that came from it. Today well over a third of all the world's Roman Catholics arose from the struggle to graft Iberian Catholicism onto the pre-Columbian cultures, despite the many dehumanizing features of the *conquista*.[37]

A key term for reflection in Hispanic theology is *mestizaje*, meaning the mix or creation of a new people.[38] The mix that gave rise to the Mexican American people and experience, however, is one that took place through conquest and colonization. The economically motivated military conquest is coupled by the imposition of a world vision that crushes the culture of those conquered and thus destroys their meaning system. Even after recovery, the native culture never returns to pre-conquest days. Over and above the material and psychological destruction that occurs in being conquered, when the conquest involves the imposition of religious symbols, and these symbols are associated with the conquering group, the devastation to the people is magnified. Distinctions of "superior" and "inferior" are given a religious basis, as all that is associated with the conquered is to be despised and all associated with the conqueror as "civilization."

The people who were "born" of this conquest, its rapes and its marriages, were of both classes. Elizondo remarks, "Mestizos are born out of two histories and in them begins a new history."[39] Hispanic theology is the effort to explore the meaning of this new Christian identity and to articulate the distinctive sense of faith and church to which it has given rise. It is the starting point to inquire into the meaning of Jesus Christ, the identity of Mexican American Christians and their mission.

Hispanics draw an analogy between Jesus' socio-cultural identity as a hybrid—a Jew of Galilean descent—and the present experience of

---

[37] Allan Figueroa Deck, S.J., "Culture," in *The New Dictionary of Catholic Social Thought*, op. cit., 261. See also *Frontier of Hispanic Theology in the United States* (Maryknoll, N.Y.: Orbis Books, 1992).

[38] Virgil Elizondo, "*Mestizaje* as the Locus of Theological Reflection," in *The Future of Liberation Theology*, Marc H. Ellis and Otto Maduro, eds. (Maryknoll, N.Y.: Orbis Books, 1989) 358–74. See also Elizondo, *Galilean Journey: The Mexican American Promise* (Maryknoll, N.Y.: Orbis Books, 1983).

[39] Elizondo, "*Mestizaje* as a Locus of Theological Reflection," 362.

being "mixed" or between cultures that is prevalent among Mexican Americans and Chicanos. This Christology would encourage Hispanics to affirm their cultural identity despite the rejection they may experience in the United States. Hispanic theology also takes popular religious symbols and practices seriously as expressions of its people. Hispanic theologians place great emphasis on issues related to cultural memory and self-cultural identity.[40]

Mujerista theology is the theological reflection done by Hispanic women whose roots are in Central and South American countries, but who now live in the United States.[41] Hispanic women reflect on their experience trying to understand the many oppressive structures that define their lives and seek to define for themselves a new future. Key to their reflection is the understanding of how racism and ethnic prejudice, economic oppression, and sexism work together and reinforce each other.[42]

In 1971 the Mexican-American Cultural Center was founded to encourage dialogue between Latin American and U.S. Latino/a religious leaders. This center was founded by Virgil Elizondo, who continued to serve as rector of the San Fernando Cathedral in San Antonio. The center has been a focal point in fostering the articulation of a U.S. Hispanic/Latino/a theology and vision of evangelization. In 1983 the National Conference of Catholic Bishops issued *The Hispanic Presence: Challenge and Commitment,* along with pastoral plans in 1987 and 1989 to better meet particular Hispanic needs in the Church.[43] Today there are Hispanic members in the leadership of the Church, an Association of Catholic Hispanic Theologians in the United States, as well as the *Journal of Hispanic/Latino Theology.* Today 56 percent of Hispanics/Latinos in the United States consider their religious background to be Catholic.[44]

[40] Bejamin Valentin, "Strangers No More: An Introduction to, and Interpretation of, U.S. Hispanic/Latino/a Theology," in *The Ties that Bind,* 38–53. See also *From the Heart of Our People: Latino/a Explorations in Catholic Systematic Theology,* Orlando Espin and Miguel H. Diaz, eds. (Maryknoll, N.Y.: Orbis Books, 1999).

[41] See Ada Maria Isasi-Diaz, *Mujerista Theology: A Theology for the Twenty-First Century* (Maryknoll, N.Y.: Orbis Books, 1996).

[42] See also Maria Pilar Aquino, *Our Cry for Life: Feminist Theology from Latin America* (Maryknoll, N.Y.: Orbis Books, 1993).

[43] Sandra Yocum Mize, "National Conference of Catholic Bishops in the United States," in *The New Dictionary of Catholic Social Thought,* op. cit., 668.

[44] Bryan T. Froehle and Mary L. Gautier, *Catholicism USA: A Portrait of the Catholic Church in the United States* (Maryknoll, N.Y.: Orbis Books, 2000) 17.

The Women's Movement

In 1963 Pope John XXII recognized the woman's movement as part of the "signs of the times." "Since women are becoming more conscious of their dignity, they will not tolerate being treated as inanimate objects, or mere instruments, but claim, both in domestic and public life, the rights and duties that befit a human person" (PT 41). This awareness was reaffirmed at the Second Vatican Council, where lack of social justice for women was specified as an issue in the modern world to be addressed (GS 9 and 29). The women's movement, as the civil rights and Chicano movement, has challenged the Church and vice versa. This dialogue has an essential role in understanding social Catholicism after Vatican II.

Feminism is a movement that challenges sexist economic, political, or cultural structures that systematically subordinate and exclude women from full participation in the life of the society. Feminist thought arose out of the emancipation movements that took on new life in the 1960s in the United States and had their own expressions on every continent. In first-world situations feminist thought has two foci: equal access to society and an equal stature with men, and an exploration of the distinctive gifts of women that recovers the silenced voices of women in the culture and society.[45] Feminism is not necessarily a Christian movement. Some women in fact have abandoned Christianity or organized religion because of their belief in its close association with patriarchy, a society ruled by the "law of the father." Patriarchy refers to systems of legal, economic, and political relations that legitimate and enforce relations of dominance in a society.

Feminist consciousness has arisen from various social classes, races, and worldviews. Liberal feminism is rooted in the Enlightenment ideal that women as individuals should have legal and political rights within current systems. Marxist and socialist forms of feminism see the transformation of the capitalist system as necessary for the liberation of all women in all classes. Radical feminism considers gender discrimination as the root cause of all other forms of oppression. Women's control over their bodies is a core issue in their liberation. Radical feminists favor cultivating a women's culture through women-centered alterna-

---

[45] For feminism as a global theological flow, see Schreiter, *The New Catholicity*, 18. For a feminist interpretation of Catholic Social Teaching and its attention to the needs of women see Christine Gudorf, *Catholic Social Teaching on Liberation Themes* (Washington, D.C.: University Press of America, 1981).

tives. Some radical feminists suggest the natural, especially moral superiority of women. These are referred to as cultural feminists.[46] Most feminists across the world emphasize structural connections among sexism, racism, classism, abuse of the environment, militarism, and all other forms of oppression.

Many feminists have chosen not to abandon the Christian tradition but to transform it. They seek to show that Christian religions operate with the same gender blindness that occurs in the culture. There, man is the norm of human nature and who defines the meaning of existence. Women are defined only as complementary to men. What is associated with being male is the norm, and what is associated with being female is the exception. Maleness is not just one kind of human experience; it is human experience.[47]

Feminist theologians point out that the Christian churches fail to promote the full humanity of women in their structures of theology and legitimize the subordination and victimization of women by recourse to Scripture and tradition to show that this was part of God's plan for creation.[48] Feminists have reinterpreted traditional Christian views of the human person, especially in how they can reinforce patterns of female passivity and male activity. They charge these undermine women's moral agency, make the domestic sphere almost exclusively the responsibility of women, and sabotage the participation of women also in public life.[49] In systematic theology feminist theologians have set up a dialogue between the lives and experiences of women and the structures of systematic theology. This is especially true when feminists consider how Christian theology has named God and made maleness constitutive of divinity.[50]

[46] For an overview of the feminist movement, see Maria Riley, *Transforming Feminism* (Kansas City: Sheed and Ward, 1989). For an excellent insight into feminism and its relationship to Christianity, see Anne M. Clifford, *Introduction to Feminist Theology* (Maryknoll, N.Y.: Orbis Books, 2001).

[47] See ibid., 16–21, for a description of the role of paternalism, dualism, and andocentrism in the worldview that feminists seek to change.

[48] Elizabeth Schussler-Fiorenza, "Feminist Theology as a Critical Theology of Liberation," in *Theological Studies* (1975) 606–26; reprinted with new introduction in *Discipleship of Equals* (New York: Crossroad, 1993) 53–79.

[49] Barbara Hogan, "Feminism and Catholic Social Thought," in *The New Dictionary of Catholic Social Thought*, op. cit., 394–98.

[50] Elizabeth Johnson, *She Who Is* (New York: Crossroad, 1993). Sallie McFague, *Models of God* (London: SCM, 1987). Anne E. Carr, *Transforming Grace: Christian Tradition and Women's Experience* (San Francisco: Harper and Row, 1988). Sandra

When feminists take the insights into society and culture, which are recognized by the women's movement and apply them to the Church, the most controversial issue is women's ordination. Women have been ordained in Protestant churches, but within the Catholic Church this remains a contested issue.[51] A global search for justice unites women across the globe that makes connections between feminist theology and liberation theology. Here women learn that social location, race, and class qualify how gender discrimination is experienced.

Women seeking bathroom breaks in textile mills in the South in the U.S.A. have different feminist agenda than upper class women in the North who seek social or cultural recognition. Those concerned with female genital mutilation in Africa, status questions in India, domestic abuse in Europe, access to medical care and education in Asia not only correct a feminist agenda that strays from the issues of real women but enlarge the vision in the Church as to what it means to make an option for the poor, including women, amid the massive inequalities of wealth and power worldwide.[52] Feminists add their voices to those who name the poor and specify the cry for structural change in the dominant economic, political, cultural, and religious institutions of society.

Women have been especially strong in their advocacy for the ecological movement.[53] They contribute to the Church's reflection on institutional violence, naming it as it resides in the most intimate of institutions, the human family. They call into question any claim to some "universal" view of humanity that ignores or distorts the experience of women and those in the third world.[54] This critical function

Schneiders, "Feminist Spirituality," in *The New Dictionary of Catholic Spirituality,* op. cit., 395. Joann Wolski Conn, "Women's Spirituality: Restriction and Reconstruction," in *Women's Spirituality: Resources for Christian Development,* Joann Wolski Conn, ed. (New York: Paulist Press, 1986).

[51] See Clifford, *An Introduction to Feminist Theology,* 140–48. For an excellent study of the issue of ordination of women to the diaconate in the Catholic Church, see Phyllis Zagano, *Holy Saturday* (New York: Crossroad, 2000).

[52] See *With Passion and Compassion: Third World Women Doing Theology,* Virginia Fabella and Mercy Amba Oduyoye, eds. (Maryknoll, N.Y.: Orbis Books, 1988); and *Beyond Bonding: a Third World Women's Theological Journey,* Virginia Fabella, ed. (Manila: EATWOT, 1993).

[53] *Women Healing Earth: Third World Women on Ecology, Feminism, and Religion,* Rosemary Ruether, ed. (Maryknoll, N.Y.: Orbis Books, 1996).

[54] Mercy Amba Oduyoye, "Christian Feminism and African Culture: The 'Hearth' of the Matter," in *The Future of Liberation Theology,* op. cit., 441–49.

in the Church is augmented as a new women's spirituality is articulated in the Church and a retrieval of the wisdom of women in the tradition goes on.

Not all women think alike, as not all blacks or Hispanics think alike. The bishops of the United States discovered this as they attempted to draft a pastoral letter that responded to the concerns of women.[55] In preparation for the writing of a document on women, bishops invited various groups of women to speak with them. They were to address conditions that contribute to the alienation of women and those conditions that fostered their reconciliation.[56] However, after four drafts, the bishops and this process were not successful in completing this pastoral letter.[57] Issues regarding the status of the discussion regarding ordination of women, debate among women themselves regarding their role in the Church, and questions regarding how to integrate the pluralism of perspectives regarding women and theology plagued a letter written at a national level.[58] Individual bishops in the United States, however, have successfully addressed the concerns of women in pastoral letters, and the Canadian bishops issued fourteen public statements on women's issues between 1971 and 1990.[59]

Voices from Africa and Asia

African and Asian liberation theologies are not simply clones of Latin American liberation theology. Rather they arise from diverse and rich cultures, unique experiences of Christianity, and issues of their own contexts. Africa has been a center of Christianity since the

[55] Mary Ann Donovan, S.C., "Women's Issues: An Agenda for the Church?" *Horizons* (Fall, 1987) vol. 14, no. 2, 283–95. Sandra M. Schneiders, "The Risk of Dialogue: the U.S. Bishops and Women in Conversation," *Journal for Peace and Justice Studies* 2, no. 1 (1990) 49–63.

[56] See "Comments on the First Draft of the NCCB Pastoral Letter: Partners in the Mystery of Redemption," issued by *The Center of Concern* (Washington, D.C.: June, 1988).

[57] "Support Fading for Document about Women," *New York Times* 141:8 (June 19, 1992); Peter Steinfels, "New Fire in Bishops' Debate over Document on Women," *New York Times* 142:13 (November 18, 1992).

[58] See "One in Christ: Toward a Pastoral Response to the Concerns of Women for Church and Society," 1992, in *American Catholic Social Teaching*, op. cit., no. 17.

[59] Mary Ellen Sheehan, I.H.M., "Roman Catholic Bishops on Women's Equality: Some Post-Vatican II Developments," in *The Church in the Nineties: Its Legacy, Its Future*, Pierre M. Hegy, ed. (Collegeville: The Liturgical Press, 1993) 158–71.

early Church. It experienced colonialization from the fifteenth to the nineteenth centuries through Western imperialism, as well as loss of contact with their cultural roots through slavery and dislocation. African theology is therefore more sensitive to indigenous religion and the need to retrieve their African heritage and to express their Christianity through their unique cultural traditions. A question in African theology is whether the direction of African religion looks ahead to how traditions have been reconstructed in the cities or back to the more original expressions in the villages.[60]

Not all expressions of theology arising out of an African context are identical. For example, the struggle against apartheid in South Africa was a focal point for theologians to express the political ramifications of Christian beliefs over their usual interest to recover African culture in expressions of the Christian life. They condemned its practice and how it was condoned by white parent churches in the first world.[61] Africans share with Latin Americans the inheritance of colonialism and post-colonial structures that continue to disempower their people.[62] More recent reflection in the African church reveals its consciousness of how its place in the world capitalist system, its colonial inheritance and post-colonial interventions in its life and culture, affect its capacity to serve a people confronted with massive poverty, unemployment, illiteracy, and epidemic levels of infection by AIDS.

In 1994 the African bishops gathered in Rome for a synod to discuss the pastoral needs of their continent.[63] Seeking a Church that is both African and Catholic, the bishops focused on the cultural symbol of family as a way to approach the unique sense of the Church in Africa. Through strengthening the relationships within the Church, the Church will better evangelize a "continent of marginal peoples whose cries

[60] Benezet Bujo, *African Theology in Its Social Context* (Maryknoll, N.Y.: Orbis Books, 1992). For an introduction to African Theology, see *Faces of Jesus in Africa*, Robert Schreiter, ed. (London: SCM, 1992); Aylward Shorter, *The Church in the African City* (London: Chapter, 1991). Vincent J. Donovan, *Christianity Rediscovered: An Epistle from the Masai* (Notre Dame: Fies, 1978).

[61] Albert Nolan, "Theology in a Prophetic Mode," in *The Future of Liberation Theology*, op. cit., 433–40. Deane William Ferm, *Third World Liberation Theologies* (Maryknoll, N.Y.: Orbis Books, 1986) 62. Allan Boesak, *Finger of God: Sermons on Faith and Socio-Responsibility* (Maryknoll, N.Y.: Orbis Books, 1992).

[62] Marie J. Giblin, "Taking African History Seriously: The Challenge of Liberation Theology," in *The Future of Liberation Theology*, 129–38.

[63] *The African Synod: Documents, Reflections, Perspectives,* Maura Browne, ed. (Maryknoll, N.Y.: Orbis Books, 1996).

sometimes go unheard."[64] This requires an evangelization process that emphasizes option for the poor, small Christian communities, permanent deaconate, authentic African liturgy, Christian literature, and efficient church leadership.

New expressions of Christian faith arising from Asia come from a context different from all other churches discussed so far, in two ways. First, Christian faith in Asia encounters on a daily basis other major religions. Second, Christians are a minority in all Asian countries, except the Philippines where they comprise the majority. Korea also is unique in Asia in that there are statistically a growing number of Christians. Asia is made up of distinct countries, each of which has had its own encounter with Western colonialism and its own forms of resistance to it. In fact, Christian missionary efforts in Asia have historically been rejected, not necessarily because of a rejection of Christianity itself, but because of its association with Western European culture. When the message was wrapped in Euro-American cultural patterns, it was rejected, or integrated with great difficulty, in situations where other major world religions set the cultural base.[65]

Because each country in Asia has its own history, there are distinct expressions of Asian theology arising from each major center.[66] However, there are two concerns that are shared by Asian authors. First, the great poverty across Asia is a great challenge to the practice of religion. More than 85 percent of all Asians suffer from abject poverty and oppression.[67] Second, the dialogue between Christianity and the

[64] Chukwudum B. Okolo, *The African Synod: Hope for the Continent's Liberation* (Kenya: AMECEA Gaba Publications, 1994) ix.

[65] For an account of this encounter in Japan, see the novel by Shusaku Endo, *Silence* (London: Owen, 1976).

[66] Examples are the work of Kosuke Koyama in Japan, *Mount Fugi and Mount Sinai: A Critique of Idols* (Maryknoll, N.Y.: Orbis Books, 1985); Choan-Seng Song in Taiwan, *Third-Eye Theology: Theology in Formation in Asian Settings* (Maryknoll, N.Y.: Orbis Books, 1990); Carlos H. Abesamis in the Philippines, "Faith and Life from the Grassroots in the Philippines," in *Asia's Struggle for Full Humanity* (Maryknoll, N.Y.: Orbis Books, 1990); and Mary John Mananzan also from the Philippines, "Theological Perspectives of a Religious Woman," in *The Future of Liberation Theology;* and *minjung* theology in Korea, *An Emerging Theology in World Perspective: Commentary of Korean Minjung Theology,* Jung Yung Lee, ed. (Mystic, Conn.: Twenty-Third, 1988); in India the work of Samuel Rayan, S.J., "The Search for an Asian Spirituality of Liberation," in *Asian Christian Spirituality. Reclaiming Traditions* (Maryknoll, N.Y.: Orbis Books, 1992).

[67] Ferm, *Third World Liberation Theologies,* 76.

major world religions is forming a new expression of Christianity in Asia.[68]

It is important to note that while Asian theology is interested in inter-religious dialogue, the subject of the poor and oppressed in Asia, and resistance to unjust structures are also central to its thought.[69] In the Philippines reflection on the personal commitment required for social transformation developed as a "theology of struggle."[70]

In other places in Asia, the religio-cultural context qualifies the struggle for liberation. The over-whelming majority of the poor and the oppressed in Asia are non-Christians, many of whom adhere to a wide variety of popular religious traditions which have some connection with the great religions that have shaped dominant Asian cultures. Despite the wide differences among Asian countries, certain themes emerge in theology that focus on social concerns: the persistence of mass poverty, the ongoing threat to democratic rights, and the ambiguous role of religion as liberator and supporter of the status quo, ecology, and women's issues.[71]

The bishops of Asia met for a synod in Rome in 1998. The synod reinforced the vision of the Asian Church for the twenty-first century as building the Kingdom of God through dialogue.[72] As all churches, the Asian Church is varied and no one voice speaks its diversity. Yet as it grapples with poverty as the contextual issue of all Asian churches and engages in dialogue with the great religions of Asia it will enrich the whole Church in a new way of being church that arises from its unique context.[73]

---

[68] See Aloysius Pieris, *Love Meets Wisdom: A Christian Experience of Buddhism* (Maryknoll, N.Y.: Orbis Books, 1988) and *Fire and Water: Basic Issues in Asian Buddhism and Christianity* (Maryknoll, N.Y.: Orbis Books, 1996).

[69] For attention to sources of Asian theology, see Peter C. Phan, *Christianity with an Asian Face* (Maryknoll, N.Y.: Orbis Books, 2003).

[70] Mary Rosario Battung, *Religion and Society: Toward a Theology of Struggle* (Caloocan City, 1988). For this expression in the Protestant church, see Eleazar S. Fernandez, *Toward a Theology of Struggle* (Maryknoll, N.Y.: Orbis Books, 1994).

[71] Bastiaan Wielenga, "Liberation Theology in Asia," *The Cambridge Companion to Liberation Theology,* Christopher Rowland, ed. (Cambridge University Press, 1999) 39–62. Chung Hyun Kyung, *Struggle to be Sun Again. Introducing Asian Women's Theology* (London: SCM Press, 1991).

[72] *The Asian Synod: Texts and Commentaries,* Peter Phan, ed. (Maryknoll, N.Y.: Orbis Books, 2002).

[73] For a description of major themes in other Asian theologies: Chinese, Malaysian, Myanmar, Taiwanese, and Vietnamese theology, see *Dictionary of Third*

The Church in the United States:
Pastoral Letters on War and Peace, and the Economy

The two major pastoral letters from the United States, *The Challenge of Peace* (1983) and *Economic Justice for All* (1986) touch on issues that were imperative in the domestic life of the United States, nuclear arms and the economy respectively, as well as had bearing on the place held by the United States in the world.[74] However, these two documents are theological documents in that the American bishops acted out of the vision of the role of the Church in society voiced by Vatican II.

The council saw the Church as a defender of human dignity and the rights that flow from that dignity. These tasks are not just social roles of the Church but have ecclesial significance. The role of the Church in public affairs follows its nature. The Church is primarily a religious organization. However, since its religious ministry involves fostering the Kingdom of God, the Church addresses itself to issues that defend human dignity, promote human rights, build the unity of the human family, and provide meaning to every aspect of human activity (LG 40). The Church in America did not seek to be identified with any political system; however, it did want to enter into dialogue with society in terms of contemporary problems as called by Vatican II. In the U.S. context, these pastoral letters reflect the American Church retrieving the meaning of Christianity within its own borders, thus expressing a dimension of Social Catholicism after Vatican II. In the U.S. context, the meaning of the human person and his or her dignity and how that dignity is fostered or challenged in the current situation was treated through the issues of peace and the economy.

The bishops saw the Catholic social tradition as a resource in their reflection. The pastoral letter sees the tradition as, ". . . a mix of biblical, theological, and philosophical elements which are brought to bear upon the concrete problems of the day" (*The Challenge of Peace*, 14). The bishops contributed to the social tradition, extending current church teachings on war and peace to the problem at hand. The "new moment" that the bishops wanted to address in their pastoral, *The*

World Theologies, Virginia Fabella, M.M., and R.S. Sugirtharajah, eds. (Maryknoll, N.Y.: Orbis Books, 2000).

[74] See both documents in *Catholic Social Thought: The Documentary Heritage*, David J. O'Brien and Thomas A. Shannon, eds. (Maryknoll, N.Y.: Orbis Books, 2002) 489–680.

Challenge of Peace: God's Promise and Our Response (1983) was the arms race in postwar America. Danger arose from two sources: first, from the kinds of weapons that were in the hands of the great powers of the world and their destructive capabilities, and second, the fact these were being stockpiled. The arms race in a cold war atmosphere was coming to a point of crisis.[75]

The pastoral letter on war and peace seeks to interpret the recent teaching of councils and popes in light of American experience and insight. It deals fundamentally with three issues: reflection on the morality of war, moral norms concerning the use of nuclear weapons, and the question of the morality of "deterrence" or the policies by which states forestall the use of nuclear weapons by threatening nuclear retaliation.

To understand the way Catholicism approaches war, one needs a proper idea of peace. "Peace is not merely the absence of war" (GS 78). Peace requires justice, and a just society requires the willingness to love. Discussion of war takes place within the context of peace. Traditionally peace is reflected in a social order where lives are well ordered, human dignity fostered, and the common good sought.

The American bishops were aware that discussion of war occurs within two major traditions in the Church: the just-war theory and the pacifist tradition. Just-war thinking usually offers criteria to treat two moral dilemmas that surround war: whether to wage war *(jus ad bellum)* and how war ought to be waged *(jus in bello)*. According to the pastoral letter, criteria governing why and when it is permissible to go to war are: (1) just cause, (2) competent authority, (3) comparative justice, or do the grievances involved and their values justify killing others, (4) right intention, or do you seek peace as the ultimate goal and thus avoid undo destruction, (5) last resort, or have you sought non-military means to right grievances, (6) probability of success, (7) proportionality or is the damage inflicted or the costs of war in proportion to the good that you hope to achieve by waging war (*The Challenge of Peace*, 85–99).

The *jus in bello* criteria deal mainly with proportionality and discrimination between the military and noncombatants as a war is conducted (*The Challenge of Peace* 101–10). The *jus in bello* principle of proportionality requires an assessment of the good and evil con-

---

[75] Brian Hehir, "From the Pastoral Constitution of Vatican II to The Challenge of Peace," in *Catholics and Nuclear War*, 71–87.

sequences that can reasonably be foreseen as resulting from specific actions in warfare. Discrimination protects the immunity of non-combatants from direct military attack by restricting direct targeting to combatants, military installations, and factories whose products are directly related to the war effort.[76]

At the time of the writing of the pastoral letter, the pacifist movement in the United States was strong and visible in the public debate on the arms race.[77] The Catholic social tradition offered both the just-war tradition and pacifism as gospel responses to the reality of war. The American bishops called on both as a context for thinking about war in the continental situation of the United States. They saw, "just-war teaching and non-violence as distinct but interdependent methods of evaluating warfare."[78] They encouraged that these methods not be considered as opposed to one another, rather as complementary and necessary for a full moral vision. There were Catholics who held these two views and belonged to movements that supported them in the public arena.

Traditionally there is a strong moral presumption against war in Catholic moral thought; however, the non-violence tradition questions whether there is ever really a moral reason for the costs of war. This type of thinking gained momentum after people experienced the devastating effects of the atom bomb at the end of World War II. The disproportionate nature of nuclear war captured the public imagination. John Paul II stated in 1981 on a visit to Hiroshima, "In the past it was possible to destroy a village, a town, even a country. Now it is the whole planet that has come under threat."[79] The bishops saw the pacifist position as important, yet also wanted to recognize a realist position, that in a fallen world, force exerted by governments to preserve their citizens can be necessary.

When the bishops incorporated both the pacifist and just war tradition in the same document, they also commented on their relationship. They felt the two positions shared values, and the two positions served to correct and balance each other. However, the main difference between the two positions was not only in their conclusion on

---

[76] For background on current issues, see J. Milburn Thompson, *Justice and Peace: A Christian Primer* (Maryknoll, N.Y.: Orbis Books, 2003) chs. 5, 6, and 7.

[77] See Gordon C. Zahn, "Pacifism and Just War," in *Catholics and Nuclear War*, 119–31.

[78] Ibid., 120–21.

[79] John Paul II, "Address to Scientists and Scholars," *Origins* (1981) 621.

the use of force but how they functioned in the moral community. The nonviolent position is treated in the pastoral letter as a personal position, while the just-war position is regarded as both for individuals and states (*The Challenge of Peace,* 111–21, 34–37).[80]

When the bishops addressed the moral norms for use of nuclear weapons, they had to interpret the teaching of Vatican II for the United States context. The teaching of the council is clear: "Any act of war aimed indiscriminately at the destruction of entire cities or of extensive areas along with their population is a crime against God and humanity itself. It merits unequivocal and unhesitating condemnation" (GS 80). However, the question remained if there could be a discriminate and proportionate use of nuclear weapons. Could there be a limited use of nuclear weapons to achieve justice? The bishops take three positions in the pastoral. First, it rejects the use of nuclear weapons against population centers, even in retaliation. Second, it strongly rejects any first use of nuclear weapons, no matter how just the causes or how careful the intent to act in a limited manner. They feel that the danger of escalation is so great; it would be morally unacceptable to initiate nuclear war in any form (*The Challenge of Peace,* 152).

The bishops consider a third use of nuclear weapons: retaliatory use in a limited counterforce exchange. This use of nuclear weapons differs from counter-population warfare. In this case counterforce strategies target missiles directly against the enemy's combatant forces, military bases, and defense-related industries. Is a "limited nuclear exchange" possible? While it may be possible on a theoretical level, the bishops express skepticism about the possibility that any use of nuclear weapons really can be kept limited. The question of the practical feasibility of waging limited nuclear war is "inconclusive" in the public arena. However, the bishops remark that the burden of proof remains on those who assert that meaningful limitation is possible (*The Challenge of Peace,* 157–61).[81] Though they do not condemn all possible use of nuclear weapons, they see no moral justification for

---

[80] See Brian Hehir, "Catholic Teaching on War and Peace: The Decade 1979–1989," in *Moral Theology: Challenges for the Future,* Charles E. Curran, ed. (New York: Paulist Press, 1990) 370.

[81] See also "The Challenge of Peace and the Morality of Using Nuclear Weapons," in *The Catholic Bishops and Nuclear War,* Judith A. Dwyer, ed. (Washington, D.C.: Georgetown University Press, 1984) 5–21.

submitting the human community to such a risk (*The Challenge of Peace,* 159).[82]

The third major topic of the pastoral is the question of the morality of deterrence, the attempt to reduce another's incentives to act in undesirable ways by threatening to carry out harmful, sometimes punitive responses to their actions. Nuclear deterrence is a means of preventing the outbreak of war by threatening to use nuclear weapons in response to aggressive military actions.[83] The Cold War view of nuclear deterrence was based on Western perceptions that communism had inherent to its ideology activities that exceeded its vital interests. These imperialist interests and aspirations had to be checked. Both the United States and Russia stockpiled nuclear weapons at such a level that the magnitude of their capacities set a risk of retaliation that no aggressor would challenge. The "unacceptable damage" to an aggressor would outweigh any possible gain in a nuclear war.

The moral problem associated with deterrence is that in the Catholic moral tradition, the intention to act immorally is immoral, even if the action is never carried out. Thus, whether it was permissible to stockpile nuclear weapons was questioned, even though one never intended to use them, unless provoked. The bishops gave a "conditional acceptance of deterrence" (*The Challenge of Peace,* 186). The bishops accept the paradoxical situation that nuclear weapons are maintained in order to prevent first use. However, the ambiguity of this position resulted in ongoing debate within the Catholic community regarding the type of international transformation necessary to reverse the arms race. This included advocacy for arms control, attempts to improve international relations, strengthen international treaties and associations, like NATO, and in general, lessen the reliance and need for nuclear weapons in world politics. David Hollenbach claims the real debate about nuclear deterrence is not about intentions, but about the relative merits of whether a particular weapon system, targeting doctrine or strategic plan, ". . . will actually make the world more secure from nuclear disaster or less so. There is no such thing as deterrence in the abstract."[84] Deterrence in

---

[82] See David Hollenbach, "*The Challenge of Peace* in the Context of Recent Church Teachings," in *Catholics and Nuclear War,* 12.

[83] See Richard B. Miller, "Deterrence," in *The New Dictionary of Catholic Social Thought,* 276–78.

[84] David Hollenbach, *Justice, Peace and Human Rights: An American Catholic Social Ethics in a Pluralist Context* (New York: Crossroad, 1988) 147.

the pastoral letter is thus framed within a theology of peace (*The Challenge of Peace,* 217–18).

The writing of the pastoral letter involved a process of dialogue, shared reflection, and consultation with average Catholics, experts, and testimony from the political and military sectors. The bishops in this letter adopted the teaching style of setting forth principles from the Catholic social tradition on the subject of nuclear war and then illustrated their application as part of the public debate on this issue. Other secular institutions also participated in this debate and shared the conclusions of the bishops. However, when the bishops entered the public debate, they engaged from the basis of their faith and its relationship to the structuring of society, using the Catholic moral tradition and commenting on issues from a religious-moral perspective. The Catholic bishops thus furthered the Catholic social tradition on nuclear war.[85]

Economic Justice for All:
Catholic Social Teaching and the U.S. Economy

The American Bishops addressed issues in the U.S. economy in their pastoral letter written in 1986, just three years after the peace pastoral. The economic letter, focused on the U.S. economic reality, yet because of the international and interdependent nature of the world economy, the bishops also called on the United States to take a morally responsible role in international economic relationships.

The bishops used both biblical themes and ethical principles from the Catholic social tradition to reflect on the economy. The fact that they attempted to comment on the American economy communicated that the economy can be an object of ethical reflection. One can have a better or worse economy in terms of its moral capacity to (1) encourage the participation of all persons, (2) guarantee a number of economic rights, including food, clothing, shelter, medical care, and basic education (*Economic Justice for All,* 80).

Perceptions of the economy in American culture can be that economy has a life of its own, impervious to intervention or ethical analysis. The fact that the bishops reflected on the state of the economy challenged this cultural presumption. The bishops avoided the ethical

[85] For a discussion of the ecclesial issues, see Hehir, "Catholic Teaching on War," 376–79.

matrix that was used in Latin America, the debate over capitalism or socialism, rather they focused on the new state of the American economy in the 1980s and its problems.

There was an unemployment rate of 8.8 percent, a sagging productivity, with a mere 1.75 percent real growth, and a need for more participation in economic planning, so that the goods of the economy could reach a broader spectrum of people. However, the general health of the economy, rather than its decline, urged the bishops to write their pastoral. Culturally, the economic debate was focused on necessity and burden. "We are told that we must curtail social programs, that we cannot assist the poor, that we do not have resources enough to assist other nations." Yet, economists claimed this forecast was nonsense. The same author, representing this alternative position, goes on to comment: "Given our extraordinary wealth, the question of what we choose to make of this great nation's economy is not primarily a technical one. We have what it takes to provide a decent life for all members of our society."[86]

The bishops shared this more positive view of the economy and entered into this debate calling for economic planning that adequately met the needs of the people. They articulated broad principles to assess an adequate economy and suggestions for policy directions, rather than specific plans for economic intervention. Economic planning is morally evaluated by who participates in the planning, in what ways and for what ends. The thrust of their letter is to call attention to those who were slipping through the cracks of American prosperity, to offer to the American debate values and norms from the Catholic social tradition that indicate normative goals of a just economy, and to provide input on four concrete policy problems: unemployment, poverty, food and agriculture, and the relationship between the United States and developing nations.

The highest priority of the bishops was full employment, which in the U.S.A. setting is less than 5 percent unemployment (*Economic Justice,* 156). Unemployment is not just personal misfortune or a result of laziness. The bishops addressed planned unemployment, that which results from the complex interactions between technological change and the shifting patterns of the international division of labor.

---

[86] Gar Alperovitz, "Planning for Sustained Community," in *Catholic Social Teaching and the U.S. Economy,* John W. Houck and Oliver F. Williams, eds. (Washington, D.C.: University Press of America, 1984) 332.

This dynamic was causing a type of de-industrialization of the U.S.A., with plants closing all over the country. Jobs were being exported to countries where there were lower wage demands, companies were being built abroad, and industrial jobs in the U.S.A. were being replaced with a smaller number of service and high tech jobs at home. The people most likely to lose jobs when these economic shifts occur were minorities and women (*Economic Justice*, 182, 179). Among the policy recommendations of the bishops are increased retraining programs (159), government support of job creation programs, and conversion of military production to peaceful purposes (169).

In 1962 Michael Harrington published *The Other America* calling attention to the substantial poverty that existed in a nation that enjoyed economic prosperity.[87] The bishops put a face on this poverty in their letter. One in every seven Americans lived below the poverty line (170). In the last decade, the poverty rate had increased by one-third (171). The bishops stated as pastors that the face of poverty was not a stranger to them; they knew many who lacked the material means for a decent life (173). People likely to be poor were children, one in four; women, who made 61 percent of what men earned; and racial minorities (*Economic Justice*, 174–81). They also noted great disparities in income distribution in the country. In 1983, 54 percent of the net assets of the country were held by 2 percent of the population (183).

The bishops noted that Catholic Social Teaching does not require equality in the distribution of income and wealth, but it does require provision for the basic needs of all (185). *"The obligation to provide justice for all means that the poor have the single most urgent economic claim on the conscience of the nation"* (*Economic Justice*, 86). Among the recommendations of the bishops are a call for social solidarity that will assist the poor without creating a dependency imposed by paternalistic programs, a raise in the minimum wage (197), a reevaluation of the tax system in terms of its effects on the poor, and a stronger commitment to the education of the poor and the stability of families.

The American bishops also addressed the topic of agriculture in their pastoral letter on the economy. During the 1980s farmers faced bankruptcy as incentives received in the 1970s to expand their production backfired. Money borrowed to expand farmlands became debts whose payment was due. Farmers could not meet these debts,

---

[87] Michael Harrington, *The Other America* (New York: Macmillan, 1962).

nor face the rising costs of production and absorb the decreased yield for their products on the world market (*Economic Justice*, 218–27). People lost farms that had been in their families for generations, and rural communities were destroyed. Small family-owned farms were absorbed by big conglomerates. Farming as a way of life was disappearing. The bishops expressed concern for the rights of migrant workers and minorities in the goods production in the United States (229–30). The bishops called for the establishment of federal farm programs to remedy this situation.

In the last section of the pastoral, the bishops called for a morally responsible role for the United States in international economic relations. They criticized a policy of selective assistance in the third world, based on "an East-West assessment of North-South problems, at the expense of basic human needs and economic development" (*Economic Justice*, 262). They spelled out concerns in the U.S. policies on development assistance (265), trade (267), finance policies (271), private investment (278), and the international food system (281).

As a "planning vision" the bishops called for cooperation between the government, leaders of major industries, labor and management within industries, labor unions and shareholders to be fiscally responsible and plan for a U.S. economy that can form international partnerships based on justice (*Economic Justice*, 322). The bishops concluded their letter with a reminder that personal conversion is key to moral responsibility in economic life.

The pastoral letter on the economy was a type of "public theology" by which the official Church sought to enter into the public debate by bringing insight gleaned from the Catholic Social Tradition to matters of current urgency. Yet the bishops advanced those insights in a language aimed at building a public consensus.[88] Critics of this letter from the left felt the bishops stopped short of condemning the capitalist system as evil and thus were too conciliatory. Critics on the right did not like the bishops calling for a more communal structuring of the economy, beyond that called for by the economic system itself.[89] Yet for the public, as well as for the members of the Church, the bishops

---

[88] Lisa Sowle Cahill, "Can Theology Have a Role in 'Public' Bioethical Discourse?" in *On Moral Medicine: The Theological Perspectives in Medical Ethics*, Stephen E. Lammers and Allen Verhey, eds. (Grand Rapids, Mich.: Eerdmans, 1998) 57–83.

[89] Daniel Rush Finn, "Economic Order," in *The New Dictionary of Catholic Social Thought*, op. cit., 326.

offered a forum for discussion and guidance on the priorities that should govern the trade-offs involved in public policy as well as future business directions in the United States. Their work however was supported and deepened by John Paul II and his own economic vision.

Chapter Ten

Social Teaching of John Paul II

John Paul II was born Karol Josef Wojtyla near Cracow, Poland, in 1920. During the German occupation of Poland, he studied for the priesthood clandestinely in a make-shift seminary in the palace of the archbishop. After ordination, he studied in Rome. John Paul II later returned to Rome for Vatican II, though he played a small part in its proceedings. He became archbishop of Cracow in 1965 and a cardinal two years later. He was elected pope on October 16, 1978. John Paul II's concern for the poor, and call for the necessity of solidarity if human dignity is to be preserved and advanced in the world, is expressed mainly in three social encyclicals: *Laborem Exercens,* On Human Work (1981), *Sollicitudo Rei Sociales,* On Social Concern (1987), *and Centesimus Annus*, On the Hundredth Anniversary of *Rerum Novarum* (1991). To understand the contribution of John Paul II to the Catholic social tradition, we need to grasp important changes in society that occurred during the 1980s and 1990s.

Liberal Capitalism

The encyclical *Laborem Exercens* was the formal beginning of John Paul II's dialogue with liberal capitalism during his pontificate. The Church's interaction with capitalism has a long history, and insight into it fosters understanding of John Paul II's thought and the world that he addressed in the beginning of the 1980s. First, we will examine liberal capitalism as a traditional conversation partner with the Catholic social tradition, and then we will look at John Paul II's contribution to this exchange.

Liberal capitalism, in the social encyclical tradition, refers to a particular economic system as well as to the theory or ideology that stands behind it and justifies it. An economic system is called liberal capitalism when the free market is the one essential mechanism for regulating the production and distribution of goods.

Liberal capitalism is the self-regulating market system. It is this system with which the social encyclical tradition has wrestled with since the beginning. The Church has seen the market as a useful tool, but at the same time demanded that the market be embedded in a culture of generosity and virtue, opposed to greed and the excessive desire for profit. The market is also to be regulated by public norms specifying what could be bought and sold and where and when these exchanges could take place. Labor movements have also been seen as having a role in constraining the market economy.

In *Laborem Exercens* John Paul II questions the market economy in a way that is both traditional and new. The Church's traditional questioning of the market rejects the eighteenth-century belief that an unrestrained market will naturally provide economic development, generate enormous wealth, and raise the material well-being of the entire society.[1] The Catholic social tradition also rejects an "economistic" view of the human person as having the essential characteristics of a drive to constantly improve the material conditions of one's life. While Catholic social teaching always appreciated the institution of the market, it also demanded that the drive for material success be restrained by virtue and that public authorities limit the market for the sake of the common good.

The Church supported welfare capitalism after World War II as a balanced use of government in the economy promoting the common good. Governments were to introduce welfare legislation and laws protecting labor from exploitation. However, this form of capitalism in the 70s and 80s seemed incapable of coping with the economic problems of Western society. Western capitalism returned to the principles of liberal capitalism or the self-regulating market system. This system called "monetarism" has been applied in Britain and the U.S.A. and in most of the nations of the West. With this change came increasing deregulation, new free trade agreements, and a previously unheard of globalization of the economy.

---

[1] Gregory Baum, *Essays in Critical Theology* (Kansas City, Mo.: Sheed and Ward, 1994) 207. My description of liberal capitalism follows Baum's analysis.

Laborem Exercens: On Human Work (1981)

Laborem Exercens was published in 1981, commemorating the nine-tieth anniversary of Leo XIII's *Rerum Novarum*. At the same time it was published, the *Solidarnosc* movement in Poland, a worker's union, was struggling against the labor practices of an authoritarian regime. John Paul II had worked in the steel mills in Poland and understood the struggle of these workers.[2] Through solidarity this movement was transforming Polish society through their cohesion over against an authoritarian Communist Party and the place Poland held in the world labor market. It is no wonder that under these conditions the main theme of the Pope's first major social encyclical is the dignity of human work (LE 14).

John Paul II charges that the power of the corporate actors in the global economy has become so great that national governments must curry their favor and have less power to protect the economic well-being of their own people. This new phase of capitalism, a cruel phase, is characterized by dislocation and widespread human suffering. Human beings generally experience work as difficult. However the world of work is unnecessarily difficult because ". . . of the harm and injustice which penetrate deeply into social life within individual na-tions and on the international level" (LE 1).

During the postwar period, the free market philosophy and the corresponding public policies encouraged the reorganization of the economy around privately-owned, internally diversified, giant corpo-rations, operating on the global level without ties of loyalty to the societies to which they belong. This created a widening gap between rich and poor nations, and between rich and poor within these na-tions (LE 7), and the surrender of decision-making power affecting the well-being of society to a small economic elite. Governments help this process through privatization and deregulation and by removing institutions designed to constrain the market to protect the common welfare. Labor under these conditions had been restructured on an international level, and the fallout of this structural change was felt at every level of society.

In face of these institutional developments, John Paul II offers several principles about the meaning of work and human dignity in this new situation of the internationalization of labor. The first is,

---

[2] George Weigel, *Witness to Hope: The Biography of Pope John Paul II* (New York: Harper, 1999) 46.

'the basis for determining the value of human work is not primarily the kind of work being done but the fact that the one who is doing it is a person (LE 6). Second, work cannot be treated simply as a tool, or factor, in the process of production. If labor is considered just another "raw material" in the production of goods, it is just an item to be bought and sold, like any other element in the production cycle. More importantly, it is not respected in itself but is under the control of those who control the means of production (LE 7, 8). The Pope does not deny that new structures in industry might mean that some will be unemployed for a time, or others will need retraining to adjust their skills to new developments in technology.

John Paul II's claim of "the priority of labor over capital" (LE 12), goes to the very foundation of this capitalist system, stating that labor arrangements have to be based on values deeper than the consideration of work as "a special kind of 'merchandise' or as an impersonal 'force' needed for production" (LE 7). The pope does more than call for a better organization of the labor market; he states that the human element in the production process should be treated differently than the things. Human subjectivity, the dignity of the human person, has to be respected in modern systems of the organization of labor and production (LE 9).

John Paul II describes work as more than something that produces articles to be bought and sold. It is part of the process by which a person becomes a human being, raises a family, fosters education, and participates in the wider culture and society. To deprive someone of work or to create conditions in which work is not secure or is monotonous and dehumanizing is against the fundamental meaning and purpose of the role work is meant to have in life.

John Paul II also attacks the operative belief that capital and labor are inherently opposed, and its consequence, that the Church's call for improved labor conditions is simply idealistic and not economically realistic. Capital, considered apart from labor, is an illusion, since capital comes from labor. Labor and capital are "inseparably linked" (LE 13). The error of economism is that it separates capital and labor. This is not just a philosophical error, but one which is mirrored in a society that arranges the production process in such a way that labor is treated simply as an ingredient in a material process, and not as a human element.

In contrast to his predecessors, John Paul II does not argue for capitalism over socialism. He criticizes both systems to the degree they fail to respect the human element in labor. Both systems have their flaws (LE 7, 8, 11, 14). Both international systems abuse labor. Because of this, the labor movement has to struggle for social justice through solidarity (LE 8). The Church supports these efforts.

If one gives a priority to labor over capital, there will be consequences. Such reordering requires a revision of the meaning of private ownership (LE 14). John Paul II argues that "the only legitimate title" to capital "whether in the form of private ownership or in the form of public or collective ownership" is that it "should serve labor" promoting the "solidarity" of laborers and of the poor (LE 32–37, 63–69). Whether citizens and those involved in the production have sufficient means for a decent livelihood must be factored into an economic vision based solely on accumulation and profit. Material things are to serve human freedom in all its dimensions. An aspect of this deeper human freedom is the ability of a person to reach his or her potential through work. This is not simply the "freedom" understood in society as the right to make a profit.

John Paul II recognizes the legitimacy of labor unions, of worker's participation in policy formation, management, and ownership, and of socializing certain means of production (LE 64–69, 94–100, 102).[3] The concept of the "indirect employer" is used by John Paul II to bridge, ". . . the values surrounding work and the structural change to put these values into practice."[4] Many relationships—states and their legal systems, corporations, international agencies and alliances, among others—form the structures that determine labor practices across the world. To create a family wage in the third world, employment of the handicapped, or trade relations that foster better wages and working conditions require the willingness to change at a structural level. The Pope uses the term "indirect employer" to distinguish these forces from the "direct" employer, as we commonly understand this term. The "indirect" employer is the systems that "exercise a determining influence on the shaping of both the world contract and, consequently of just or unjust relationships in the field of human labor" (LE 16).

When workers are unjustly treated, the person hiring them may only be partly to blame. The system in which the employer acts may

[3] See William O'Neill, "Private Property," in *The New Dictionary of Catholic Social Thought*, op. cit., 785–90.
[4] Dorr, *Option for the Poor* (Maryknoll, N.Y.: Orbis Books, 1992) 290–94.

structure the economy in such a way that it becomes impossible for a just wage to be paid and to remain competitive. A common viewpoint in such a situation is to blame "the system." The Pope acknowledges the system but also calls us to take responsibility for these systems and to change them.

While the concept of "indirect employer" takes the employer-employee relationship beyond the interpersonal, it also points to the fact that structures were created by human beings, and they have the responsibility to change them. This involves sacrifice, solidarity, and the readiness to face the factors that keep the poor in poverty. At this level everyone has some degree in complicity, and all are called to work toward change. When the concept of indirect employer is taken to the international level, it can illustrate how the policies of a first-world country can impose impoverishment on another entire country. The very structure of this impoverishment denies access to the material goods necessary for human dignity and the participation in decision-making that flows from being human (LE 17). The social teaching of *Laborem Exercens* indicates these structures are not "carved in stone," rather they will be changed only when peoples and governments are willing to take the legal and political means to change them.

Sollicitudo Rei Socialis: On Social Concern (1987)

In 1987 John Paul II published *Sollicitudo Rei Socialis* to commemorate the twentieth anniversary of *Populorum Progressio,* Paul VI's encyclical on development (1967). John Paul II had the advantage of a twenty-year perspective and the chance to comment on the political arrangements in which the development debate was taking place. Among these were the lack of development in the world, in spite of a growing international economy, and the adequacy of ideas used to describe it.

Key to John Paul II's analysis of development is the persistence and the widening of the gap between the North and the South and the conflicts between the East and the West that explain the retardation and stagnation of the South (SRS 22). Developing nations, instead of being able to concentrate on national development, simply become "parts of a machine, cogs on a gigantic wheel" of a world economic and political system that serves the interest of the members of the East-West bloc. The capitalist bloc and the socialist bloc, the two contenders in the world system, both tend toward imperialism and neocolonialism. Smaller nations must "side" with one or the other. The Pope sees the smaller nations caught in a battle which is not their own. It is a battle between the two superpowers. "Seen in this way, the present division of the world is a direct obstacle to the real transformation of the conditions of underdevelopment in the developing and less advanced countries" (SRS 22). John Paul II adds the voice of the Church to a growing body of critique on notions of development.

Development

Social critics at the time questioned the meaning of a purely economic notion of development. It did not attend to the fragmentation in community and destruction of cultures caused by development initiatives based on the economic model alone. This was coupled by a growing body of concerns over the ecological state of the world. John Paul II brought his own critique of development to this international criticism, and he increased calls for solidarity as a remedy to the growing isolation of people from ties that would generate concern for the neighbor.

The critiques of John Paul II tend to be cultural and moral with political and economic consequences.[5] The formation of a new form of community through solidarity has an important role to correct a vision of life for the next millennium. Sustainable development and sustainable community are contrasting paths to the future, carrying with them different notions of the structure of human society and responsibility. The World Council of Churches added their critique that under reigning approaches to sustainable development, formation of community is often ignored.[6] Domestic and global wealth is generated without eradicating poverty or making local communities more viable and sustainable. In reigning development approaches, the image of a good society is equated solely with a growing gross domestic product.

Economic growth alone does not make a good society. We can observe this on two fronts. For those above the poverty line, human happiness does not necessarily correlate with increased consumption

[5] See John A. Coleman, S.J., "The Culture of Death," in *The Logic of Solidarity*, Gregory Baum and Robert Ellsberg, eds. (Maryknoll, N.Y.: Orbis Books, 1989) 90–109.

[6] *Earth Habitat: Eco-Injustice and the Church's Response*, Dieter Hessel and Larry Rasmussen, eds. (Minneapolis: Fortress, 2001) 87ff.

and incomes. Growth in the gross domestic product does not necessarily bring a better quality of family life and friendship, satisfaction
with work, more leisure, and a sense of spiritual richness. Pursuit of
money alone is more easily correlated with the greed, weakening of
family relationships, and the psychological and spiritual emptiness
that characterize the current first-world culture.

As to those below the poverty line, reigning views of development
do not provide a viable vision of their future. Even at a 3 percent
growth rate, a growth impossible for many poor countries, yet an
optimal development index, only seven poor countries could close the
development gap with the first world in a century, and only nine
countries in one-thousand years! A truer picture of the world's development has one billion like us, living a good quality of life, 3.6 billion
as the managing poor, and one billion at the bottom living on less
than $1.00 a day. The World Bank predicts that the real future will
mark a growth in the bottom two divisions.[7]

John Paul II called for a moral understanding of development, or
the world's drive toward an economic development alone will actually
corrupt real development. Having "super development" side-by-side
with the "miseries of underdevelopment" will destroy the international order (SRS 28), just as "having" can destroy the deeper aspirations of "being" in an individual caught in the consumer rat race
(SRS 28).

Development is more than an economic reality; it includes the
trajectory of human growth toward otherness and depth that is
inherent in the Catholic social tradition. Rich people can be "underdeveloped" in this sense. John Paul II reaffirms the vision of authentic
human development called for by Paul VI (SRS 28; P.P. 20–21).

When people argue over views of development, they are actually
in debate about the direction of the world. It is common to think that
a globalizing economy will save the world. John Paul II joined his
voice to many across the world to say an economic vision alone was
insufficient. Core issues regarding attention to the sustainability
issues essential to human dignity, such as life expectancy, housing,
drinking water, unemployment, the international debt (SRS 14, 17,
18, 19), and respect for culture (SRS 14) were needed to make explicit the human results that should flow from economic growth.

[7] Rasmussen, *Earth Community, Earth Ethics* (Maryknoll, N.Y.: Orbis Books,
1996) 149–50.

The Pope recognized that the global economy is here to stay. However, a more adequate view of global development must concern not just economics but also the distribution of power among peoples of the world. As power shifts from local communities to transnational capital and institutions that wield and regulate it, a vision of development that fosters community responsibility, ecological sensitivity, economic productivity, religious freedom, and political responsibility is needed. This means replacing, "corrupt, dictatorial, and authoritarian forms of government by democratic and participatory ones." This is an essential ingredient for the development of "the whole individual and of all people" (SRS 44).

Contrasting views of development emerged in the 1980s that addressed the issue of sustainability. Sustainability is the capacity of natural and social systems to survive and thrive together. If human life is not just economic, then sustainability had to be conceived in ways that were more than economic. The challenge was to maintain the deeper meaning of the inherent connectedness between human persons and economics and not to spiritualize the problem.

John Paul II contributed to this debate theological terms that linked the essential social vision of human nature contained within the Catholic social tradition to problems in the sustainability debate. The world vision was over-focused on the economy and lacked a language to address how people were connected in a fragmented and economically segmented world. What John Paul II saw, along with others in social movements and churches, was that without a deeper sense of what was at stake in our language of development, North and South would serve to describe totally different ways of life based on class and culture rather than indicating geography.[8]

John Paul II offered some characteristics of an alternative view of development. They increase local economic self-reliance within a framework of community responsibility and ecological balance, along with developing webs of social relationship that define human community (SRS 26). A more complete vision of development goes beyond the economic alone and takes into consideration both the regeneration of the earth, and of human communities who depend upon it (SRS 38). While John Paul II did not write specifically on the environment until the World Day of Peace in 1990, we see the beginning of an integration

[8] Ibid., 132.

of these concerns in his efforts to build with others in the world an alternative view of development (SRS 34).

When women critique prevailing theories of development, they concur with the broad analysis of John Paul II, but would say more. They engage in a gender analysis, which they find weak in the encyclical, highlighting the failures of development in the lives of women and children. They focus on three areas usually overlooked in development theory: the household, women's work, and women's multiple roles. They would add to the awareness of the "demographic problem" (SRS 25) and the growing body of analysis on the linkages between birth rates and women's educational levels. In other areas addressed by the encyclical, they would connect militarism to patriarchal social structures and stress the role of mutuality in solidarity.[9]

Solidarity

John Paul II offers a vision of solidarity that not only calls for moral renewal in the world but a revision of spirituality within the Catholic Social Tradition. Solidarity means more than living interdependently. It is the movement toward the "other" that respects the other and his or her good as carrying the face of one's own moral obligation. Solidarity is "a firm and persevering determination" to commit oneself "to the common good; that is to say to the good of all and of each individual because we are all really responsible for all" (SRS 38).

Desire for profit and thirst for power contradict the posture of solidarity. Solidarity implies that the goods of the earth are destined for all. Equally destined for all are the riches produced or processed by our work. "That which human industry produces through the processing of raw materials, with the contribution of work, must serve equally for the good of all" (SRS 39).

Desire for profit and thirst for power ignore the fundamental equality of all and the purpose of creation and the goods of the human economy. These are more than destructive personal attitudes; they are structures of sin that reside in cultural visions of what it means to be an adequate human being. These structures are rooted in

---

[9] Maria Riley, "Feminist Analysis: A Missing Perspective," in *John Paul II and Moral Theology*, Charles E. Curran and Richard A. McCormick, S.J., eds. (New York: Paulist Press, 1988) 276–90.

personal sin and are linked to the acts of individuals who socially reproduce them and make them difficult to remove (SRS 36). Structural sin goes beyond observations of human limitation made by social analysis, according to John Paul II.

A theology of structural sin indicates that these behaviors are linked to the mystery of evil, a heritage of sin that goes beyond the life of an individual. The thirst for power and the desire for profit "at any price" make human attitudes absolute in a manner that is really religious in nature. They are a form of idolatry. To see them as human short sightedness does not grasp their depth (SRS 36–37). John Paul II remarks that "hidden behind certain decisions, apparently inspired only by economics or politics are real forms of idolatry: of money, ideology, class, technology" (SRS 37).

If that which blocks development are not just inadequate theories or structures for human flourishing but human sin itself, genuine development requires a conversion. Here the virtue of solidarity is connected to the spiritual nature of all humanity and to Christian spirituality. In the case of the former, men and women "without explicit faith" can see that the obstacles to full human development are not only economic, "but rest on more profound attitudes which human beings can make into absolute values" (SRS 38). People must change their attitudes and work toward a change in ethos in their societies in order to ensure a more human life on the planet. They should assume these negative attitudes reside in the depth of the human heart, and thus require vigilance to eradicate.

For those who are Christian, this process involves all the intensity of Christian spirituality. It is a call to conversion on a moral, affective, intellectual, and religious level. "This conversion specifically entails a relationship to God, to the sin committed, to its consequences and hence to one's neighbor, either an individual or a community" (SRS 38). The spiritual conversion is not just an interior one; it has concrete manifestations in the individual and in society. A sign of conversion is a growing awareness of interdependence among individuals and nations and evidence that people "care" about injustices and violations across the world (SRS 38). The spiritual path of solidarity is reflected in a new imagination that creates systems that are more interdependent in economic, cultural, political, and religious ways. These moral changes reflect a deeper growth in this spiritual path of solidarity.

For the Christian, living the virtue of solidarity has a political-mystical dimension; it gives one access to God. As we find worth in our neighbor, respond to her or him as "other," we find God. As we see in the enemy, friend, and the unknown person who is allowed to impact our life, the image of God, we discover bonds with others deeper than the natural or human bonds we hope bind the world (SRS 40). In the midst of a fragmented world and individualist spiritualities, John Paul II offers a vision of spirituality that goes deep in order to forge the model of unity needed to build the world, a model of communion (SRS 40). This vision does not address the policy issues for this new unity, but it does address the issue of the lack of moral will to do anything about the problems of the new millennium. "The 'evil mechanisms' and 'structures of sin' of which we have spoken can be overcome only through the exercise of human and Christian solidarity to which the Church calls us and which she tirelessly promotes" (SRS 40).

The Church in this sense does not offer technical solutions to the problems of development; rather she is an "expert in humanity" who through fulfilling her mission to evangelize contributes to its solution. John Paul remarks that "she offers her first contribution to the solution of the urgent problem of development when she proclaims the truth about Christ, about herself and about man, applying this truth to a concrete situation" (SRS 41). The condemnation of evils and injustices and the examination of alternatives are aspects of the ministry of evangelization. Problems such as development are moral problems in the Church. This connection takes such moral teaching beyond the private realm, and the solution to the development problem to the capacity of the human community and its structures for conversion. In this light John Paul II explains the meaning of Catholic Social Doctrine.

Social Doctrine

John Paul II sets the social doctrine of the Church in a framework of moral theology. He distances social doctrine from the approach that sees it as Catholic social theory or political or economic programs espoused by the Church. While there is no "moral equivalence" among alternative social or political positions, the Church's position is not posed as an alternative to them. It is not an ideology among others in this sense (SRS 41). John Paul II also distances himself from the position that the Church's Social Doctrine is a "third way" between liberal capitalism and Marxist collectivism.

Catholic Social Doctrine is the "accurate formulation of the results of a careful reflection of the complex realities of human existence, in society and in the international order, in the light of faith and of the church's tradition" (SRS 41). This tradition has produced a "set of principles for reflection, criteria for judgment, and directives for action" (SRS 41; OA 4), which help in the task of "promoting both the correct definition of the problems being faced and the best solution to them" (SRS 41). Today social doctrine has to be international in its outlook (SRS 42) with option for the poor having a primacy in the exercise of Christian charity, the meaning of Christian spirituality, and the vision of social responsibility. This option applies "to our manner of living, and to the logical decisions to be made concerning the ownership and use of goods" (SRS 42). In other words, option for the poor is part of the "transcendent data" and epistemological premises of the Christian life.

Sacramental life in the Church

Sollicitudo Rei Socialis addresses the relationship between spirituality and ethics. At its end John Paul II extends this reflection to the sacramental life of the Church. The liturgical movement in the Catholic Church has addressed its social mission, although this theme has at times remained in the background of liturgical literature.[10] The liturgical renewal that began before Vatican II sought to correct an over emphasis on the awe and transcendence of the liturgy and its privatization, toward an inclusion of the historical and public dimensions that are also proper to the liturgy.[11] Toward the end of the encyclical, John Paul II, reminds the Church, "All of us who take part in the Eucharist are called to discover, through this sacrament, the profound

---

[10] See *Liturgy and Justice*, Anne Y. Koester, ed. (Collegeville: The Liturgical Press, 2002); *Living No Longer for Ourselves, Liturgy and Justice in the Nineties*, Kathleen Hughes, R.S.C.J., and Mark R. Francis, C.S.V., eds. (Collegeville: The Liturgical Press, 1991); David Hollenbach, "A Prophetic Church and the Sacramental Imagination," in *The Faith that Does Justice*, J. Haughey, ed. (New York: Paulist Press, 1977) 234–63; Mary Evelyn Jegen, "Theology and Spirituality of Non-Violence," *Worship* 60 (1986) 119–33.

[11] See Walter J. Woods, "Liturgy and Social Issues," in *The New Dictionary of Sacramental Worship*, Peter E. Fink, S.J., ed. (Collegeville: The Liturgical Press, 1990) 1198–201. See also Peter Fink, "Sacramental Theology after Vatican II," Ibid., 1107–14.

meaning of our actions in the world in favor of development and peace; and to receive from it the strength to commit ourselves ever more generously, following the example of Christ, who in this sacrament lays down his life for his friends (cf. John 15:13)" (SRS 48).[12]

Centesimus Annus:
On the Hundredth Anniversary of Rerum Novarum (1991)

Published in 1991, John Paul II's third social encyclical, *Centesimus Annus*, commemorates the centenary of Leo XIII's *Rerum Novarum,* as well as celebrates the century of Catholic social teaching. A significant event that frames this encyclical is the fall of the Berlin Wall in 1989 and the transformation that swept Eastern Europe and other parts of the globe as a result. These changes were both economic and political. Steps were taken to dissolve the Soviet bloc and to begin market economies in Eastern Europe. Politically there was a move away from totalitarian or dictatorial regimes and a movement toward more limited, participatory, and democratic forms of government.[13]

The collapse of communism meant also the transformation of the bi-polar world of the United States and the Soviet Union in 1989. Power had to be distributed in a multi-polar world. The global dominance of transnational economic institutions and corporations, which could evade governance by national states or international bodies, provided a new context for thinking about governance. These new forces dimmed the hope for a single world authority that could promote relations among peoples across the world in a cooperative way.[14] As territory and contiguity became less important as a way to map reality, even major powers had to accept that unilateral action was unwise.[15]

[12] See Monika Hellwig, *The Eucharist and the Hunger of the World* (New York: Paulist Press, 1976); Kenneth Himes, "Eucharist and Justice: Assessing the Legacy of Virgil Michel," *Worship* 62 (1988) 201–24; Robert Hovda, "The Mass and Its Social Consequences," *Liturgy* 90 (April, 1991) 9–12.

[13] See Patrick T. McCormick, "Centesimus Annus," in *The New Dictionary of Catholic Social Thought,* op. cit., 132–42.

[14] See Lisa Sowle Cahill, "Toward Global Ethics," in *Theological Studies,* vol. 63, no. 2 (June, 2002) 324–44. See also Joseph S. Nye and John D. Donahue, eds. *Governance in a Globalizing World* (Cambridge, Mass., and Washington, D.C.: Visions of Governance for the 21st Century and Brookings Institution, 2000).

[15] Robert Schreiter, *The New Catholicity: Theology Between the Global and the Local* (Maryknoll, N.Y.: Orbis Books, 1997) 4–8.

The end of socialism in all but a few countries allowed for a world-wide expansion of market capitalism. This brought about a second shift, the move to a single world economy. This new economy could ignore national boundaries, move capital quickly and engage in short term projects that maximize profits. In many ways global capitalism provided its own vision of reality. In spite of new insights into common purposes shared by people across the globe, fostered by global communications, deep economic disparities continued to be an impasse in coming to a vision of the global good.[16] The end of communism did more than clear the playing board for all capitalist markers. It meant that one-third of humanity and one-fourth of the world's land mass moved from communism to capitalism. Digesting this world would change capitalism as we know it.[17] John Paul II realized that the direction of this change required ethical reflection. *Centesimus Annus* contributed to this needed global process.

John Paul II was not an observer in this world. Dorr comments that no less an authority that the former Soviet president Mikhail Gorbachev testifies to the role John Paul II played in the collapse of communism. He remarks, ". . . everything that happened in eastern Europe during these last few years would not have been possible without the presence of this pope, without the leading role—the political role—that he was able to play on the world scene."[18]

Centesimus Annus was written out of the pastoral experience of the Pope and his deep involvement in the struggle against totalitarian regimes in Poland. In some of the commentaries that followed its publication, those who had lived through the difficulties of the confrontation and conflict between the social doctrine of the Church and communist ideology or who were still facing communism in their countries could readily grasp why John Paul II was so affected by the intensity of the events in Europe.[19]

---

[16] William Greider, *One World, Ready or Not: The Manic Logic of Global Capitalism* (New York: Simon and Schuster, 1997).

[17] Lester C. Thurow, *The Future of Capitalism* (New York: William Morrow, 1996) 8, see also ch. 3.

[18] As cited in Dorr, *Option for the Poor* (Maryknoll, N.Y.: Orbis Books, 1992) 342.

[19] See, for example, Francois-Xavier Nguyen van Thuan, "Historical and Pastoral Aspects of the Encyclical *Centesimus Annus*," in *Centesimus Annus: Assessment and Perspective for the Future of Catholic Social Doctrine*, John-Peter Pham, ed. (Libreria Editrice Vaticana: 1998) 3–13.

Throughout the encyclical John Paul illustrates how certain principles and insights upheld in Catholic social teaching since Leo XIII remain key to the Church's mission in society, even in these radically changed circumstances of the time. He reflects on two contrasting models of life, capitalism and democracy and socialism and totalitarianism in order to comment on the proper role of the economy and the state in this new situation. Two main issues are addressed. The capitalist system is assessed in light of the failure of socialism and the meaning and the basis of Catholic social doctrine centered on its vision of human dignity is reexplained.

The first part of the encyclical is devoted to how the principles put forth by Leo XIII in *Rerum Novarum* have in the long term proven valid and important in making judgments about social issues. John Paul II stresses the continuity more between Leo XIII and today, than areas of discontinuity, where the magisterium had made shifts in teaching in order to respond to new situations.[20]

The Fall of Socialism and the Future of Capitalism

The third chapter begins John Paul II's reflection on the events of 1989. While the Pope is aware of the multiple economic and political factors that led to the fall of communism, he dwells on the symbolic issues of this radical political shift. The fundamental problem with communism or "real socialism" was not its economic mistakes. Communism failed because it denied the truth about the meaning of human freedom. In his words, "Not only is it wrong from the ethical point of view to disregard human nature, which is made for freedom, but in practice it is impossible to do so. Where society is so organized as to reduce arbitrarily or even surpress the sphere in which freedom is legitimately exercised, the result is that the life of society becomes progressively disorganized and goes into decline" (CA 25). He criticizes a bureaucratic control that "dries up the wellsprings of initiative and creativity" (CA 25). Communism's failures were first and foremost moral failures.[21] For John Paul II, the events of 1989 had symbolic importance for the world (CA 26–27).

---

[20] McCormick, *"Centesimus Annus,"* 134.

[21] George Weigel, "The New 'New Things,'" in *John Paul II and Moral Theology*, op. cit., 315.

However, the fall of socialism does not mean that capitalism has "won," that capitalism and the free economy are now above criticism. Despite the fact that capitalism is now the only viable economic system and the ideology of market capitalism makes it impervious to such critiques, John Paul II applies to capitalism similar questions as posed to socialism. Does it insure or contract the basic truth about the human person: the right to freedom, to initiative, to human rights, to "being" rather than just "having" (SRS 36–39)?

The economic freedom afforded by capitalism is not enough to give it validity unless the culture created by capitalism also fosters integral human development. In John Paul's words, economic freedom is only one element of human freedom. "When it becomes autonomous, when man is seen more as a producer or consumer of goods than as a subject who produces and consumes in order to live, then economic freedom loses its necessary relationship to the human person and ends up by alienating and oppressing him" (SRS 39).

John Paul distinguishes between various forms of capitalism that have functioned over time. He asks, should capitalism be the goal of third-world countries, since capitalism is the only system left in the world. Will it by itself bring economic and civil progress?

He affirms capitalism as "an economic system which recognizes the fundamental and positive role of business, the Market, private property, and the resulting responsibility for the means of production, as well as free human creativity in the economic sector" (CA 42). He rejects however a capitalism that operates only on the market economy, in which, "freedom in the economic sector is not circumscribed within a strong juridical framework which places it at the service of human freedom in its totality." Such a system must respect that the human person at his or her core is also ethical and religious, not just economic (CA 39).

John Paul II affirms capitalism: ". . . it would appear that, on the level of individual nations and international relations, the free market is the most efficient instrument for utilizing resources and effectively responding to needs" (CA 34). The Pope, however, also describes situations where capitalism falls short: he emphasizes three. First, many human needs are not met by the workings of the market: for example, the ethical and cultural system that stems from a market economy can promote a culture of death (CA 39), or destroy the environment (CA 40). Second, there are groups of people without the resources to enter the market, namely, the poor within countries who are marginated without jobs and skills or whole nations who barely survive on the fringes of the market (CA 35, 48). Third, there are goods that "cannot and must not be bought and sold."[22] In this last instance John Paul is referring to the issue of "commodification," placing things into a market economy that should not be bought or sold.

John Paul II does not criticize coordinated governmental policies to bring assistance to the poor, but he does question the failures of Welfare State to the degree it fosters dependency rather than gives individuals impetus to take their place in the economic life of the country through employment (CA 48). He calls for solidarity and subsidiarity as directions for the formation of policy by which government intervenes in economic processes and supports its citizens (CA 10, 15, 48). He affirms the development of "mediating structures"—religious institutions, voluntary organizations, unions, business associations, neighborhood groups, service organizations, and the like—to express a public moral culture that can reach out to the deeper values of a humane society.[23]

John Paul II affirms democracy as a system with the best potential to ensure the participation of men and women in society, as their freedom dictates. "The church values the democratic system inasmuch as it ensures the participation of citizens in making political choices, guarantees to the governed the possibility both of electing and holding accountable those who govern them, and of replacing them through peaceful means when appropriate" (CA 46). However, democracy is valued when it is ruled by deeper principles than simply the rule of the majority. Instead, "authentic democracy is possible only in a State ruled by law, and on the basis of a correct conception of the human person" (CA 46).

John Paul II cautions that the market must be placed in the broader context of state and society, and in some instances global society. "The individual today is often suffocated between two poles represented by the state and the marketplace" (CA 49). Society however "has neither the market nor the state as its final purpose" (CA 48). Life in society is to be aimed at the fulfillment of deeper human

---

[22] See J. Bryan Hehir, "Reordering the World," in *A New Worldly Order: John Paul II and Human Freedom,* George Weigel, ed. (Washington, D.C.: Ethics and Public Policy Center, 1992) 87.

[23] Weigel, "The New 'New Things,'" 325.

needs than fulfilled by the market and the state, such as the search for truth and the experience of solidarity.

At the same time, the rights of the state are qualified by the interdependence of all nations and the need to construct a moral world order that recognizes and respects an international relationship that works for the common good and respects the "subjectivity" of every nation. In this sense John Paul II appears to offer more of a vision of a global society than that of a global political entity in the strict sense.

Within this wider context of concerns, the market must take advantage of what it does well and create the wealth needed to sustain communities across the world. Negatively, it must supplement and acknowledge its limits. John Paul II calls for a "juridical framework" within which the market will function. This framework must set law and policy that will contain the market and address the human needs it leaves unattended.

On an international level John Paul II points out that many countries are just beginning to choose the market mechanism as a means for their sustainability. However, the decentralized nature of international politics makes the establishment of a regulatory framework very difficult. The vision of how this will be done remains general rather than specific in this encyclical. It appears to be closer to a framework of coordinating transnational and global institutions and communities into a moral sphere that has expanding circles of relationship and influence.[24]

Both public and private entities can be promoters of values that form the ties that provide a new type of regulatory framework. John Paul II calls for a global system of values, which can provide direction that cannot be provided only by the market or just by force or state power alone. Labor unions, corporations, nongovernmental organizations (NGOs), religious groups all have a contribution to make. This new network needs to reflect on and be directed by the deeper meanings of human life, values that mirror the deepest desires of the human heart. However, these values need to be institutionalized, not necessarily by a world government but by coordinated global responses and strategies to address and contain problems at a global level.[25]

---

[24] See Cahill, "Toward Global Ethics," for a reflection on such efforts.

[25] Michael Camdessus, "Church Social Teaching and Globalization," *America* (October 15, 2001) 10.

The sentiments of John Paul II have been echoed by Vaclav Havel, the past president of the Czech Republic. "We often hear about the need to restructure the economies of the developing or the poorer countries. But I deem it even more important that we should begin to also think about another restructuring—a restructuring of the entire system of values which forms the basis of our civilization today."[26]

John Paul II reflects on how changed communication and patterns of travel have created shifts in cultural and political identity. Political borders traditionally mark boundaries of sovereignty, identity, and responsibility (CA 46). They indicate where social investments are made and administrative guidelines are enforced, where tariffs are collected and legal systems applied. However, shifts in technology, transportation, and communication dictate that things can be made and sold anywhere. Governments are involved already with affairs far beyond their borders. The notion of national economy and identity is transformed as the tension between global business, which focuses on markets and national governments and which are to focus on the welfare of the voters, grows. John Paul II calls therefore for a new type of governance in the world.

Goverance differs from government. Governance is "the framework of rules, institutions, and peaces that set limits on the behavior of individuals, organizations and companies" because the imbalances in today's world are cause for concern. Goverance involves a coalition of parties that would include governments, but would also include corporations, non-governmental organizations, and other networks of people involved with policy making and care.[27] In the new world situation, issues of justice go beyond how one country treats another. Any economic or political crisis can affect the entire global marketplace and peace. This makes every country and agency responsible in some way for the stability and quality of world development.

For countries that are well off commitments to the elimination of poverty across the world are not just an "option," they are a necessity to ensure world peace. "If large numbers of poor are left helpless, their poverty will undermine the fabric of our societies through confrontation, violence and civil disorder."[28] For countries moving away

---

[26] As quoted in an article by Michael Camdessus, former managing director of the International Monetary Fund, Ibid., 6.

[27] See June O'Connor, "Making a Case for the Common Good," *Journal of Religious Ethics* 30 (Spring, 2002) 160.

[28] Ibid., 8.

from "national security" regimes, it is necessary in reforming their systems to give democracy "an authentic and solid foundation" through explicit recognition of human rights (CA 47). The coordination of global governance rather than government is surfacing in the world as the impact of actors beyond governmental state apparatus becomes integral to global development.

A traditional complaint of independent states is that global governance might meddle with national sovereignty. However, the purpose behind a different kind of authority is to address problems impacting sovereign states across the world, which no state can address properly. If done well, respecting subsidiarity, such governance would enable states to do more effective governance at their level of influence. John Paul II offers a general but symbolic image of new world coordination where subsidiarity would guide international coordinating efforts. This vision needs the help of those in the sciences and those already working toward this coordinating effort for its practical construction.

For these reasons John Paul II sees the old international order as morally unacceptable in this new situation. *Centesimus Annus* continues themes in *Laborem Exercens* (1981) and *Sollicitudo Rei Socialis* (1987). The new world toward which we must strive is one less controlled by the superpowers. In it there is a United Europe, separated from the "logic of the blocs." The peoples and nations of the developing world will have a different status from the one accorded them by the Cold War. A new type of citizenship is required; one at all levels of government: local, regional, national, and global. For members of the Church, this requires a new type of spirituality built on solidarity and love toward ever widening responses to the "other."

We need to note that John Paul II's affirmation and criticism of market capitalism is more than a commentary on social policy. His insights are part of a whole vision of how one integrates faith and life in the changed circumstances of global society. In this sense his remarks have meaning within his wider vision of what Social Catholicism might contribute to a deeper and profound global effort.

Discerning the Social Good in Today's Culture

The American context provides special challenges in respecting the "freedom" and search for the "truth" encouraged by social teaching. Stephen Carter, in his *Civility*, claims Americans have a problem understanding what it means to be free. The freedom that humans possess is not the freedom to do what one likes, but the freedom to do what is right. Freedom requires the truth of transcendence that draws us toward the needs of the other. By forgetting what it means to be free, our "collective amnesia" puts at risk our claim of civilization.[29] John Paul II concurs. A notion of freedom, which detaches itself from obedience to the truth, absolves itself from the duty to respect the rights of others. The wars of the last century testify to this (CA 17).

A similar problem arises in the search for the "common good" in society. John Coleman states the common good "looks to both some objectivity of the good and a concomitant societal consensus" about public goods and the institutional relationships necessary for human flourishing.[30] Since Vatican II the Catholic social tradition is more attentive to the fact that human experience and its context have bearing on a vision of the social good. Experience and place in society impact one's sense of the truth, the common good, or even perceptions of what is good. However, Catholic tradition affirms that this does not place us in an impossible position. Practical reason does address the truth in contingent matters, and moral truth is a practical truth, what is the good in this situation.[31] The challenge is to accept people have different perceptions of truth and what is right, without sinking into a relativism or hopelessness that "truth" can never be found.[32] When people can ask how a proposed solution affects the "other," those most in need, uphold human rights, or protect human dignity, they are pursuing the path of truth outlined in social teaching. Pursuit of truth and good in the political order challenges members of the Church both to listen to voices that challenge and to bring into public dialogue the core values of human flourishing fed by their tradition.

---

[29] Stephen Carter, *Civility: Manners, Morals and the Etiquette of Democracy* (New York: Basic Books, 1998) 78.

[30] John A. Coleman, S.J., "Retrieving or Re-inventing Social Catholicism: a Transatlantic Response," in *Catholic Social Thought: Twilight or Renaissance?* J. S. Boswell, F. P. McHugh, and J. Verstraeten, eds. (Leuven: Peters, 2000) 289–92.

[31] For a discussion of Aquinas and moral reason in social ethics, see Cahill, "Toward Global Ethics," 333–44. For another treatment, see Jean Porter, *Moral Action and Christian Ethics* (Cambridge: Cambridge University Press, 1999).

[32] David Hollenbach quotes James Gustafson on the relevance of historical understanding in ethics. See "Tradition, Historicity, and Truth in Theological Ethics" in *Christian Ethics: Problems and Prospects,* Lisa Sowle Cahill and James F. Childress, eds. (Cleveland: The Pilgrim Press, 1996) 61.

John Paul II cautions that detaching human freedom from its essential and constitutive relationship to truth leads to contemporary relativist thought.[33] Failure to search for the truth of human dignity in its transcendent and permanent nature undermines the vision needed for essential political conditions in our world. Only a belief in the transcendent nature of human life, for instance, grounds openness in public administration, the rejection of illicit means in order to gain or increase power, respect for the rights of political adversaries and others.[34] Contrary to those who hold religion is extraneous to public debate, the Church's Social Tradition teaches it is central. Religion takes seriously that human beings have a transcendent goal. Without attention to the ethical relevance of transcendence, which religion is meant to uphold, society is at peril.

Even though freedom must be related to truth and human autonomy has to be related to community, groups also can be blind to the truth. The history of war testifies that any human community can make absolute a cultural sense of truth or freedom. The idea of a "holy war" or a necessity of "national security" places on a human conflict a dignity it might not deserve. Distortion of the truth in community can be fed by need for identity or protection of current status. A national community must be in dialogue with others to address how their own interests might blind them to a greater truth in their midst. When a community is not open to dialogue, its sense of freedom and truth can be simply tools to protect the status quo, or made irrelevant to practical affairs.

Lure of Easy Solutions

Vaclav Havel, reflecting on the "correct system" of the communist regime, claims there is a wary alliance between truth and a historical human system. The *Power of the Powerless* is a reflection on the experience of the totalitarian communist system. Communism offered ready answers to any questions whatsoever. It was a totalitarian system, which could not be accepted in part. To accept it had profound implications for human life. In an era when metaphysical and existential certainties were in a state of crisis, communism provided a home for

[33] John Paul II, *Veritatis Splendor* (Vatican City: Libreria Editrice Vaticana, 1993) no. 4:8.
[34] Ibid., no. 101:151.

the mind. All one had to do was accept it and suddenly what was dark and anxious became clear. Havel remarks, "one pays dearly for this low-rent home: the price is abdication of one's own reason, conscience, and responsibility, for an essential aspect of this ideology is the consignment of reason and conscience to a higher authority."[35]

The center of power in the communist system is the center of truth. In the communist block the loss of the transcendence of truth also meant a subsequent loss of freedom. Havel cautions that the freedom that people under communism lost through accommodation to the system can also be lost in the West. The numbing force to freedom and truth in the West is not the state, but the soul owning market. While the West enjoys a type of political freedom not afforded in the communist bloc, it too can only live the illusion of freedom, for it can make the market its center of truth.

The only corrective for freedom in either system, according to Havel, is living in truth. For the West, moral purpose and commitment to the truth are necessary to sustain its own freedom. The question is, does the West have this ethical commitment, and does its religion foster it? John Paul II echoes Havel's concerns as he remarks that the free market economy can actually resemble Marxism in the sense it totally reduces humanity to the sphere of economics and the satisfaction of material needs (CA 19.5-20). This operative "truth" of the modern age slips into American culture and must be challenged.

Thinking or rationality in first-world culture can easily be limited to technical rationality. This translates into utilitarianism, what works is what is right. Reason in this sense is not called upon to deliberate ends and norms that ought to govern our lives. Means and ends get confused (CA 41). Theologian Juan Luis Segundo echoes this concern. He claims the greatest dilemma of modern times is not ordering means to ends, but deciding on what scale of means is appropriately human.[36]

The scale and complexity of the means utilized in our world today often makes it impossible to decide exactly what ends these mechanisms are serving. We lose track of our goals and purposes. For example, at what point do nuclear stockpiles cease serving needs of security? Religion is called upon to work with the social sciences, to

---

[35] Vaclav Havel, *The Power of the Powerless* (New York: M.E. Sharpe, 1985) 25.

[36] Juan Luis Segundo, *Faith and Ideologies*, John Drury, trans. (Maryknoll, N.Y.: Orbis Books, 1984) 260.

create communities of concern where such questions can be asked, and to help construct tools for communities to determine whether both ends and means are in harmony with values. Technical rationality alone can not achieve this goal. The Catholic Social Tradition calls for continuing communal discernment at various levels of local, national and global issues.

Cultural biases can also dim the capacity to think about issues of a public nature. Theologian Shawn Copeland charges that accepted standards of racism, sexism, and classism undermine people's ability to think and feel and thus dim the public vision of a wider public good.[37] The cultural individualism of the modern age, or the sense that only the individual is real, is a social blindness that also hides the truth. Sociologist Robert Bellah claims it is hard for the average American to even think at the communal level.[38] Individualism so captures the modern mind that communal issues such as how shall we live and for what shall we live can not be considered beyond choices made in private. Pursuit of personal goods is affirmed in the mentality of the market. However, this climate leaves social goods to be imposed and enacted by force. John Paul II praises modern culture's achievement but also acknowledges the negative effects of a market culture: a culture of death, atheism, and political cynicism concerning our capacity to seek important human values.

Finally, the search for truth in society also depends on our sense of the "given" world around us or nature. Much emphasis has been placed in the recent past on the moral imperative to "subdue nature." The earth in this view is considered a resource to be used according to human will. Nature, considered only in this mentality, is reduced to a means to be exploited. Today we cannot ignore the consequences of our use of nature for the future.[39]

The term "natural" is used often in conversation, but its meaning is ambiguous. What is referred to as "nature" might in the social realm simply be the status quo. People say "it is natural" to mean, "do not change it." Calls on nature can also be used to postpone action. References to nature can suggest that a harmony of social and natural

---

[37] Anne E. Patrick, *Liberating Conscience* (New York: Continuum, 1997) 222.

[38] Robert Bellah et al, *Habits of the Heart: Individualism and Commitment in American Life* (Berkeley: University of California Press, 1985).

[39] John Haught, *The Promise of Nature* (New York: Paulist Press, 1993) 110–12, 113–14 as referenced in Rasmussen, 240.

interests exists somewhere just below the surface of life. Solutions to difficult problems will simply evolve in time, rather than require the diligence of human attention and work. History shows that descriptions that link "nature" and social life have supported social theories like the "survival of the fittest" or deemed it "natural" that some races and peoples are "genetically inferior." Gender studies based on "nature" can legitimate a subordinate role to woman. Nature can be used to dominate others, as well as exploit natural resources.[40]

A status quo that is racist, elitist, militaristic, sexist and destructive of peoples and cultures is related to nature, but negatively. The same activities that create these social dysfunctions also undermine the future of the earth. A status quo based on imbalance of power and oppression does not serve nature in its balance and diversity; rather it destroys it. Facts of nature are relevant in setting norms for human behavior; however, the facts of nature rarely specify the material norms of social behavior entirely.[41] Issues raised by the new science challenge current views of nature and how they relate to our vision of social life. Understanding how nature and human behavior relate is a continuing challenge in Catholic social teaching.

In the midst of these problems of discerning the truth in modern society, religion and theology help by retrieving from the Christian life values that are accessible to all and speaking about them in the public domain.[42] When religion functions in the public realm, the goal is not to create a civil religion but to discern and point to signs and calls of transcendent meaning in the nation's public life. The social encyclicals of John Paul II stand within this call to attend to wider questions of human freedom and truth within the public realm of global society.

How then do we honor the biblical tradition to dwell in the Wisdom of God and maintain God's covenant with us in the social conditions of our times? We do this by understanding, pondering, evaluating, and judging the human goods and values in our social conduct in relation to others, located in concrete social situations, yet conditioned

[40] Larry Rasmussen, *Earth Community, Earth Ethics* (Maryknoll, N.Y.: Orbis Books, 1996) 240.

[41] Josef Fuchs, *Moral Demands and Personal Obligations* (Washington: Georgetown University Press, 1993) 41.

[42] Michael J. Himes and Kenneth R. Himes, O.F.M., *The Fullness of Faith: The Public Significance of Theology* (New York: Paulist Press, 1993) 21–22.

by and influencing problems of humanity interpersonally, societally, and globally.[43] We ask, given these conditions, what is the modicum of freedom of which humans are capable to promote the greatest good and eliminate the greatest evils in this situation, and to in fact, promote human dignity. John Paul II offers a model of an ethic that respects the variability of people's experience, yet it moves beyond relativism when he proposes the "humanistic criterion." This is a standard for evaluating and choosing between social systems, institutional reforms, or legal reforms in terms of how they enhance human dignity.

> The humanistic criterion is, ". . . the measure in which each system is really capable of reducing, restraining and eliminating as far as possible the various forms of exploitation of man and of ensuring for him, through work, not only the just distribution of the indispensable material goods, but also a participation, in keeping with his dignity, in the whole process of production and in the social life that grows up around that process.[44]

Conclusion

The social teaching of John Paul II is more theological and moral than that of some of his predecessors. In his last two social encyclicals, he makes fewer comments on strict policy proposals and more connections between Catholic social doctrine and moral theology. Does this more theoretical orientation make his work irrelevant in secular society? The answer is no. First, he continues the orientation given by Vatican II to the place of the Church on the socio-political order. The principles in the Pastoral Constitution of the Church in the modern world are (1) the ministry of the Church in society is religious, it has no specifically political charism, (2) the religious ministry has as its primary goal the achievement of the Kingdom of God—the Church is in a unique way the "instrument" of the Kingdom in history, (3) the power of the Kingdom is to permeate every dimension of life, (4) as the Church pursues its properly religious ministry, it contributes to four areas of life that have direct social and political consequences,

---

[43] Ibid., 35.

[44] John Paul II, "Address to the United Nations on the Declaration of Human Rights" *AAS* 1156, para. 17, as quoted in Dorr, *Option for the Poor, 100 Years of Catholic Social Teaching*, 275.

and (5) these four religiously rooted but politically significant goals are (a) the defense of human dignity, (b) the promotion of human rights, (c) the cultivation of the unity of the human family, and (d) the provision of meaning to every aspect of human activity (GS 40, 42).[45]

Vatican II specified that two characteristics should mark the place of the Church in society: transcendence and compenetration. It is marked by transcendence because of its religious ministry; the Church transcends every religious system. When John Paul II criticizes both socialist and capitalist forms of the economy as to their capacity to structure economic activity to provide for human flourishing, as well as respect human initiative, he takes this posture. The second characteristic, "compenetration," a term used by John Courtney Murray, states that as the Church is engaged in its religious ministry, it should be engaged in the daily life of every socio-political entity. There is a tension between these styles of ministry. Different forms of language are used depending whether the theological categories that define the depth dimension of issues such as human rights are used or whether more secular language is needed. When interpretations are made, in the calling for policy reform, or in comparing schools of thought on development, secular rather than theological language is needed. Within this broad view of the Church's role in society, the use of theological language does not necessarily equal "begging the question" or moralistic rhetoric that cannot be translated into insight for policy.

A second issue that has bearing on the interpretation of the style of this pope in his contributions to social doctrine is Paul VI's call for regional discernment. Rome relinquished the role of handing down solutions to international problems in the face of a growing awareness that the complexity of the world had surpassed that of the industrial times. It was assumed prior to Paul VI that different parts of the world experienced social questions in relatively similar ways. Few today would venture to define material and social welfare in the same way for all societies.[46] John Paul II is the first pope to write in this "new era" of social teaching. His style might not be the only one expressed as future popes contribute to the tradition, with their own gifts and resources. However, it seems that one cannot interpret the

---

[45] See J. Bryan Hehir, "The Peace Pastoral and Global Mission," in *The Church and Culture Since Vatican II,* Joseph Gremillion, ed. (South Bend, Ind.: University of Notre Dame Press, 1985) 99–103.

[46] Cahill, "Toward Global Ethics," 325.

social teaching of John Paul II without assuming that its meaning for policy direction also has to be worked out at continental and regional levels and by international bodies who function within the framework of specific disciplines.

For this reason it is important for the mission of the Church that all know the Catholic Social Tradition, especially the laity. All Catholics should study this tradition, have it as a light within their own realms and professions, translate its values into operative policy, and contribute to its formation. Continued use of processes such as those by which pastoral letters were written in the United States point to the broad consultation and involvement of experts necessary to form the Catholic Social Tradition of the future.[47]

Today in the Church there are variant models of this mission. It is challenged to accept different, at times even the discordant voices that intrude in its prevailing worldview. In John Paul's words, "We are concerned with such a structure of community that permits the emergence of opposition based on solidarity."[48] The Pope has as a centerpiece of his anthropology interdependence and relatedness to the other that is imperative in forming new roles of the members of the Church in its mission in the world. It is a challenge to search for new expressions of these principles within the Church and to foster both an integrative and globalizing concept of culture that is imperative in this process.

If members of the Church are to do this task beyond that as individuals in their realms or professions, then how their activity is linked to the formal activity of the Church requires more thought. This "missing link" of ecclesial renewal is crucial for a social teaching tradition that is moving away from specific proposals toward a powerful language of human rights and global solidarity. However, these principles need translation and "carriers" into the public realm where decisions are made.

This challenge to "carry" the social mission of the Church into society will be the basis of new forms of associations of consecrated life within the Church and new forms of ministry. It will stimulate

[47] See Kenneth R. Himes, O.F.M., "*The Challenge of Peace* and *Economic Justice for All*: Twenty Years Later," in *The Proceedings of the Catholic Theological Society of America* 56 (2001) 77–96.
[48] As quoted in Dorr, *Option for the Poor,* 305. This is an excerpt of John Paul's writing on *The Self and the Act,* 49.

new links between the Church and secular movements, para-ecclesial groups who function institutionally to carry the vision of social Catholicism into the middle-range work of policy formation.[49] The creation of new social carriers for the social teaching of the Church, however, is essential to its tradition.[50] It is likely that these groups will follow the pattern suggested by Hehir and take up either an educational-cultural, legislative-policy making or prophetic or "confessing church" stance to the social policy debate. The broad principles given during this pontificate for the development of the global society can also provide the basis of a "new church" in Catholicism. In these two tasks, we will find that the impact of John Paul II will be felt for many years ahead.

---

[49] Coleman, "Retrieving or Re-inventing Social Catholicism," 284–86.

[50] Johan Verstraeten, "Re-thinking Catholic Social Thought as Tradition," in *Catholic Social Thought: Twilight or Renaissance?* op. cit., 59–77.

PART THREE

The Future of the Catholic Social Tradition

Chapter Eleven

Communities Formed
in the Heart of the Church:
A Thought Experiment

Some ecologists say it is not the general conditions of an ecosystem that ultimately determine its capacity to sustain itself, but that single factor that is in short supply in a given system that determines its carrying capacity.[1] Is community that single factor that marks the Church's capacity to transform Social Catholicism for this new century? Some caution that the Church must link the social encyclical tradition to new social carriers, or face irrelevance in the social realm.[2] These carriers might occupy different places along the sociological matrix of community: from associations, to movements, or groups, yet as collectives within the Church, all have a communal dimension in some degree.

Martin Luther King, Jr. once asked, "Where do we go from here, chaos or community?" King questioned the possibility of community in society. But he more seriously pondered the chance for a society without community. Does the Church have a chance to carry out its

---

[1] Larry Rasmussen, *Earth Community, Earth Ethics* (Maryknoll, N.Y.: Orbis Books, 1997) 39.

[2] John A. Coleman, "Retrieving of Re-inventing Social Catholicism," in *Catholic Social Thought: Twilight or Renaissance?* Jonathan Boswell, Francis P. McHugh, Johan Verstraeten, eds. (Louvain: Peeters, 2001) 281ff.

social mission without community? If the formation and engagement of community is a serious challenge facing Social Catholicism today, we must inquire about the state of the moral ecology of community. Is it an endangered species in the Church, or a reality forming in new ways?

To search for community is not to return to the community of the past. The changed social conditions of today will not recreate it. The rational quest of self-interest alone will not create community, since community requires sacrifice. Coercive external authority cannot form community that lasts. Community today must be built from within as a new type of community, free from the limitations of the past, yet able to form the humanity of the future.

What is community? Community is a center of multi-layered interactions among people. There traditions and rituals are preserved and developed. Life skills are learned and called forth. Discipline is nurtured and expected. Fidelity and accountability to the community are practiced. At its best community is a way of life that shapes and defines member's identity. True community shows itself in an alliance for a common cause, a life beyond itself. Community is also a moral stance towards one neighbor. The parable of the Good Samaritan (Luke 10:25-37) defines a neighbor or a community member in terms of compassionate behavior.

Community is required for the social conscience. The human spirit must have experiences that hold the historical forms of the criteria that will provide ethical guidance in social interactions. It is only by participating in the truth of values such as equality, respect, and dignity that one understands them. Bonds created with significant others form the data about life and its transcendent values that ultimately form the values we shape in the world.[3] We learn values in relationship. We cannot separate the moral values of the Church from the church community because it is here, in family, parish, school, and wider associations that the pre-moral attitudes so important in moral formation are communicated.

At one level community is a network of humanizing relationships. Community is lived locally, yet modern communications, governance, economics, and the fact we live on the "one earth" makes it possible to speak of community in a wider society and across the

---

[3] Juan Luis Segundo, *The Liberation of Theology*, John Drury, trans. (Maryknoll, N.Y.: Orbis Books, 1976) 150.

globe. Theologically sharing one humanity and one creation grounds all life in community.

Americans tend to place the burden of ethical behavior on the development and sanctity of individual conscience. Yet, Robert Bellah reminds us that even our respect for conscience in American society is vulnerable without a sense of community. Addressing the American Academy of Religion, he cautioned that culture does not float free from institutions.[4] To validate the sacredness of the individual conscience in society, we must face that our capacity to imagine a social fabric that would hold individuals together is vanishing.

Americans hold their sense of conscience in high esteem, yet conscience stands on shaky ground. It is not based in a proper relationship between the individual and the group. Americans ground conscience in a religious individualism that does not need church. This religious individualism, in turn, is fed by a climate of economic individualism that, ironically, knows nothing of the sacredness of the individual. Its only standard is money, and the only thing more sacred than money is more money. What economic individualism destroys and what religious individualism cannot restore is solidarity, a sense of members being in the same body, an essential for establishing a sense of obligation to another. Bellah cautions that as religious people seek to retrieve a necessary respect for the individual in their churches, families and societies, they engage in a futile effort if they simply mimic a cultural individualism that cannot save.

Without a minimal degree of solidarity, amid the argument, controversy, conflict, and pluralism indigenous to community living, the project of greater recognition of individual dignity is dead. The group collapses in on itself. Without community, real individuality is lost. The only ones who have "dignity" in such conditions are the minority who have access to money and decision-making power.

Today the Church lives in conditions that do not foster community. It lives in a culture highly influenced by the state and the market with their agencies of socialization: the media and education. Neither is hospitable to the notion of community. In simpler societies kinship and religious communities could withstand cultural pressure and provide models of difference. But in modern society, families and churches are often too colonized by the market and the state to provide much

---

[4] Robert Bellah, "Is There A Common American Culture?" *Journal of the American Academy of Religion* (Fall, 1998) vol. 66, no. 3, 613–25.

of a buffer. Bellah charges that churches and families are fragile in their capacity to provide a radical alternative to modern culture or even a perspective to criticize it and alter it. To uphold a sense of transcendence in society religion is responsible to engage in cultural criticism.[5] Yet religion must be lived in a community capable of the task.[6] In this light, the creation of community is central to the practice of Social Catholicism in this century.[7]

Community and Social Catholicism: The Future

If we desire a community that is different than the past and able to be sustained in the conditions of the future, what would be its characteristics? Theorists claim that a shared history, identity, mutuality, plurality, autonomy, participation, and integration mark modern community.[8] We recognize in these values a changed type of community elicited from and for a new set of circumstances. If our capacity to continue the Catholic social tradition is as strong as the

---

[5] How one engages in societal criticism marks differences in schools of thought surrounding the social encyclicals. For example, those in a prophetic school might see institutions as the problem or unnecessary. The "right" is often more organized than the "left" in the Church. Those in a social-principle understanding recognize the need for stable social carriers. This chapter is closer to the latter in its intent.

[6] Ideas have impact in history and on society only through a distinctive institutionalization and carrier units. If older forms of these have been lost in Social Catholicism, there is no way that an evocation of Catholic anthropology alone will have much contemporary impact on politics or social policy. New forms of community are needed, and new agents of translation are necessary.

[7] See Bran Stiltner, *Religion and the Common Good: Catholic Contribution to Building Community in a Liberal Society* (Lantham, Md.: Rowman and Littlefield, 1999). Stiltner argues that the Catholic tradition argues for the values of freedom, tolerance, and pluralism by references to the good of political communities and its sub-communities, not just by reference to the rights of individuals, as liberalism. Community in this sense is not just a stage for human becoming, but engagement in community is essential for human flourishing. We could say there is a procedural and substantive good within the tradition in the creation of community itself.

[8] The following analysis is based on and adapted from the work of Larry Rasmussen, *Moral Fragments, Moral Community* (Minneapolis: Fortress Press, 1993) 110ff., and his use of the work of Philip Selznik, *The Moral Commonwealth: Social Theory and the Promise of Community* (Berkeley: University of California Press, 1992) 183–90, 357–65.

quality and direction of our communities, what vision of community can direct our future? Let us engage in thought to explore some qualities of community living and the call such a vision places on us in Church and society.

Communities of a Shared History

A shared history assumes that customs, language, geography, shared events, and crises bond a community more than abstract ideals. A community shares a Story through which each member's story is interpreted. Ethical vision is latent in a community's shared culture. Yet today a community's history has to be multi-cultural, first to bond the real people on the move in the world and second to create a social vision that respects diversity, racial, ethnic, economic, age, and religion. Shared history alone is not sufficient to bond a community.

Aspects of a shared history can be pathological, as we see in various ethnic divisions in the world, rising fundamentalism and wars of ethnic cleansing. Shared history and a sense of belonging are important for community, but the content of that belonging has to be open to moral criticism and ongoing reflection by all the members. The community of the future has to be built differently if it is to be more than a tool for hatred or an enclave for group preservation.

How we live in community affects our approach to social transformation. Brian Johnstone claims that moral methods are processes "by which a community of persons adopts, founds, and communicates a moral way of life."[9] These processes must be clear enough that they can be followed intelligently in a way of life. They also must be coherent in that the starting points, sequences, and conclusion are in practical harmony with one another. In Christian morality, the internal order of a method is not just academic. It is integrally bound to its capacity to coherently direct a way of life in community.[10]

The style of practical living in a community, whether family, parish, religious community, civic or movement/association, nation, or globe

[9] Brian Johnstone, "Moral Methodology," in *The New Dictionary of Catholic Social Thought,* Judith Dwyer, ed. (Collegeville: The Liturgical Press, 1994) 597.

[10] Michael J. Schuck reminds us that social teaching ". . . coheres around a theologically inspired communitarian social ethic, which has yielded a cluster of shared, integrated insights concerning religious, political, familial, economic and cultural relations in society." *That They Be One: The Social Teaching of the Papal Encyclicals, 1740–1989* (Washington: Georgetown University, 1991) 180.

is a social construct. It involves a balance in the play of human power, whose history counts, who speaks, who sits at the table, whose issues are addressed, who votes, whose values and character mark the decision and whose generation is represented and who speaks for the future. Today, a sense of shared history includes awareness of the history of the earth upon which it depends for sustainability.

A community vision with a shared history is one marked by *participation,* which is the optimal inclusion of all involved voices in a decision and in the sharing of the burden as well as the benefits of life together in a given locality.[11] Participation is not just a quality of community, but a goal of integral human development (*Economic Justice for All,* 71). The experience of participation fostered in community forms the capacity to advocate for the conditions necessary to participate in society: access to work, health care, housing, education as well as a call to responsible citizenship. Participation grounds a shared history in real benefits and shared burdens.

Communities of Identity

Identity refers to the kind of persons being formed by a community. The formation of identity in community involves a sense of "we" that does not destroy individuality or is based on a hostile moral tribalism where "we" is seen always opposed to a "they." Identity has to be pluralistic in modern community. A climate of civility must exist where individuality and identity are centered in a respect and loyalty that creates healthy boundaries among people who respect difference.

Unlike the nineteenth century where geography, ethnic ties, and common values bonded community, modern community will be more diverse and pluralist. Pluralism, however, can hide incivility, where "your" truth and "my" truth grounds culture wars.[12] Old calls for pluralism in American religion called for Catholics, Protestants, and Jews to unite around shared beliefs. These no longer define the real battles in religion and in the name of religion in society today.

Modern communications generate true or false pluralism. They can open the mind to a great variety of thought, yet also generate

---

[11] Rasmussen, *Earth Community, Earth Ethics,* 172. I draw on Rasmussen's reflections on a vision of sustainability in this section.

[12] James W. Fowler, *Faithful Change: The Personal and Public Challenges of Postmodern Life* (Nashville: Abingdon Press, 1996) 162ff.

focus groups for hate, which hide behind its freedom. When reality is created through communications rather than reflected, pluralism does not foster identity, it thwarts it. The web does not substitute for the healthy pluralism of community because alone it cannot supply the ingredients for identity.

Identity requires that community be a place of manifold engagement.[13] Community is an inclusive whole where people live interdependently with one another, sharing both a private and a public life. In community, one generation initiates the next into a way of life. As center of manifold engagement, community gives each member a significant place in day-by-day participation. Manifold engagement creates important bonds that tie the members together and gives them a sense of identity in the group. Successful use of the web to build community occurs in groups that already have the ingredients for identity in ties beyond the web.

In the Catholic community identity is fostered by its *sacramental character.* The liturgy is the possession not of individuals but of the Church; it is fundamentally a communal entity.[14] The liturgical community recognizes the world as it is, both fully redeemed and incomplete and affected by sin. The world, creation, and community itself is not yet fully transformed by the redemption God has accomplished in Christ. Christians in the eucharistic assembly find their identity now as continuing the "passage" from death to life. As Jesus was in that passage on the night he gave them a share in his very life, he shares his mission of self-emptying service to humanity in fidelity and communion with God. The liturgy is the manifestation and proclamation of God's faithfulness and love to the servant Jesus, whom God has now raised up in glory. As we participate, that same promise is extended to the Christian community. We take up this ministry with joy and confidence.[15]

The Christian who lives in the sacramental vision shares the identity of a socially engaged life and mission. This vision is oriented

[13] Rasmussen, *Moral Fragments, Moral Community,* 139.

[14] Bruce T. Morrill S.J., *Anamnesis as Dangerous Memory: Political and Liturgical Theology in Dialogue* (Collegeville: The Liturgical Press, 2000) 196.

[15] Morrill remarks that "joy and confidence" might not be the personal experience of everyone celebrating the Eucharist (ibid.). It is the meaning rendered, offered, and conferred by what is celebrated. This belongs to the whole Church. In this sense, we can say, even when we as individuals do not "feel" this meaning, the Church prays it for us.

toward seeing God in all things. All can be actual or potential carriers of divine presence: other people, communities, movements, events, places, objects, the world at large, the whole cosmos. Objects that are visible, tangible and finite can mediate God's presence.[16] The community itself is a sacrament of God's presence, an expression of the Church as sacrament in the world.

Theologian Yves Congar remarked that the "monuments" of the tradition could not be reduced to the Bible, patristic sources, and Denzinger. They include as well: liturgy, worship, gestures, and the lifestyle of believers.[17] The sacramental identity of the community that has carried Social Catholicism is an essential part of its meaning. Social tradition is best understood as a tradition of belief, teaching, practice, and committed action. Its sacramental vision places the ethical pursuit of justice within the scope of God's gratuitousness.

A community of identity is marked by *responsibility.* Consequences are not lost in scales of action whose range of impact makes no one responsible. A workable community creates responsibility on a scale that people can handle, and it makes plans that are subject to alteration and correction by the members.[18] A community with a sense of identity overcomes the modern pathology of authority, perceived as uninhibited power and non-approachable disinterestedness. Public scandals in the Church feed an alienated sense of authority that is fostered in culture. Violence that cripples schools, families, congregations, dioceses, and society erupts as an authority model of "power over" others that is acted out in relationships. Those who seek to heal these problems do so by fostering broader responsibility among members.

Responsibility in the Catholic community is supported by the principle of *subsidiarity,* which holds that nothing is done by a higher or larger organization that cannot be done as well as a lower or smaller one.[19] In this sense subsidiarity is a call for pluralism of participation. The individual in community or a smaller community has a right to take active part in shaping their social world, and larger entities should

[16] Richard McBrien, *Catholicism* (New York: Harper Collins, 1994) 10.

[17] Yves Congar, *Tradition and Traditions: An Historical Essay and a Theological Essay* (New York: Macmillan, 1966) 425–58.

[18] Richard Sennett, *Authority* (New York: Knopf, 1980) 168.

[19] Michael E. Allsoop, "Principle of Subsidiarity," in *The New Dictionary of Catholic Social Thought,* op. cit., 927–29.

not block this responsibility. They foster such participation by addressing problems that transcend the power of local effort or an individual. Subsidiarity calls all to responsibility.

Experiences of responsibility in community where members make, break, and remake meanings that guide their lives and live in groups that are clear about what can and cannot be done will demand structures of responsibility at both local and higher levels of society and the globe. Without a sense of identity and responsibility learned in community, the human community will not create the global systems of checks and balances required for its survival. In this spirit, the Catholic Social tradition has argued for the protection of cultural groups as centers of identity, and for new structures of world governance (CA 58).

The principle of subsidiarity also directs that the function of authority in the Church should foster the responsibility of its members. This involves a continuing striving toward openness to circles of conversation previously omitted from its hearing. This will foster also a new openness and imagination in relating to the public domain. History shows that major church initiatives in opposing racism, denouncing weapons and strategies or war, and defending conscience were begun by individuals and movements that at first were denied official recognition and support.[20] The call to participate calls all professionals within the Church to be willing to collaborate in fostering its social consciousness through their disciplines. It urges all members to stay in the conversion, especially concerning contested issues that challenge a common ground.[21] Social Catholicism will have carriers in the future that will arise from new types of enablement within the Church and new bonds with those who share its values.

Communities of Mutuality

Mutuality is the atmosphere of interdependence and reciprocity in a group. People sense they need one another in some way and gain from cooperating with each other. In a world order where race, class,

---

[20] Gordon C. Zahn, "Social Movements and Catholic Social Thought," in *One Hundred Years of Catholic Social Thought*, John Coleman, S.J., ed. (Maryknoll, N.Y.: Orbis Books, 1991) 53.

[21] Joseph Cardinal Bernardin and Oscar H. Lipscomb, *Catholic Common Ground Initiatives* (New York: Crossroad, 1997).

and gender relationships need restructuring, a community of mutuality provides the life experience for this vision. In the Catholic community, mutuality is an aspect of the relationship of solidarity. Solidarity sees the neighbor "on par with ourselves" (SRS 39).

Solidarity carries mutuality to the willingness to go beyond oneself, to sacrifice in order to recognize the worth of another (SRS 40). It implies a spirituality of the cross, the self emptying that attentiveness to the other requires. Solidarity and mutuality form their own logic. Living with solidarity and mutuality in communities and movements means to live beyond current "structures of sin" and to live with a new imagination (SRS 40). Such imagination is needed also at the global level. The interdependence at the heart of world peace demands abandonment of international structures that thwart mutuality in the world today: politics of blocs, economic, military, and political imperialism, and the lack of collaborative trust (SRS 39). The roots of these structures reside also in the human heart and can be faced in real communities of mutuality.

The feminist community points out that mutuality counters a dominating attitude that others know what is good for women and minorities, without including them in the conversations that defines the problems and proposes their solution. "Mutuality moves beyond equality to recognize the reciprocity of giving and receiving, caring and being cared for. In its negative expression, it recognizes the reciprocity of evil, of harming and being harmed, of hating and being hateful."[22] Mutuality is recognition of the diminishment of spirit that occurs to both parities in racist or sexist relationships. It is recognition that twisted relationships are a two-way street.[23] Mutuality frees us from cloaked paternalism, maternalism, and racism under the guide of solidarity.

Mutuality builds on a sense of responsibility and creates a climate of *accountability*. As the structuring of responsibility, both to others and to the earth, accountability marks a community vision with structures and procedures for holding decision makers accountable. It checks a growing world reality where the weak have no influence on those in charge. In this climate the "weaker" can only resist by nega-

[22] Maria Riley, O.P., "Feminist Analysis: A Missing Perspective," in *The Logic of Solidarity: Commentaries on Pope John Paul II's Encyclical on Social Concern*, Gregory Baum, ed. (Maryknoll, N.Y.: Orbis Books, 1990) 199.

[23] Denise Lardner Carmody, *Virtuous Woman: Reflections on Christian Feminist Ethics* (Maryknoll, N.Y.: Orbis Books, 1992) 52.

tion of whatever the powerful want them to be, whether this negation is expressed through terrorism, germ warfare, or paralyzing cynicism.[24]

A community grounded in mutuality builds structures that are accountable before new problems, such as the changing nature of war. Here goals are not just to win conflicts but to absolutely dominate the other side by destroying the other's capacity to resist, through propaganda, lies and terror tactics (CA 15). The social ecology of the globe, where conflicts must be worked out, is destroyed. To create in the midst of international conflicts protections that insure accountability and mutuality among nations calls for a new imagination that can reframe pacifist and just-war traditions for an interdependent world. The seeds of this reflection lie in the experience of real communities.

Mutuality is also supported by the Church as it fosters family life for a new millennium.[25] In family life sex differences can be used to ground differences in power and role. The mutuality between the sexes can be defined so that the biological differences between them overshadow the interpersonal mutuality they should share. The tendency to focus the meaning of parenthood on physiological process can feed into a biological view of women's maternity, "asymmetrically emphasized over the fatherhood of men." Use of gender stereotypes can cloud the parallel participation by men and women in both the social and the domestic aspects of marriage.

When sexual morality in the Church is defined only through an analysis of acts of sexual intercourse rather than in a matrix of relationships that links parenthood, kinship, and social roles to the integrity of sex, the mutuality that is the ground of marital intimacy is lost and its relationship to larger roles of parenting and the community is clouded. "Spousehood and parenthood must be linked together as ongoing personal and embodied relationships that have a definitive sexual-procreative dimension."[26] While Christian views of

---

[24] Michael Lerner, *The Politics of Meaning: Restoring Hope and Possibility in an Age of Cynicism* (New York: Addison-Wesley, 1996).

[25] Christine E. Gudorf, "Mutuality," in *The New Dictionary of Catholic Social Thought*, op. cit., 655. See also Kenneth R. Overberg, *An Inconsistent Ethic? Teachings of the American Catholic Bishops* (Washington, D.C.: University Press of America, 1980).

[26] Lisa Sowle Cahill, "Marriage: Institution, Relationship, Sacrament," in *One Hundred Years of Catholic Social Thought*, 117. See also *Family: A Christian Social Perspective* (Minneapolis: Fortress Press, 2000). See ch. 4 on family and Catholic social teaching.

marriage have in recent years moved to harmonize its physical and inter-subjective aspects, there is much work to be done.[27]

Family is the fundamental community within the Church and the primary place mutuality is learned. Social issues surrounding the family go beyond questions of divorce. Reproductive technologies move into mainstream society basic questions about the purpose of sexuality, the nature of parenthood, and the definition of the family.[28] Public debates that have bearing on how reproductive technologies will enter into a vision of marriage and family life require communities to learn mutuality in the heart and see it is etched into policy.[29] The church community will also be called upon to check market-driven initiatives into the intimacy of family life in order to insure the family, as a community of mutuality, is protected.

Communities That Are Pluralistic

Plurality is perhaps the most "modern" of the characteristics of community. It connotes that people will belong to more than one community at the same time. Modern community is not a totalizing one. Membership in a variety of groups does not threaten a group but enhances it. It extends the community into wider spheres of influence and brings to the community the well being of family, occupational, recreational, ethnic, and religious groups other than its own. Plurality is held in relationship to the other values of community, identity and mutuality. Plural membership has to be balanced with sufficient presence to make community life a reality.

The pluralism of today contrasts with Catholic life of the past. The ultramontane Church, characterized by strong papal influence on the mindset of Catholics, special forms of Catholic organizations in society, and a monolithic approach to Catholic life and doctrine, is not the Church of today.[30] By Vatican II Catholics in the first world

---

[27] Lisa Sowle Cahill, "Marriage," in *The New Dictionary of Catholic Social Thought*, op. cit., 568.

[28] Margaret Farley, "Family," in *The New Dictionary of Catholic Social Thought*, op. cit., 371–81. See also *Personal Commitments, Beginning, Keeping, Changing* (San Francisco: Harper and Row, 1990).

[29] Sidney Callahan, "The Family: The Challenge of Technological Change," in *One Hundred Years of Catholic Social Thought,* 174–88.

[30] Staf Hellemans, "Is There a Future for Catholic Social Teaching?" in *Catholic Social Thought: Twilight or Renaissance?* op. cit., 20–24.

lived in a pluralistic society. Pluralism suggests that a variety of viewpoints, explanations or perspectives are offered as accounting for the same reality.[31] Pluralism entered theology as theological reality was expressed by many tools, methods, and approaches to understand reality which were incorporated into theological expression.[32] After Vatican II, Catholics "mixed" in society outside Catholic circles.

The voice of the Church in this climate appears as one voice among many vying for impact on one's reality. In a world that is increasingly complex, claims to authority based on "certitude" have less appeal as the experience of change makes it the only constant. Secularization shifts even the criteria by which the Church is judged.[33] Measures of success valued in the society are applied to the Church. Can it keep pace with technology and shifts in cultural consciousness? These questions become very important in the eye of the public, at times even more than whether or not the Church lives the Gospel.

In the freer atmosphere of a pluralistic culture one does not have to rebel against religion, because it cannot be imposed. One simply ignores it. In a pluralistic climate modern forms of atheism are often expressed not as violent denials of God, but as indifference.[34]

Awareness of pluralism will help the Church find its place in the policy debate. Religious institutions in a democracy operate at the nexus of public opinion and public policy decisions. They rarely form decisions, rather they contribute to the framework that sets limits for policy choices and provides indications of policies desired by the public. For the Church to be effective in this role in a pluralistic society, it has to speak in terms that members of the public can understand. In order to be heard in the wider public debate, the Church needs to express values in non-religious terms so that others can find them morally persuasive.[35]

Today the voice of the Church has to be pluralistic: various lobbying groups, advocacy committees, and community organizations

[31] William Henn, "Pluralism," in *The New Dictionary of Theology*, Joseph A. Komonchak et al., ed. (Wilmington, Del.: Michael Glazier, 1989) 770–72.

[32] Karl Rahner, "Pluralism in Theology and the Unity of the Creed in the Church," in *Theological Investigations* XI (New York: The Seabury Press, 1974) 3–23.

[33] Franz-Xavier Kaufmann, "The Sociology of Knowledge and the Problem of Authority," in *Journal of Ecumenical Studies* (Spring 1982) 30–31.

[34] Michael H. Crosby, O.F.M., "Relationships of the Sacred and the Secular," in *The New Dictionary of Catholic Social Thought*, op. cit., 857–60.

[35] Joseph Cardinal Bernadin, *A Moral Vision for America*, John P. Langan, S.J., ed. (Washington, D.C.: Georgetown University Press, 1998) 15.

sponsored by single, religious and married people have to be more involved in shaping its public voice in American society. When members of the church add their expertise so that this public voice can be heard, they do so by freely committing their energies to this important dialogue. In a former church model, this public dimension was done by the clergy, with members of the laity as "silent partners." New models of church responsibility and jurisdiction are needed to include a variety of voices in official church advocacy.

Limits to plurality also exist for Catholics in the public arena where their plurality and identity can clash. Personal conviction, formed within the Church, has to be translated into public actions. Personal conscience is free to judge strategies about public policy as to their effectiveness, but moral stances taken by the Church that are clear and consistent on public issues cannot be abandoned in the public arena. This can be a complex dilemma for health care workers, public officials, and those who work in industries that are materially connected to abuses to human dignity.[36] Plurality alone is insufficient as a norm in carrying the values of Social Catholicism. It is a value that has to be held in tension with others.

Equity marks the ways of proceeding for a pluralistic community. As basic fairness in distributive and procedural justice, equity bridges the gaps between the ways of living and being human that exist in Church and society today. Divisions of race, class, and gender; tensions between clergy and laity; growing divisions between generations and their needs; chasm between rich and poor nations, and the need between species to respect their biotic integrity call for equity in measuring these relationships.

Equity in the Catholic Social Tradition is nuanced with a *preference for the poor.* Communities within the Church should integrate a preference for the "least" to foster equity, since equity in society is only approximated. Advocacy for those marginated from current arrangements of equity moves a group or society closer to its reality. Communities foster equity by a preference for the poor in a way different than governments. Governments and other political entities hold the current balance of conflicting interests in social arrangements. While programs in place might care for the poor, and governments have a responsibility to the poor, the restructuring required by an option for the poor must have power in the wider society before it has governmental impact.

[36] Ibid., 90–91.

Donal Dorr remarks that traditionally the Church has promoted "Christian ethos" in societies by influencing "instruments of culture" such as schools, hospitals, newspapers, and other media. However this very strategy invests the Church in mainstream interests, not the radical stance that the option for the poor suggests.[37] In other words, Dorr finds a tension between the three models of church ministry: educational-cultural, legislative, and prophetic. For Dorr, recent Catholic social teaching does not support the type of radical/prophetic action connoted by "option for the poor."

However, if option for the poor, and the spirituality that upholds it, informs the educational-cultural and legislative actions of the Church, they will be more attuned to transformation on behalf of the poor than accommodation to the current state of affairs. The challenge for communities, it seems, is not between prophecy and legislative/cultural action as it is a choice between something and nothing. Option for the poor should be the criteria to judge what strategy is the most effective to bring about greater equity. Action based on equity provides a stance from which the effectiveness of prophetic actions could be judged, but is not identical with it.

A group responds to injustice with attention to option for the poor in a series of steps: it must understand a problem, reflect in faith, learn how it colludes in maintaining the injustice, foster protest, search for realistic alternatives, and devise strategies to carry them out.[38]

Response may involve short-term solutions, long-term commitment, a life work, a commitment to a corporate ministry by a group bound for life, and collaboration with others. The successes and defeats involved require both spirituality for the "long haul" and the posturing of some groups in the Church to continue a tradition of service that is trans-generational.[39] From a faith perspective, human energies and optimism alone are not sufficient. The support of a community centered in a hope and trust in God, belief in God's ultimate promise of the Kingdom celebrated in word and sacrament, along with an effective bond with the marginalized is the spiritual power that reanimates the journey for the long term.

[37] Donal Dorr, "Option for the Poor Re-visited," in *Catholic Social Thought: Twilight or Renaissance?* 252, 254–56.

[38] Ibid., 253.

[39] At the first level, this ministry is centered in the community of the Church. At a second level, this is one reason for the need to institutionalize social response: for example by societies of consecrated life and the formation of new institutes in the Church.

The "poor" are those who taste the reality of material poverty and those who carry the emotional, cultural, political, and religious deprivation that the forces that underlie material poverty share with other "structures of sin" in society. Victims of abuse, lives paralyzed by addiction, those cut off from society by illiteracy, isolated by racial, ethnic or religious hatred, singled out for derision by homophobia, sentenced to death by lack of access to health care, vulnerable to maltreatment because they are young or elderly, left out because they are immigrants, all share in some way this concern.

Pluralistic communities that strive for equity within a horizon of option for the poor, as a "church from below" can reimage Catholicism as well as draw on its strengths. Rome can promote and coordinate world-wide discussion of what local communities address and the patterns that cut across structures of alienation across the globe. It can unite these stories, provide links to the tradition, and synthesize their common elements in its documents and teachings. Conferences of bishops can focus these discussions on national and continental realities. Catholic communities, with their ties to people of good will, can overcome the "nothing of significance can be done anymore" malaise in Church and society. In the process Catholics can "opt" for the Church and for better societies as they opt for the poor. Structures that promote this quality of change will require the Church to strive itself toward equity in the midst of pluralism as new voices are integrated in significant ways into the scope of the consciousness that underlies its social teaching.

Communities That Are Autonomous

Autonomy is the ability of a community to develop responsible individuals as it incorporates them into a complex of relationships, which gives them a social self or "we." Genuine autonomy is the capacity to foster self-direction that avoids both the illusion of unlimited choices within the group and the brutal crushing effect of the group on the individual.

Autonomy fosters in the individual a sense of self, which includes the group in its well-being and a sense of the group that includes the flourishing of its members. Loyalty helps the group take the individuals seriously and supports the individuals to make the emotional investment necessary to incorporate the group into their self-identity.

In American society autonomy is highly valued. It is often interpreted as the right of an individual to pursue his or her goals. In medical decisions, it translates into the right of the patient to make decisions regarding his or her care. Autonomy, however, can be regarded as the only value. Alone it only indicates where the locus of decision making lies, it does not exhaust the values at stake in a moral decision.

Richard McCormick points to two dangers in absolutizing autonomy.[40] Little thought is given to other values that should guide and inform the use of autonomy. The fact that a decision is made by an individual, or a group, can falsely become the sole element that makes a decision right. The question that is not addressed is what other values would make a decision right or wrong?

Also a cry for autonomy can claim an independence from others that is unrealistic, "absolutizing autonomy is an intolerance of dependence on others." It can undermine or avoid a climate of trust and care that is meant to provide support during times of frailty and dependence in life. McCormick discusses how autonomy enters into decisions at the end of life, but analogously similar issues are experienced in groups.

In the Catholic community autonomy is nuanced by the principle of *mediation*. Mediation is the belief that created realities mediate the grace of Christ. As Richard McBrien puts it, "the universe of grace is a mediated reality: mediated principally by Christ, and secondarily by the Church and by other signs and instruments of salvation outside and beyond the Church."[41] This includes institutional elements of the Church, ministries, its communities and members, the "signs of the times," the poor, and the reality of the neighbor who is at hand.

The value of mediation nuances autonomy by directing that the autonomy of the group is not for itself alone, but for a purpose in the wider life of the Church and society. It challenges all communities and movements within the Church to take up their mediating function. All share in Christ's mission given to each Christian at baptism, the source of the identity of all social action within the Church. Groups are called to be attentive to their mission as an icon of their identity,

---

[40] Richard A. McCormick, S.J., "Physician-Assisted Suicide: Flight from Compassion," in *On Moral Medicine,* Stephen E. Lammers and Allen Verhey, eds. (Grand Rapids, Mich.: Eerdmans, 1998) 668.

[41] Richard P. McBrien, *Catholicism* (San Francisco: Harper, 1994) 1196–97.

rather than focus on their autonomy alone. Consensus by itself is not enough to validate a group decision, as attention must be given to data mediated by other elements within the matrix of Church and society.[42] Grounding autonomy within the horizon of mediation empowers a group to own its own mediating role in Church and society and to contribute its voice.

Groups that "carry" the Catholic Social Tradition share in the meaning and function of "church" in varying ways. A local parish and a group of professional bankers advocating for change in policies for debt reduction differ in this mediating function.[43] When a group functions within the matrix of Catholic life, it receives transference of credibility from the wider Church that carries with it a reciprocal call not to misname its autonomy as absolute.[44] The values of its autonomy as well as the reality of mediation must be held in tension. They are also joined by the necessary sufficiency to function as an entity in the Church.

Sufficiency fosters the autonomy of a community. Sufficiency is the commitment to meet the basic material needs of all. It requires careful organization of exchange and a vision of economic life that involves both ceilings and floors for consumption. It takes into consideration the eco-efficiency of its life and sees sustainability as involving both material simplicity and the maintenance of communal spirituality. Major disparities of wealth and poverty generate instability of the human community, but so do situations with no soul or life vision that address people's spiritual needs.

Sufficiency nuances the value of autonomy and mediation with the principle that all activities and roles of the Church are qualified by the norm that the goods of the earth are meant for all (SRS 42). Recent social teaching has placed the teaching on private property

---

[42] See chapters on obedience in Judith A. Merkle, *A Different Touch: A Study of the Vows in Religious Life* (Collegeville: The Liturgical Press, 1998).

[43] See McBrien, *Catholicism,* 723–24, for characteristics of local church.

[44] In a formal manner this is addressed by canon law. Beyond this, the values of autonomy, mediation, and sufficiency provide one horizon in which to consider these relationships. At the heart of the *mandatum* discussion in the United States, is the delineation of an ecclesial relationship. See National Conference of Bishops, "*Ex Corde:* An Application to the United States," *Origins* 29:25 (December 2, 1999). New forms of participation will require ongoing reflection on new ecclesial relationships. To some degree there is always a transference made to a group or an individual and the institution with which they associate in human interactions. For an example of this in spiritual direction, see Janet K. Ruffing, R.S.M., *Spiritual Direction* (New York: Paulist Press, 2000) esp. ch. 6.

under a "social mortgage," claiming it has an intrinsic social function, nuanced by the principle of the universal destination of goods. By extension this principle also applies to the property of the Church. What if this norm were extended not just to the material property of the Church but all its resources? If communities within the Church took this norm to heart, three areas of concern would be addressed. The transfer of funding and expertise, reexamination of ministerial roles in the light of the right to the sacraments, and refocusing of Catholic spirituality to its relevance for service to the world, yet grounded in deep traditions of Catholic worship. Let us treat these in reverse order.

Catholic spirituality needs to ground its justice activity in its deeper spiritual life. Catholic spirituality today can miss the mark by being too worldly or too other-worldly. Groups focused on justice can be self-righteous, tending toward polarization, isolation, and intolerance toward others in the Church. The person of Christ can easily lose its decisiveness for the identity of the group. Others can retrieve a Catholic spirituality focused on selected aspects of pre-Vatican life, reexpressing them in the current cultural matrix of the Church and society. This posture can promote a new type of lay dependency, a totalitarian version of Catholic orthodoxy not nuanced by a sense of the hierarchy of truths, and an approach to Catholic identity in the public realm that is inhospitable to dialogue. This too drifts toward self containment, but under different auspices. Both spiritualities promote enclaves that have little to do with others in the Church and have limited resources for dialogue with society. Both have an inability to communicate with others outside its framework of meaning.

If early "justice" orientations of Catholic spirituality overstated the horizontal dimension of Christian faith, leaving out its transcendent symbols, latter forms, in the effort to retrieve these symbols, eliminate its capacity for "compenetration" in the society because of the church-world construct in which it operates. A former approach idealizes the world, while the latter can drift toward demonizing it. Spirituality is important for the future of Social Catholicism. It informs the conscience and choices of the individuals and groups and conveys a vision of the role of the Church and its groups within history and society. The above are broad approaches that link Catholic identity to the public realm, as caricatures; they describe no group in particular. However, they point to the need of a solid Catholic spirituality that promotes justice.

Sufficiency as a value directs that a group must maintain a communal spirituality that provides real nourishment to its members, not culture wars within the Church. To create this common ground involves linking justice work to deeper symbols and practices of Catholic life and tempering efforts to restore the more transcendent dimensions of Catholic practice with a focus on social responsibility. A this-worldly spirituality that does not feed the mystical dimensions of Christian life or an other-worldly spirituality that avoids the complexity of dialogue and compromise will prove "insufficient" for a Social Catholicism of the future.

The challenge of forming an adequate Catholic spirituality is further challenged by the problem of postmodern times: how to speak about the mystery of God when many plausibility structures that have grounded our notions of God no longer function in society. The first resolution of a Catholic spirituality of justice was sensitive to issues of plurality and religious liberty. It tried to dialogue with modern atheism and agnosticism, choosing at times a silence about God, instead pointing to the gestures of an ethical life as a common ground among those working for a better world. The second resolution of a Catholic spirituality of justice tries to reclaim a needed sense of transcendence with pre-modern notions of reality. The latter are not in dialogue with modern sensibilities that arise from investment in justice work: a sense of context, the importance of this world, future as hope, and attention to suffering.[45] If neither are enough, what is open to us?

Is it possible that existing communities can enter in the vulnerability that real openness to the other demands? Can they speak the name by which each one knows God, and can they celebrate that name in word and sacrament? Can such faith sharing, arising from action for justice, become integral to the life of the Church? Can theology capture and express this faith experience? Do Catholics who are involved in social commitment have to remain "anonymous Catholics" or can they retrieve the deep traditions of their sacramental life, celebrate and proclaim the God they know in Jesus Christ and the Spirit as the source of all communion? What blocks to this renewal in sacramental life exist in the Church, and how committed are we to their resolution? Can Jesus Christ, God who became incarnate, also share

[45] Lieve Boeve, "Thinking Sacramental Presence in a Postmodern Context," in *Sacramental Presence in a Postmodern Context,* L. Boeve and L. Leijssen, eds. (Leuven: Peeters, 2001) 14.

in the profile of the Inexpressible God of the mystical tradition, who the testimony of sacramental visibility does not diminish?[46] Can this sacramental visibility also provide in a renewed way the meaning structure of engagement in the world within the church community?

New structures of authority and ministry are also called for by the value of sufficiency. Controversies surrounding public misconduct in the Church hide deeper issues involving authority and the designation of ministry. Questions concerning the direction institutional arrangements about authority should take in the Church and who is called to ministry today are significant for the future of Social Catholicism.

Debates about the nature of authority in the Church can distract us from the concern of the sufficiency of authority in face of the growth and complexity that all organizations face. As the Church becomes more complex because it lives in a pluralistic society, the skills needed to lead the Church are multiple. The notion of the one authority, one who could be "all things to all," remains a good spiritual ideal but a managerial and pastoral impossibility. The options in this situation are two. Either limit the field of focus, so that the authority can still be credible, or expand one's function of authority so a more complex situation can be led well.

One author puts it clearly: "An authoritarian management might "succeed" while the complexity and uncertainly of the social environment remained weak, that is, while the possessors of authority could control this complexity and uncertainty."[47] In face of the new complexity of its social mission, the Church can move in one of two directions. It can attend to the notion of sufficiency in its authority structure by a more participatory model, or it can drift and limit its scope and effectiveness to rituals and routine.

Parishes that are able to incorporate lay leadership in their functioning can minister to a wider range of pastoral needs than those who do not. On a continental and global level, recognition of particular churches and greater trust of individuals and groups within these churches is a logical conclusion to the call for regional discernment given in the 1970s.

Concern for the sufficiency of authority extends to the widening of the vision of who is called to minister in the Church. "According to

---

[46] M. C. Luchetti-Bingemer, "Postmodernity and Sacramentality," ibid., 104–5.

[47] Pierre Delooz, "Participation in the Catholic Church," in *Authority in the Church*, Piet F. Fransen, ed. (Leuven: Peeters, 1983) 188–89.

their calling, members participate in the mission and work of the Church and share, to varying degrees, the responsibility for its institutions and agencies" (*Justice in the World,* 41). Contested issues regarding to whom the call to ordination is given, the restoration of the permanent diaconate of women, the discipline and charism of celibacy, the meaningful association of lay people and religious orders, the role and function of new associations in the Church, the inclusion of women and cultural and ethnic minorities in the formation of church policy, institutional supports for the growing number of laity in church ministry, ministry relevant to the cultural impasse of new generations, are beyond issues of containment, their resolution is directional for the future of the Church. These issues are further intensified when viewed in the light of the right of the Catholic faithful to the sacraments, and the drift toward a congregational Church that can result without adequate provision for sacramental ministry.

Because of the information explosion, and the rise in the educational level of members of the Church, it will be hard to construct a model of authority in the future based on power that is not shared. Without meaningful ways for all members to participate in the life of the Church, the tradition of linking Catholic life and social involvement will continue to drift toward extinction.[48] The effectiveness of social teaching involves practical judgments, and practical conclusions and recommendations. Structures have to be fostered which enable these to be made by those affected by the decision, and who have the expertise to make them. The discipline of shared authority calls members of the Church, not just the hierarchy, to a communal sense of responsibility that transcends a cultural vision based on autonomy alone.

Finally, questions of sufficiency provides norms for the *church as a economic actor* in a transitional phase of its life. The bishops of the United States describe the institutional situation of the Church well. "Catholics in the United States can be justly proud of their accomplishments in building and maintaining churches and chapels, and an extensive system of schools, hospitals, and charitable institutions (*Economic Justice for All,* 348). Because of changes in demographics, parishes and institutions are left empty or under-used (355). Decisions regarding these resource must be made that often hinge on their effectiveness for the poor or working class and an optimal return of

---

[48] This is really the question posed by the symposium represented by the text *Catholic Social Thought: Twilight or Renaissance?* Boswell, McHugh and Verstraeten, eds. (Leuven: Peeters, 2000).

the sponsoring body's investment. These decisions are also steps toward a renewed economic model in the Church that supports the diversity of its ministers.

Migration patterns are changing the face of the Catholic Church in the United States. Planning and policies are needed to see that sufficient transfers of expertise and institutional support are given to new peoples both within and beyond the Church. Since material sufficiency is inadequate without spiritual sufficiency, this transfer of resources must also be directed toward the integration, preservation, and enhancement of these distinctive cultural traditions in Catholic faith life. The enablement of new Catholics in the United States, and the integration of minorities not previously given voice, will change the face of Social Catholicism in the future.

Communion

Communion is a call to integration. It is a quality of community as well as the goal of community, and theologically a work of the Holy Spirit. Communion balances and mixes the values that norm community. No one value alone is a mark of an adequate community. All communities will involve a mix and match of the above qualities. It is the relationship of the qualities to one another that makes a sustainable community and gives identity. One can even speak of a community charism as a manifestation in the life of a community, not of one quality, but a unique constellation of qualities that marks its place in the whole.

A shared history has to be balanced by a sense of pluralism or there will be a closed group. Autonomy needs a good sense of mutuality and participation. Identity alone is insufficient because it must be open to change in the world. Communion is that sense of integrative capacity to keep a healthy tension between qualities of community in a manner that is unique to the group, the culture, and the context.

This move toward communion and integration is the opposite of dysfunction, that is, when elements of the group's life live in contradiction to one another and reduce the effectiveness of its mission and its reality as a context of human flourishing. Communion and integration will bring about intimacy instead of fragmentation in a community, and ultimately foster the ground by which Divine-human intimacy can be known and the love of that relationship brought to the world.

As Martin Luther King, Jr. noted, without community, we have only chaos to look forward to. This chaos can ignite our world, as well as the church itself. The choice is ours. A community requires intimacy to ground its members as lack of intimacy is experienced as no community, the state of affairs in many of our churches, neighborhoods, and cities today. A climate of distrust and accusation, watchdogging rather than appreciation, scandal and dereliction of duty rather than witness, biting criticism rather than support, self-righteous finger pointing rather than collaboration, mark our Church today. The chaos of drive by shootings, brutal racist murders, militant religious suicides, our elderly living in fear in the high rises of our towns, our children fearful to go to school or our families racked by addiction, divorce, and economic insecurity will continue unless we rebuild our communities.

The need to create community today is relevant for a vision of Social Catholicism in the future because community has always been at the heart of the Catholic Social Tradition. Community in this sense is not based just on technical or organizational skill but on a sense of responsibility, care, and commitment that resides in characters already formed and forms characters entrusted to it. The climate of learning "how to learn" forms the pre-moral values that have always been the conditions of hearing any formal social message by the Church. Tolerance, respect, and loyalty are insufficient to hold a community together unless these qualities are evident in a group that has sufficient face-to-face relationships so that people can experience trust and mutuality. While the effectiveness of Catholic Social Teaching in the next century requires technical and political and economic analysis of the multiple factors influencing our globe, without the availability, investment, witness and credibility of community formation in the Church, and with the Church and others with whom we share concerns in society, Social Catholicism will have little impact. The Church has always been a place where the experimentation with community needed in society always occurs.

To go beyond the utilitarian ethic of our culture will require a capacity for solidarity that is only learned in community. For some Catholics this will call them again to "opt for the Church" in new ways, and for the Church it will require a new openness to voices, competencies, questions, and peoples that to date have not held a significant place in its communion. If the solutions to our problems today require a "new logic," new communities of meaning within the

Church are key to the translation of the values fostered by the Catholic Social Tradition to the transformation of the pubic realm.

The Catholic Church can no longer provide an encyclopedia of answers to these pressing problems. However, as Jesus Christ gives new meaning to existence, then it is logical to hold that this new meaning will have markers in history and a community life that grounds people in a conscience capable of social investment. The "answers" then given by the Church to the world are its members, animated in spirit, nourished by the sacraments, as non-poor formed with an option for the poor; as poor, ready for voice and enablement, both competent and open to the new challenges before us. In being faithful to this call outside itself, to the Other, the Church will continue to become anew and carry out its mission. This then is a continuation of the Catholic Social Tradition as its members and its mission arise from the heart of the Church. May those who have the privilege to be alive at this challenging time in history do what we can to set the course of our new age to a fuller humanity for all people.

Index

human action (significance of), 48, 159, 162
human dignity, 77, 80
human rights, 117–18
humanistic criterion, 235

identity, 246–47
ideological suspicion, 155
idolatry, 219
inculturation, 14, 31, 59
indirect employer, 213–14
industrial revolution, 87–88
integral human development, 79, 124, 216
international economy, 207
international order, 120, 227, 229
international systems, 112
Isasi-Diaz, Ada Maria, 191

Jedin, H., 71
Jegen, Mary Evelyn, 72, 221
John XXIII, 16, 74, 110–12, 116–18
John Paul II, 15, 48, 79, 80, 201, 209–38
Johnson, Elizabeth, 47
Johnstone, Brian, 57
Judd, Stephen, 169
just war, 200–02
justice
    biblical roots, 50–52
    early Church, 52–53
    related to peace, 120
    types, 54, 93

Kaufmann, Franz-Xavier, 253
Ketteler, Wilhelm Emmanuel Von, 91, 100
Keynesian economics, 102
King, Martin Luther, 241
Kingdom of God, 55–59, 162, 199, 235, 255
Kohler, Oskar, 68
Koyama, Kosuke, 197

labor
    dignity of human work, 211
    full employment, 205
    internationalization, 121
    living wage, 96, 98
labor unions, 71, 96, 99, 213, 227
Laborem Exercens, 210–14
laity, 71, 72, 75, 79, 107, 237
Lamb, Matthew, 140
Land, Philip, 126
Lasch, Christopher, 33, 134
latifundia, 121
Latin American Church, 149–50
Leo XIII, 67, 68, 92–93, 96–97
Lerner, Michael, 251
Lernoux, Penny, 150
liberal capitalism, 209–10, 211, 213
liberalism, 7, 88, 96, 129, 210
liberation, 126–28
liberation theology
    church documents, 168
    hermeneutical circle, 155–58
    kinds: African, 195–97; Asian, 197–98; Black, 185–88; feminist, 192–95; Hispanic/Latino, 188–91; Latin American, 147–74; *Mujerista,* 191
    themes: *conscientization,* 158–60; faith, 148; moral norms, 161–64; praxis, 49, 139, 157, 162; poor, 152–54, 159
Liptak, Dolores, 182
Lumen Gentium, 46, 64, 65, 199

Manansan, Mary John, 197
Martinez, Gaspar, 160
Marx, Karl, 19, 89
Marxism, 7, 128–29
Massaro, Thomas, 98, 176
Mater et Magistra, 16, 76, 114, 116
May, Gerald, 21